'Adele Gladman and Angie Heal ⟨ individuals who understood what ⟨ long before the world did, and work people and make others take action… This book is therefore of great significance as the authors, once again, bring the experiences of children and young people themselves to the fore.'

— Anne Longfield, OBE, Children's Commissioner for England

'This is a comprehensive work by two practitioners who were at the heart of the Rotherham CSE case. It is without doubt the defining work on sexual exploitation of children in the UK and is a text that all social workers and practitioners in the field should read. It has been important to chart the history of Rotherham. It has enabled the authors to provide much needed guidance for us all on how best to recognise and deal with this scourge of our towns and cities.'

— David Greenwood, Head of the Child Abuse Department, Switalskis Solicitors

'Adele Gladman and Angie Heal have taken on a daunting task in writing a book about organised sexual abuse and intimate terrorism, with input from survivors, victims and professionals. The result is an extraordinary achievement, full of direct testimony and of real practical use to families, practitioners and managers in sustaining a proactive, community-wide approach to these social evils. The worst of human behaviour is here, and yet to counter this we also see amazing courage, resistance and love, and excellent practice to counter the failures. Anyone can benefit from reading this book, because we all need to understand what makes communities vulnerable to networks of abuse and the continuous steps that are needed to help keep them safe.'

— Ruth Gardner PhD, FRSA, Honorary Senior Research Fellow, Centre for Research on Children and Families, University of East Anglia *of related interest*

Not My Shame
A Graphic Novel about Child Sexual Exploitation
T.O. Walker
ISBN 978 1 78592 184 1
eISBN 978 0 85701 294 4

Learning from Baby P
The Politics of Blame, Fear and Denial
Sharon Shoesmith
ISBN 978 1 78592 003 5
eISBN 978 1 78450 238 6

Tackling Child Neglect
Research, Policy and Evidence-Based Practice
Edited by Ruth Gardner
Foreword by David Howe
ISBN 978 1 84905 662 5
eISBN 978 1 78450 165 5

Safeguarding Black Children
Good Practice in Child Protection
Edited by Claudia Bernard and Perlita Harris
Foreword by June Thoburn
ISBN 978 1 84905 569 7
eISBN 978 1 78450 011 5

Risk in Child Protection
Assessment Challenges and Frameworks for Practice
Martin C. Calder with Julie Archer
ISBN 978 1 84905 4 799
eISBN 978 0 85700 8 589

Challenging Child Protection
New Directions in Safeguarding Children
Edited by Lorraine Waterhouse and Janice McGhee
ISBN 978 1 84905 395 2
eISBN 978 0 85700 760 5

Child Sexual Exploitation After Rotherham

Understanding the Consequences and Recommendations for Practice

Adele Gladman and **Angie Heal**

Forewords by T, Survivor of organised child sexual abuse in Rotherham and Anne Longfield, OBE, Children's Commissioner for England

Jessica Kingsley *Publishers*
London and Philadelphia

First published in 2017
by Jessica Kingsley Publishers
73 Collier Street
London N1 9BE, UK
and
400 Market Street, Suite 400
Philadelphia, PA 19106, USA

www.jkp.com

Copyright © Adele Gladman and Angie Heal 2017
Forewords copyright © T, Survivor of organised child sexual
abuse in Rotherham and Anne Longfield 2017

All rights reserved. No part of this publication may be reproduced in any
material form (including photocopying, storing in any medium by electronic
means or transmitting) without the written permission of the copyright owner
except in accordance with the provisions of the law or under terms of a licence
issued in the UK by the Copyright Licensing Agency Ltd. www.cla.co.uk or in
overseas territories by the relevant reproduction rights organisation, for details
see www.ifrro.org. Applications for the copyright owner's written permission to
reproduce any part of this publication should be addressed to the publisher.

Warning: The doing of an unauthorised act in relation to a copyright work
may result in both a civil claim for damages and criminal prosecution.

Library of Congress Cataloging in Publication Data
A CIP catalog record for this book is available from the Library of Congress

British Library Cataloguing in Publication Data
A CIP catalogue record for this book is available from the British Library

ISBN 978 1 78592 027 1
eISBN 978 1 78450 276 8

Printed and bound in Great Britain

*To the victims, survivors and their families of the
Rotherham child sexual abuse scandal.*

*Adele would like to dedicate this book to her mum and dad who first
showed her what a good relationship looked like and made her the
person she is; to Jim, her rock and the person who kept her going
through the darkest of times; and finally Nicholas and Amelie,
who are the inspiration for everything that she strives to achieve.*

*Angie would like to dedicate this book to Harry for his so solid,
unwavering support and her beloved mother Pegs, who she will
forever greatly miss. Pegs lived through the writing but not the
publication of this book; she would have been very proud.*

Contents

A Survivor's Foreword by T, survivor of organised child sexual abuse in Rotherham   9

Foreword by Anne Longfield, OBE, Children's Commissioner of England   13

Acknowledgements   15

Introduction   17

Chapter 1   The Consequences of Statutory Agency Failure in Rotherham   39

Chapter 2   Defining and Identifying Child Sexual Exploitation and Organised Child Sexual Abuse   64

Chapter 3   Understanding the Impact of Grooming and Organised Child Sexual Abuse   103

Chapter 4   Taking Effective Safeguarding Action within a Safeguarding Framework   136

Chapter 5	Key Considerations for Criminal Investigations and Tackling Perpetrators	176
Chapter 6	Child Sexual Exploitation, Organised Child Sexual Abuse and the Criminal Justice Process	209
Chapter 7	Strategic and Senior Management Responses to Child Sexual Exploitation and Organised Child Sexual Abuse	240
	Conclusion	278
	References	*292*
	Subject Index	*302*
	Author Index	*308*

A Survivor's Foreword

First, I would like to write about how this whole thing has affected my life. Before all this came out nationally I felt alone, ashamed of myself, degraded and hurt. I thought I was the only person in Rotherham that had gone through such horrific things. And all this was made more believable because the people who you are supposed to put your trust in are the very people that allowed me to feel it was my fault and that I didn't need to pursue – what would have been – the right course of action. That's why in 2001 I had to make the decision to put it in a box, buried to the far back of my memory shelf, to be able to move forward and protect me and my baby.

I was well aware of the fact that South Yorkshire Police thought they had no duty of care towards me and my family while I was pregnant and just after having the baby. The only people that was ready to protect me and my baby was my family. We had threats to me and the unborn baby, but the police wasn't concerned and passed them off as empty threats. I knew these people and I knew they were serious. They all knew that the baby was DNA evidence to convict one of them, so I had to hide away. I stayed indoors and focused on school. Once the baby was born there was threats to kidnap. But these were also passed off by the police. I had no trust in them at all. There was clearly some sort of hush hush cover up going on, but because I was 13 I didn't understand what protection should have been implemented. My family questioned the way things were, but was reassured everything was under control and not to worry. Social services and South Yorkshire Police never wanted to help my mum on the several occasions she took me to them, or the numerous telephone calls she made. We was always sent away with comments such as 'she is OK', 'she comes home eventually'. My mum informed them every time that it was older Asian men that was keeping me hidden away for days. They didn't seem to care. It was all as if nothing mattered. Me as a teenager started believing everything the perpetrators were saying, because of all this lack of protection and help from the police and social services.

The only time they came running was when my family rang to inform them – after begging for help and not receiving it – that I'd become pregnant. They were there the same day coming up with plans to 'help', but in reality they were busy creating the barriers to cover it all up – the fact that I was 12 years old and pregnant. There were injunctions, child protection, and so on. This meant by this point newspapers and television couldn't publish my name or my picture. But this also meant I couldn't talk to them and tell them my story. They got a statement off South Yorkshire Police and that statement didn't make me out to be a victim, so they plastered horrible things about me and my family all over the papers. I had to ignore it all and try to make a life. It seemed impossible but I took it day by day and I got myself to a better place without them. My family are the ones that supported me. I had to push myself so hard, every day at 13 getting up, feeding a baby, going to school and studying for exams. My life had a major change because of the failings of South Yorkshire Police, and Rotherham Metropolitan Borough Council social services' inability to do their jobs properly.

Since all of this has come to the surface again recently because of the investigation and trial that's coming up, my stress and anxiety are at a high level. I'm struggling to cope with the paranoia it is bringing out. I can't go out and be around certain people, as I'm so scared they are related or friends with the perpetrators. I start thinking they are looking at me and talking about me. But I'm a qualified youth worker now and I know my feelings aren't right and I shouldn't stereotype. It's just crazy what the mind does when under a lot of pressure.

I also don't trust police and social services. I feel that too much happened for me to ever fully have confidence in them again. They're trying to help me now as much as they can, but I've just got no trust in them whatsoever. It's just part of what I went through then. I can't change that. I like to deal with my own issues without them because they left me to sort myself out, from when I was 11 until when I was 13.

This book is an amazing opportunity to help practitioners learn more about it and ways to overcome its challenges. I believe that workers that met me around that awful time knew what was happening to me but was so scared to speak out. All I needed was to see professionals saying the same as my family, just to reassure me. My family was right in what they were trying to learn me, telling me the perpetrators were in the wrong and it was illegal. But I just didn't believe my family and when I was took to social services and police they wasn't backing my family up, which only left me to ignore what was correct.

This book will help you all to be empathetic and identify risk factors that may be a contributor. This will help you support others in future practice, and spot the warning signs. It will also help you gain an insight into how it really feels for survivors such as myself. I believe that if social workers would have listened to my mum the first time she told them what was happening to me, then my life could have been so much different – I would have put trust in and listened to professional advice. I believe workers then knew what needed to be done and had the knowledge, but was too scared to stand up and admit this was a problem and it needed addressing in fear of losing their jobs and being victimised by senior members of staff. One thing I have learnt from this whole thing is that being silent is what made this town become such a mess.

Speak out and don't be scared to challenge and stand up for what is the right thing to do. I am so happy to be able to use this very bad and unfortunate part of my life to talk about and try and change the way things went wrong. My personal opinion is that the only way to move forward is for workers to be prepared to challenge every little thing they come across. Yes, it's a lot of work, but in the long run it will come naturally and society will change the way they think about the failures that once was, and look forward to putting trust in South Yorkshire Police and Rotherham children's services again.

T, Rotherham, October 2016

Postscript

T has since had to give ·evidence in court against her attackers. Six men were subsequently convicted of offences including rape, indecent assault, sexual intercourse with a child under 13 and false imprisonment in relation to her (aged 12), and another girl aged 13. They were jailed for a total of 81 years. T said giving evidence was the hardest thing she had ever done in her life, which is significant given what she has been through. But she is glad she had done it and hopes it will help others come forward as a result.

Foreword

The terrible experiences of the children and young people in Rotherham who we now know were abused so dreadfully over two decades shocked the nation.

The findings about the abuse from the 2014 report by Professor Alexis Jay, now Chair of the Independent Inquiry into Child Sexual Abuse, shone a light into their world and challenged every one of us to stop it ever being repeated. The subsequent report by Dame Louise Casey showed that the scale of the abuse taking place in this South Yorkshire town and the extent of the negligence of professionals, agencies and civic leaders was more than had ever been imagined.

It is a terrible indictment that because many of the children who were abused and exploited were already vulnerable, the men who exploited them felt they could be confident they would never be challenged. For me, one of the most shocking aspects was how children who had been targets of exploitation were often seen as the problem – unreliable, untrustworthy and just causing trouble. These children were disregarded by authorities when they needed help the most. Poor decisions about the care and protection of children left them to face the continuing misery of sexual exploitation, their silence so often secured with threats and intimidation by the offenders.

In different roles, Adele Gladman and Angie Heal were two of the remarkable individuals who understood what was happening in Rotherham long before the world did, and worked tirelessly to support young people and make others take action. Both gave evidence to the Home Affairs Select Committee in 2014 and both continue to assist in ongoing investigations and inquiries.

This book is therefore of great significance as the authors, once again, bring the experiences of children and young people themselves to the fore. Using first-hand accounts from children about what happened to them, it explores the impact of sexual exploitation, what could have been different, and what kind of help and intervention is needed if we are to prevent these pernicious crimes from happening again.

When I speak to children who have been sexually exploited they often tell me how they tried to tell someone about what was happening to them. Others will say that they knew that things weren't okay but could not find the words to speak out, believing it was their problem – they got themselves into it, they should get themselves out.

There can no longer be any doubt that this is our problem.

Tackling child sexual exploitation is challenging but everyone working with children needs to be able to spot the possible signs – and be confident in taking effective action to stop it and bring perpetrators to account, whether that professional is a police officer, a social worker, a doctor or a teacher. Awareness of child sexual exploitation has never been higher as a result of what has happened in Rotherham, Oxford, Derby and other parts of the UK. And, of course, this is not just a book about Rotherham, but about every town where children may be being abused.

This important and powerful book understands that as adults we all have a duty to protect children and that for those in positions of power with responsibility for children's wellbeing, this must be an absolute priority. It provides a vital tool to enable them to make this happen and so ensure that every child has the protection and support they need to grow and flourish.

Anne Longfield, OBE, Children's Commissioner for England

Acknowledgements

Due to issues of confidentiality, we are not able to personally acknowledge some of the people who have participated in this book. We would like to thank 'T' and the other victims, survivors and their families who participated in different ways in the writing of this book. T is inspirational in the way she has largely been able to compartmentalise her abuse and not let it define who she is and what she wants to do with her life.

We would like to acknowledge all victims, survivors and their families of child sexual exploitation and organised child sexual abuse, not just in Rotherham but across the UK. While some are able to report their abuse and speak out, others keep their trauma hidden, unable to share the horror of what happened to them. While we know that some fare better than others, ultimately we hope that everyone can find inner strength and external support in order to recover so that they can lead the life they want.

We would like to thank Jayne Senior, who opened our eyes to what was wrong, then showed us what good practice should look like.

Adele would also like to acknowledge the work and vision of Irene Ivison, which led to the Home office funded pilot in Rotherham, and Jalna Hanmer whose support, guidance and friendship over the years has been invaluable.

We would also like to express our thanks to people who gave their time to talk to us or review some of the chapters in this book, including Temporary/Detective Chief Inspector Martin Tate, Detective Sergeant Steve Smith, Detective Inspector Helen Tate, Lucy Edwards, Ann Lucas, Jayne Senior, Detective Sergeant Andy Pollard, Detective Inspector Gemma Booth, Keith Daniel, Amber Wilson, Phil Mitchell, David Greenwood, Julie Woodhouse and one family who would prefer to remain anonymous. We would also like to thank other professionals who prefer not to be named.

In addition we would like to thank all those at Jessica Kingsley Publishers who have been great supporters of this project, especially our editor Steve Jones, Danielle McLean, Daisy Watt and Alexandra Holmes who have kept us on track and answered endless queries.

Introduction

This book is dedicated to all victims and survivors of child sexual exploitation (CSE) and organised child sexual abuse (CSA) in Rotherham and across the country. The narratives emerging from Rotherham and beyond are awful in the extreme, not just in relation to the sadism inflicted on them by the perpetrators, but also the poor and sometimes negligent practice from agencies and professionals who had a duty to protect them. This compounded their abuse. Some survivors are now coming forward, more confident in being able to tell their stories, knowing they will now more likely be heard and believed. This includes T, who wrote such a powerful Foreword and whom we shall call Tanya, who wanted to share her story after watching a *Panorama* programme about CSE and CSA in Rotherham (September 2014). Others, however, will forever remain hidden, unable to share their burden and the horrors of what happened to them.

Rotherham is not the only town affected by such stories, and it is certainly not the only town to get it wrong. Unfortunately, across the country accounts of poor and erroneous practice can still be heard. There is a very long way to go before we all get it right. We are immensely grateful to those who have been able to share their experiences with us, and with Professor Alexis Jay and Dame Louise Casey, in the hope that it will help others understand what happened and how the abuse and trauma has impacted on them and their families. This is exemplified by Tanya in the Foreword:

> I also don't trust police and social services. I feel there is too much happened for me to ever fully have confidence in them again. They're trying to help me now as much as they can, but I've just got no trust in them whatsoever. It's just part of what I went through then. I can't change that.

Her account is a clear example of how past poor practice still affects current perceptions of survivors and how even those who are complying on a practical level to get their abusers convicted, and who are being offered comprehensive care and support packages, are still very affected emotionally by the legacy of the past. It is crucial that we work with victims to give them confidence that knowledge and practice has changed and, where appropriate, to come forward and report crimes that have been committed against them. Victim and survivor accounts of their involvement with practitioners inform good practice; it is vital we continue to learn.

This book has been born out of our shared but different experiences as professionals working in Rotherham, and elsewhere, which has left us forever affected. We are committed to sharing our knowledge and expertise, learned through first- and second-hand accounts from children and adults who have been sexually, physically and psychologically abused. While it is predominantly aimed at practitioners and students working with children and young people, this book is also relevant to those working with adults who have experienced issues of sexual abuse, either as children or as young adults. They include those with learning or physical disabilities who are in residential care or supported living arrangements, or who may otherwise be vulnerable to exploitation and abuse.

This Introduction discusses the use of terminology and outlines the forthcoming chapters. First, however, we would like to take this opportunity to introduce ourselves and say something about our own experiences in order to give this book additional context.

Adele Gladman

The motivation for writing this guide stemmed from the time that I spent in Rotherham, from 2001 to 2002. The experiences I had during my time working in the town had a huge impact on me and have stayed with me ever since. I was working as a child and family law solicitor when I heard about a proposal to run a research and development pilot in Rotherham, backed and funded by the Home Office. I was then focused on my legal career, but intrigued by questions about CSE. It was an issue that I was finding more and more in my cases, particularly those involving adolescent young women who were in the care of the local authority. I was hearing stories in court about young women who had 'absconded' and 'been found' in massage parlours, brothels and red-light areas. What astounded me at the time was that no one else seemed to regard this as a child protection issue; the concern was focused on how to respond to the young person's perceived problem behaviour. No one seemed to be asking 'how did they get there', 'who facilitated them being there' and in my mind the most important question of all, 'what was happening to them while they were there?' No one apparently was seeing that these children were being abused, or asking who was abusing them and what could be done to protect them. To me, these were fundamental questions, and as time progressed I found myself looking more into the issue of CSE and being astonished that so little was known or being done about it.

Those enquiries led me to undertake a research-based Master's degree at Leeds Metropolitan University. Through that degree, I met Jalna Hamner, who was Professor at the university and a trustee in an organisation called CROP, the Coalition for the Removal of Pimping. It was an organisation that had been established by Irene Ivison, whose daughter Fiona had been sexually exploited and murdered. Through Jalna I heard about the research and development pilot. Irene had led on the development of a bid to the Home Office in partnership with Rotherham Metropolitan Borough Council but had died before the outcome of the bid was known. When the bid was successful, Jalna suggested that I apply for the post of Research and Development Officer, leading the work on the pilot. The aims and objectives of the bid matched some of the questions that I was asking around the experiences of the young people involved, and what could be done by the organisations working with them to protect them. Additionally, there was a strong focus on responding to those carrying out the abuse – the mapping and profiling of offenders, and working with the police to look at what legislation could be utilised to investigate, deter and prosecute abusers. I perceived the pilot as a real opportunity not only to increase and raise knowledge about this abuse, but also to develop systems and models to respond to it.

I took what I believed would be a leave of absence from the law to start work on what was initially a one-year funded contract. I genuinely believed that I had a good understanding of the issues of abuse and some professional resilience towards them. I was wrong. With the benefit of hindsight, I was totally unprepared for what would happen during my time in Rotherham. When the pilot ended, I felt like I had opened Pandora's Box. I wondered if children in other areas of the UK were having similar experiences. As a result I never returned to legal practice but continued working with issues around safeguarding children, child sexual exploitation and professional standards. This is something I continue to this day.

My time in Rotherham had a deep, personal impact on me. Some of the experiences I had, and the children I met, will stay with me forever. One such memory is of my first day at work on the pilot. I was the only person working on it, and it was managed by the Rotherham Youth Service, mentored by CROP and evaluated by a team from the University of Luton. I was based with a small youth service project, the Risky Business Project, which was located in a former children's home in Rotherham. On my first day, I arrived and sat in the office looking at the aims and objectives of the pilot, which were extensive. When the project manager and workers came into the office some time later, I learned that they had been responding to the case of a young woman known to the project as being involved in CSE. She had been repeatedly sexually assaulted and was the victim of the most vicious and sadistic physical attack I have ever encountered, before being abandoned by her abusers.

As I listened to the accounts of the workers, I realised that nothing could have prepared me for what I was going to hear and experience over the next year. I realised that I knew very little about the nature of CSE, what it meant for those children involved, and the levels to which those abusing them would go in order to achieve and protect their own interests. I wish I could say that this young person was an isolated case, but there were many others. What was equally as shocking was the response that the victims received from those organisations that should have acted to protect them. At that point I did not realise that a significant challenge that the pilot would face was the levels of poor practice, avoidance and denial across the services working with these children.

The pilot was extended to 18 months and during that period I learned a great deal. I achieved some positive outcomes for the pilot, the Risky Business Project and some of the young people with whom we worked. I developed a model that ultimately was replicated and developed in some of the subsequent successful prosecutions of CSE offenders in the UK. There were particular issues in Rotherham, not least because there were no red-light areas, brothels or massage parlours. The young people involved, therefore, were taken to private locations and frequently believed that they were in relationships with their abusers. They did not recognise that they were victims of grooming or abuse. There was often a lack of engagement and cooperation between the young person and the police or social care. This was often used as a reason to justify the lack of response from those services.

The tragedy of Rotherham is that much of the abuse I encountered, and that followed when the pilot ended, was preventable. The pilot never achieved its full potential and that is lamentable for the children of Rotherham. There was, and remained for quite a number of years, a strong culture of denial in the town.

Despite repeated evidence suggesting that four brothers – the Hussains – were largely responsible for much of the abuse of which the pilot was collating information, this was dismissed as 'anecdotal'. The evidence that led to two trials and the subsequent convictions of 13 offenders (including all four brothers and two of their cousins) in February and October 2016 was given to the police in 2001 and 2002 but never pursued or progressed. The young people were regarded as the problem and not identified as victims of abuse. I attended one meeting where a child protection officer clearly either did not know or disregarded the law in relation to sexual offences and children, referring to a child of 12 raped by multiple perpetrators as being 'happy to consent to have sex' with her abusers. I saw documents describing children as 'prostitutes'; there were issues of organisational cultures as well as individual denial or negative labelling of the young victims involved. While there was some isolated good work, for the most part I encountered practice that can only be described as negligent, particularly as it allowed children to continue being abused without challenge. I have no doubt that this also led to abusers feeling that they were invincible and could do whatever they liked to children in Rotherham.

As part of my work, I started considering what good practice responses would look like and trying to work with organisations to raise awareness about this. For the most part, I was ignored and later serious orchestrated attempts were made to cast doubt on my integrity and the validity of my work. I was put under pressure to suppress some of my data and present my research findings in a way that showed Rotherham in a different (more positive) light. The strain of not being able to help many of the children I encountered took a toll on my health and I left Rotherham temporarily defeated, but determined not to let this issue rest.

This is a story that remained largely untold until Jayne Senior, former manager of the Risky Business Project, took the very brave decision to contact Andrew Norfolk of *The Times* newspaper. Despite great personal risk she did so because she could no longer bear to listen to the ongoing narratives of poor practice in Rotherham, which were resulting in children continuing to be abused. Andrew then started an investigation, which ultimately led to him reporting some of the terrible stories that were emerging from the town in 2012. That, in turn, led to the establishment of a Home Affairs Select Committee inquiry into CSE and the commissioning of Professor Alexis Jay to conduct her 2014 independent inquiry. Although I had met Andrew and assisted with some of his enquiries after his first articles were published, it was through Alexis that for the first time I was able to tell someone my account of my time in Rotherham and show her the evidence and the victims' accounts that I had collected during the pilot. The publication of her report showing the sheer numbers of victims she identified in Rotherham was shocking and upset me greatly, especially as her report identified that had I been listened to, much of the abuse could have been prevented. Before reading her report, I genuinely believed that I had achieved something before I left, that Rotherham was a safer place for children and that action would be taken against their abusers. It is difficult to describe the anguish that came with the realisation that this had never happened, and that my research and warnings to the Chief Constable and Directors of Service downwards had instead been ignored or dismissed.

I have continued to raise awareness of what went wrong in Rotherham – through the Home Affairs Select Committee (2014), the Casey Inquiry (2015) and other subsequent inquiries working with the Independent Police Complaints Commission and the National Crime Agency, among others. It is through this that I met Angie Heal for the first time. I realised that she too had uncovered evidence of the scale of sexual abuse in the town as well as some of the perpetrators responsible and that she too had been disregarded and silenced. Together we continued to be determined to help others learn lessons from the terrible mistakes made in Rotherham. It is that determination that is the core foundation of this book. Responding to issues of child sexual exploitation is complex and challenging, but not impossible. This book draws together the collective experience and learning from myself and Angie over the years as we struggled to influence practice in Rotherham and beyond. It has been impossible to cover every practice issue due to the extensive nature of the abuse and its complexity. However, we hope that it is of use to those reading it and offers practical guidance on how to address some of the challenges posed by issues of child sexual exploitation, and to improve existing good practice. We know what the alternative is – lifelong damage for those abused, damage which impacts on every aspect of their lives: on their whole family, on a generation and on whole communities. Simply put, it is lives ruined.

During the pilot and afterwards I have met many survivors who have given me consent to tell their stories. We have used case examples from our own practice and experiences across the UK throughout this book to illustrate the consequences that followed some of the poor professional decisions that were made, and what could have happened if the correct response had been given. Some details have been changed to protect the person's identity. I am often asked if Rotherham is exceptional or if the same is happening in other areas of the UK. I have seen evidence of CSE across the UK. I have observed both good and poor practice. I sincerely hope, however, that in many aspects Rotherham is exceptional. I never again want to read reports as shocking as the Jay and Casey reports. I also hope that in putting this practice guide together, we can learn from the mistakes that were made in Rotherham and achieve something positive from the terrible abuse of so many children. We owe them that.

Angie Heal

I worked for South Yorkshire Police (SYP) from 2002 to 2007 as a strategic drugs analyst. It was a partnership post, funded by the four (then) Drug Action Teams (DATs) in the county. My remit was to research and report on issues of drug use and supply, and make recommendations for action to senior officers and the DATs. I had previously worked with issues of illegal drugs as a general and psychiatric nurse, a drugs worker and a researcher in crime and social policy. During my employment with SYP I was not closely managed, nor was I often given much work to do. Mostly I tasked myself with researching areas that I decided warranted investigation. I was seen as someone who knew what they were doing and so was largely left to my own devices, which enabled me to do some innovative work. I combined my knowledge of the drugs field, my Master's degree in social research methods and my training as a police analyst to produce reports that I aimed to make relevant and readable for both a tight-knit police culture and practitioners in partnership agencies. One of the problems I encountered, however, was that the majority of my managers within SYP (of whom there were quite a few over the years) either did not feel comfortable with or were not interested in my work, leaving me somewhat isolated and unsupported much of the time. I carried on regardless, as I very much believed that what I was reporting was important.

The first piece of work I tasked myself with in 2002 was researching crack cocaine in South Yorkshire, investigating the varying patterns of use and supply in different areas of the county. It was through the interviews that I conducted for this research that I first came across the issue of CSE and organised CSA. I met Ann Lucas, the Sexual Exploitation Service manager in Sheffield, who first told me about the links between CSE, sexual offending against children, drug use (given to children by perpetrators as part of the grooming process) and drug supply (a significant number of the perpetrators were involved in the supply of Class A drugs). She suggested that I also made contact with the Risky Business Project in Rotherham, which is when I first met Jayne Senior. Despite having been a drugs worker and working with women involved in street prostitution, I knew nothing about the organised sexual abuse of children by groups of men. I was deeply shocked by both what I found out and that I had not previously been aware of it, despite my professional experience. I became determined to highlight it to senior managers, who I had presumed must be equally unaware.

In my 2002 crack cocaine report, my second recommendation (of seven) was to tackle the perpetrators of organised CSA, who were also drug suppliers. I recommended that if they were unable to be prosecuted for sexual offences, they should be investigated and prosecuted for drugs offences. To me it was obvious that their child victims would then be safeguarded and their involvement in local Class A drug markets terminated. Despite knowing how widely read that report was and how well it was received, particularly within SYP, I could not believe the complete lack of interest in the information I presented regarding the organised sexual abuse of children and the links to illegal drugs. Jayne and I regularly debated the reasons why this could possibly be, but we could not come up with any solid, logical explanations. I consequently decided to keep reporting these issues as often as I could. This resulted in *Sexual Exploitation, Drug Use and Drug Dealing: The Current Situation in South Yorkshire* (Heal, 2003) and *A Problem Profile – Violence and Gun Crime: Links between Sexual Exploitation, Prostitution and Drug Markets in South Yorkshire* (Heal, 2006). In addition, I regularly included issues of CSE in the six-monthly intelligence reports I did from 2003 to 2007, which gathered information from policing units and teams, drugs agencies, CSE projects and agencies working with those involved in street prostitution. I circulated these reports as widely as I justifiably could, including to relevant frontline police officers and staff, senior police officers, relevant council staff in children's services and community safety departments, regional Home Office staff, Drug Action Team coordinators and the agencies which had participated in the research.

During the fieldwork period for my 2003 report, Jayne decided she trusted me to read Adele's report, written the previous year. She had previously told me about Adele, her treatment by SYP and Rotherham Council managers and the theft of case files from their office. We met in the canteen at Police Headquarters; Jayne believed the report to be so controversial I had to read it secretly. It was a surreal moment – sitting in the police canteen, reading a report under the table that was so explicit in events, trauma and names. I felt scared. It was only later that I realised just what a huge risk she had taken in trusting me, especially as I worked for the police. I was humbled by her faith in me, and promised myself I would do what I could to help tackle such horrendous crimes. Unlike Adele, apart from once, I did not usually meet with victims in Rotherham or their families. Given the chaos and trauma in their lives, it was mostly not appropriate for them to be asked to share their stories with me directly; their workers at Risky Business did that on their behalf. I still used to leave each visit to the Risky Business offices, however, in a state of silent shock, horrified at the acts that people were capable on perpetrating on anyone – let alone children – and the incomprehensible lack of concerted action by those with the statutory responsibilities to protect them. I could not comprehend their apparent lack of concern and compassion for these children.

By 2006 I was being warned that some officers in my department were not supportive of me or my work, and once the head of the department left later that summer all my protection vanished. The Drug Strategy Unit, in which I was located with two police officers, was swiftly disbanded and there was a plan to downgrade my post significantly and bring me in line with police management structure and culture. It was clear that my work was seen by my new managers as irrelevant, which given that I was regularly reporting the rape of children – serial rape, committed by multiple rapists accompanied by threats, physical violence, psychological intimidation of victims and their families – will never fail to astonish and sadden me. SYP, therefore, left me no option but to resign, so I found another job and left in March 2007. My post disappeared along with the partnership funding.

For the next few years I remained committed to raising the issue of CSE and organised CSA when I could, although professional possibilities for me during that time were very limited. By August 2013 things were starting to stir in Rotherham, with the announcement of the Jay inquiry, and SYP finally established a major incident team to investigate suspects. I was determined to be involved, to have my say and make sure my reports were included in the inquiry. I contacted the Jay team myself; I could not wait for them to contact me.

Despite being someone who worked with Jayne and Risky Business for years, and subsequently was part of the Jay inquiry as well as meeting regularly with a team from *Panorama*, I found that the extent of the abuse disclosed by Alexis Jay and the subsequent media and public reaction knocked me sideways. Her report was published on 26 August 2014; when I first heard the news headline on the radio that '1,400 girls had been sexually abused over a 16-year period in...' I thought the presenter was going to say Syria. I could hardly breathe when she said Rotherham; I was shocked to the core. Reading it in print, seeing it on television and listening to it on the radio was a surreal experience. I sat watching TV for a couple of days, unable to switch off the endless coverage. I cannot begin to imagine what it was like for the victims, survivors and their families or for those professionals who were far more involved than I had been, such as Jayne. As someone who was seen as trying for years to raise the alarm, I – like Adele – became caught up in a media storm. It seemed that every news outlet in the country was trying to contact us. International interest was phenomenal too, with even a request from Al Jazeera to participate in a discussion on a programme that went out to 280 million homes. As someone who does not like attention, I found it easy to reject the majority of offers, but I also felt I had a duty to speak out publicly. I chose a few: *Panorama*, *BBC News*, *The Star* (Sheffield) and also the Canadian Broadcasting Company and the *Wall Street Journal*. As Adele has mentioned, I have also given evidence to committees, inquiries and investigations, I have met with journalists, MPs and chief constables and given seminars and conferences, as well as speaking to numerous others. The release of my 2003 and 2006 reports under Freedom of Information Act requests in May 2015 even briefly knocked the general election off the headlines two days before the country went to vote.

It has become apparent that we have been involved in the biggest child protection scandal in UK history. The public and media interest has been astounding, and also something for which – for the most part – I have been very grateful. It is the pressure from the media that has resulted in major strategic and practice changes across the country; they have been able to do what we alone could not. The inaction and indifference by senior police officers and Rotherham Council staff to what was occurring on their watch is still difficult to comprehend, despite the countless attempts by social commentators to make sense of what happened. While we are still unable to come up with a definitive answer, throughout this book we discuss the different complex, contributing factors because we have to learn lessons from Rotherham and beyond. Adele and I continue to work to limit the possibilities of anything like this ever happening again.

Terminology and other issues for consideration

Having outlined our involvement in Rotherham and our motivations for writing this book, there are some issues of terminology that we would first like to consider, which should add clarity about our thinking before the discussions in the chapters.

Child sexual exploitation

First is the term child sexual exploitation. This phrase was agreed to replace the term 'child prostitute', which clearly was very inappropriate and became factually incorrect once an amendment to the Sexual Offences Act 2003 came into force in 2015 (Home Office, 2015). While 'exploitation' may be the correct use of the word in relation to the grooming stage of CSE, as will be discussed in Chapter 2, it is not appropriate in relation to the worst crimes inflicted – vaginal, anal and oral rape, actual and grievous bodily harm, attempted murder, murder, psychological intimidation and threats to kill. Offences of those type are clearly not 'exploitation' and we believe to use this term at this level does not help people's understanding of the seriousness of these crimes.

From one perspective, the term 'child sexual exploitation' does describe what happens: it involves children, it involves sexual acts and it is exploitative. But we believe that the term intellectualises and normalises what is, in reality, the abuse and rape of vulnerable children and young people by skilled and predatory adults. Nowhere in the definition of CSE is 'rape' or 'abuse' explicitly mentioned. The sexually abusive experience of the child is often accompanied by acts of unimaginable sadism, using the child's individual vulnerabilities and fears to condition and imprison them in a cycle of abuse. We appreciate that CSE is now a commonly used term and particularly in light of the media coverage as a result of the Jay report (2014) is more widely understood than ever before. A number of specialists, however, now refer to child sexual abuse (CSA) in relation to sexual offences committed against children; throughout this book we use the term 'organised child sexual abuse' in conjunction with 'child sexual exploitation'. The word 'organised' identifies it as different from other forms of child sexual abuse, such as intra-familial. It is now recognised it comes within a law enforcement definition of organised crime, as we discuss later in this book. We would like to raise awareness that the term 'child sexual exploitation' is not appropriate once sexual offences have been committed, and when perpetrators are working together it should be replaced with 'organised child sexual abuse'. Where services or publications refer to CSE, however, we have left them unchanged.

Victims and survivors

Second are the terms 'victims' and 'survivors'. A victim is defined as 'a person who has been attacked, injured, robbed, or killed by someone else' (Merriam Webster, 2015b). A survivor is defined as someone who 'continues to function or prosper despite' (Merriam Webster, 2015a); it is a term frequently used to describe former victims of sexual abuse. Essentially though, what is important is how the person feels about and defines her or himself. This is discussed in more detail in Chapter 2. The terms are often used together throughout this book, although we must stress they are not interchangeable. It should also be noted that the criminal justice system uses the term 'victim' during investigations and prosecutions, while the person may indeed consider themselves a survivor. The terms can be controversial; referring to a person as a victim who sees themselves as a survivor, or vice versa, can lead to misunderstandings. In addition, any professional misunderstanding and misuse of the terms can be damaging. In one case we encountered a young woman who referred to herself as a survivor and was, therefore, regarded by a professional working with her as refusing to accept the reality of what happened to her. Professionals working with victims and survivors of organised child sexual abuse need to ensure that they understand the finer nuances of what is, admittedly, a very complex area. It is just too important to get wrong.

The use of the term 'survivor' is often applied to those who have transcended the abuse, who despite their trauma have gone on to heal significantly or use their experiences in a positive way. This term is positive and enabling, particularly to those who chose to apply it to themselves. In contrast, and somewhat confusingly, the term is also often applied to a person who has previously been abused, but is still consumed by the trauma. Adele has heard it used in relation to former victims who are experiencing debilitating mental health issues, post-traumatic stress syndrome and substance misuse problems – those whose daily lives are still entirely consumed by the abuse. The impact of the term can be multifaceted; it can also minimise the impact the trauma has had and continues to have on the person. Their needs may be underestimated because 'survivor' implies that they need no further help, that they have overcome the abuse. Using the term erroneously or prematurely reduces professional urgency and the need to act to meet the victim's needs, which would enable them to become a survivor. The term can also be very debilitating when they have an added pressure through expectation of others to cope, to live a positive life and be – externally at least – unaffected. What it mostly does, however, is fail to recognise the ongoing torment that most victims experience on a regular, sometimes daily basis. Premature use of the term does not acknowledge that while some victims have the resilience and strength to move on, others do not and require long-term support and interventions. As one man commented, 'They call me a survivor. Why? Because I wake up every morning?'

Child and young person

Third are the terms 'child' and 'young person'. The United Nations Convention on the Rights of the Child 1999 defines a child as everyone under the age of 18; the UK has ratified this convention. Every child, therefore, up until their 18th birthday, should be afforded statutory agency protection if they are suffering or likely to suffer significant harm as a result of physical, sexual, emotional abuse or neglect (HM Government, 2015). Legally this is quite clear and all professionals and agencies should be working to this definition. It is not always so straightforward, however. There is an argument that teenagers do not like to be referred to as 'children' and that in order to respect their physical and emotional development they should be referred to as 'young women', 'young men' or 'young people'. The National Institute for Health and Care Excellence (NICE) in its guidance for healthcare professionals, *Child Maltreatment: When to Suspect Maltreatment in Under 16s*, states:

> This guidance uses the following terms to describe children of different ages:
>
> - infant (aged under 1 year)
>
> - child (aged under 13 years)
>
> - young person (aged 13–17 years).
>
> (NICE, 2009)

Herein lies an issue that can cause confusion, sometimes with dangerous consequences. The above NICE guidance shows the contrast between the treatment of children by health professionals and the legal definition. The National Health Service (NHS) usually treats children in adult services from the age of 16. Discussion with the former Rotherham Council Chief Executive, Martin Kimber at the Communities and Local Government Select Committee on 10 September 2014 is an example of such confusion. One of the MPs on the Committee made a point about Kimber using the phrase 'young women' in the session, whereas he wanted to remind him that the victims were in fact girls. He suggested Kimber's choice of language spoke volumes (Local Government Chronicle Plus, September 2014). While we cannot second guess any implication from his use of the term 'young women', in light of the above discussion in relation to the NICE guidance and NHS protocols, his choice of language may not actually speak the 'volumes' as suggested. We wish to clearly state, however, that for the purposes of this text we use the term child and young person in the legal sense: to refer to all those up to the age of 18.

Ethnicity

Fourth is the issue of victim ethnicity. As will be discussed elsewhere in this book, much has been made in media and public discourse about the ethnicity of the perpetrators of CSE and organised CSA. Far less has been written about the ethnicity of their victims. Even in 2016, those in contact with specialist services are usually white (and female). In Rotherham, the vast majority of children referred to Risky Business were white, despite there being a significant local Asian community. Practitioners and managers should not assume, however, that no contacts or referrals means there are no victims of CSE or organised CSA from ethnic minorities – quite the contrary.

Berelowitz *et al.* (2012) noted that there were 16,500 victims reported to be at risk of CSE within a one-year period; they also stated that 81 per cent of children presenting with indicators on their dataset were white or white British. This means there were approximately 3,135 children in that one-year period who were at risk of CSE who were also from an ethnic minority group. That is a significant number of children who potentially were not protected from sexual abuse and trauma, simply because of their ethnic origin.

> Undoubtedly, there are girls and young women from Asian, Black and Eastern European communities that are being sexually exploited. But this appears to be much more hidden, within families or communities, and rarely gets spoken about. This is a very covert problem. (Heal, 2003, p.45)

Berelowitz *et al.* (2015) note their concern regarding the under-identification of victims from black, Asian or other ethnic minorities including those of Gypsy, Roma or traveller origin. Where there is such an under-representation, particularly where there are different minority groups living in the local area, practitioners and senior managers should consider why this may be. For example, do services inadvertently exclude victims from black, Asian and other communities making contact and continuing working relationships by unintentionally speaking only to white victims through images in literature and a predominance of white British staff? Do links with other projects that work with children from ethnic minority communities need to be made in order to make contact with potential victims?

The language in this book is deliberately ethnicity neutral as it is also gender neutral, which will be discussed later. This is to encourage readers to avoid thinking in stereotypical terms of white female victims. We urge practitioners to think in a wide perspective and consider all when contemplating images of victims, as well as those of perpetrators. Narrow perspectives can lead to victims being unrecognised and unprotected and perpetrators being able to act with impunity, as will be discussed in later chapters.

Intimate terrorist

Fifth and finally is the term 'intimate terrorist', which we sometimes employ in relation to a particular type of perpetrator of organised child sexual abuse. Johnson and Leone (2005) state 'Intimate terrorism is defined by the attempt to dominate one's partner and to exert general control over the relationship, domination that is manifested in the use of a wide range of power and control tactics, including violence' (2005, p.323). In earlier work, Johnson referred to patriarchal terrorism – which he later renamed intimate terrorism – as violence typically embedded in a pattern of controlling behaviours, suggesting that the perpetrator is trying to control their partner (1995). He stated that such forms of violence are usually what is meant by terms such as domestic violence and spousal abuse. Although rooted in debates about adult domestic violence rather than child abuse, the term 'intimate terrorist', in just two words, immediately conjures up a very accurate picture of the *modus operandi* of one of the types of perpetrators we describe throughout this book: those who groom and exploit their child victims, form intimate and relationships with them, before dominating, controlling and sexually abusing them. It is 'the systematic use of terror especially as a means of coercion' (Merriam Webster, 2015c) and whereas its commonplace meaning is in relation to gaining political ends, it can also be used with regard to interpersonal relationships.

We reference the term 'terrorist' with some caution, however, as the majority of the perpetrators of organised child sexual abuse in Rotherham were of Pakistani heritage. Care must be taken not to misinterpret this use of the word, in a culture of heightened sensitivity to global religious extremism where acts of brutality and killings are a feature and Asian communities have been stigmatised and demonised as a result. Our use of the word is solely in relation to the methods employed by certain perpetrators to control and dominate children with whom they are intimate; we apply it to abusers of all ethnicities who terrorise children and young adults. As Chapter 2 discusses, the child may believe their abuser to be an intimate partner; the abuser knows otherwise.

Chapters

Having provided some context in relation to our own work and discussed issues of terminology which provide clarity and also explain some of our thinking, we now outline forthcoming chapters.

Chapter 1 examines the consequences of failure in relation to what we term a 'disaster' in Rotherham. While this book is dedicated to learning lessons from the experiences of victims and survivors in the town, this opening chapter considers the broader consequences of statutory agency failure. This includes the impact on parents and siblings; the town and people of Rotherham; communities; the local Pakistani community; Rotherham Council; South Yorkshire Police; professionals working in the town; and the perpetrators themselves. It discusses the reputation of the town; claims for compensation from victims and survivors; the repeated audits, inspections and inquiries; the financial impact of the scandal and the strain on existing services and professionals still working there. All of this, we purport, is a result of the failure by senior managers to respond quickly, professionally and compassionately to the organised sexual abuse of children in the town.

Chapter 2 defines child sexual exploitation, including CSA, and examines the different behaviours from both a victim and perpetrator perspective. Using illustrative real-life cases, this chapter provides detailed information to help professionals thoroughly understand the nature of organised child sexual abuse in order to be able to identify risk factors with children or families with whom they are working, and be able to respond effectively to such presenting indicators. The chapter also provides a profile of offending behaviour in relation to CSE and CSA, including individual abuse, peer abuse and organised abuse. It discusses the rise of sexual abuse that is both initiated and/or perpetrated online, and its relationship with contact abuse.

Chapter 3 discusses the impact of grooming and organised child sexual abuse. It details the concept of children's vulnerability along with the process of grooming – how they are targeted by their abusers before becoming heavily involved – and examines the impact on both victims and their families. It describes the impact and influence of the abuse on the child's behaviour and their future vulnerability. It discusses the impact on children and their families of statutory agencies' failure to act, as well as the role of agencies in supporting victims and survivors. It uses illustrative good practice and other case studies.

Chapter 4 concerns professionals taking safeguarding action at an operational level. It explains thresholds and the consequences of not adequately assessing risk, or indeed not assessing it at all. It stresses the importance of early intervention work with children and their families, including preventative work. It specifies effective child in need and child protection responses and planning. It examines how professionals should respond to a child's failure to engage with them; this includes reasons for non-involvement and strategies to address such issues. Part of taking action involves working in partnership with families, which may include responding to changing dynamics between the child and their family. The importance of regularly reviewing the effectiveness of interventions is discussed, which is particularly pertinent in a situation that is often very fluid. This chapter also discusses the professional's role in relation to ensuring effective partnership working, including challenging poor professional attitudes and practice.

Chapter 5 discusses tackling the perpetrators, in terms of both proactive and reactive responses. This includes reporting information to the police and ongoing intelligence gathering, as well as sharing information with other agencies. It highlights common problems and details what should happen, using good practice case studies from a number of police forces. It outlines the importance of developing and maintaining good relationships with victims, survivors and their families and supporting them during the investigation process, including where suspects are given bail and the subsequent vital need for effective witness protection. This chapter also examines other possible options where victims do not want to give statements, including third-party evidence. It also includes a detailed police operational case example – Operation Clover, South Yorkshire Police – which, as referenced by Adele above, resulted in significant convictions and sentences for some of the main abusers in Rotherham.

Chapter 6 concerns the criminal justice process and considers the needs of victims, survivors and their families before, during and after a trial. It discusses the provision of pre-trial therapy and the importance of this for the victim or survivor, while not jeopardising the prosecution case. The experiences of victims at court, particularly during cross-examination, are illustrated using case practice examples. Issues of safety and risk are also addressed. There is also discussion of the vital issue of communicating the outcome of trials, helping victims, survivors and their families understand trial verdicts, who else needs to be informed and future support after the trial. The chapter concludes by looking at the section 28 pilots under the Youth Justice and Criminal Evidence Act 1999 and the Barnahus model pilots and the future for victims of organised child sexual abuse giving evidence at court.

Chapter 7 examines strategic responses. This includes the roles and responsibilities of the Local Safeguarding Children Board (LSCB), the statutory agencies both as individual organisations and as partner agencies of the LSCB, and the role of other agencies. It outlines what LSCBs and partners should be doing and references good practice examples. It also specifies the importance of all agencies in challenging poor or ineffective practice and organisational and professional cultures, both internally and in partner organisations, accountability, training, the provision of policies and procedures that are embedded into daily practice, and staff supervision and support. This chapter discusses that the effectiveness of these factors needs to be regularly checked through robust quality assurance processes. Strategic responses need to include raising awareness and working with different communities and peripheral services such as taxi licensing and the leisure and hotel industries. Sharing information and learning lessons across directorates and county partnerships are discussed. This includes adult social care and other adult services, in relation to working with adult victims and survivors of organised child sexual abuse, and young adults who are vulnerable to being targeted and groomed in similar ways.

The final chapter, the Conclusion, draws together key learning from this book and makes recommendations for current and future practice.

Chapter 1

The Consequences of Statutory Agency Failure in Rotherham

Introduction

The quote below, from Dame Louise Casey, lays bare her view of the corollaries of inaction in Rotherham.

> We must not lose sight of what the failures in Rotherham have meant in practice; victims have been hurt and remain without justice, the Pakistani Heritage Community has been harmed by association, as have individual social workers, police officers, taxi drivers and other hard working people in the Council, voluntary sectors and the town of Rotherham more broadly. It has also harmed public services because what happened in Rotherham does not represent its values – of putting the needs of the most vulnerable always at its centre. (Casey, 2015, p.5)

What we know about the scale of the abuse in Rotherham is very clear: there were over 1,400 victims who were sexually abused in a 16-year period, between 1997 and 2013 (Jay, 2014). The ongoing effects of such sexual, physical and psychological abuse will be discussed in detail in later chapters, but they include mental ill health, self-harm, drug and alcohol misuse, interrupted education, poor or no job prospects, pregnancy, termination of pregnancy, adoption, family breakdown, unstable housing and economic insecurity. As referenced in the Introduction and as will be discussed in more detail later, some victims and survivors are only able to report the abuse once they reach adulthood; others can never share their experiences with professionals nor with trusted loved ones. Their distress is suppressed and hidden and they are, therefore, unsupported in the after-effects of their trauma.

While the focus of subsequent chapters in this book is rightly on victims and survivors, there are other consequences of the failures of statutory agencies in Rotherham, as noted by Casey above. These issues need to be discussed and understood in order to comprehend the full scale of what can only be called a disaster. While other people in the town may not have been raped, physically assaulted or humiliated by their abusers, this does not mean they have been unaffected. Most of the people in Rotherham have been touched in some way by this catastrophe. This chapter discusses the impact on the town and its people of the wholesale failure of agencies to address organised child sexual abuse for so long. It discusses the effects on different groups of people and organisations, including families; the town of Rotherham and its people, including local businesses; the local Pakistani community; Rotherham Metropolitan Borough Council (RMBC); South Yorkshire Police (SYP); professionals working in Rotherham; the perpetrators. It also references some of the financial costs of the disaster.

The impact of failure
Families of victims and survivors

Victims are not the only members in a family to be affected by the acts of perpetrators of organised child sexual abuse. The effects on parents and siblings of child sexual exploitation and abuse are considerable, and three-fold at least.

First is witnessing the change in the child's behaviour, particularly if grooming is involved and the skilled 'intimate terrorist' (Johnson and Leone, 2005) is successful in psychologically and physically isolating the child from their family. Such actions initially include the child being secretive, lying, coming home late and repeatedly being absent from home.

Second, as the abuse of the child escalates, is the parent/s attempt to contain the situation. This can have a significant impact on their domestic relationships as a result of desperate arguments and resorting to increasingly drastic control measures in attempting to keep their child at home, which are often unsuccessful. This includes the relationship between the parent/s and their abused child, which becomes more complex and despairing the longer the abuse continues. It can include a change in the bond with other children they may have, particularly if they are still living at home, as they may feel a lack of parental attention as the focus is always on the abused child, where they are, who they are with and what is happening to them. It includes the relationship between the abused child and their siblings, where the siblings may alternate between being angry with the abused child for upsetting the household in such drastic ways, and being very concerned and distressed when they are missing or have clearly been abused. It also includes the parent/s' own marriage or relationship, which can be put under enormous strain as a result of differing approaches to parenting a child involved in CSE for example, and similarly the relationship with a former partner – the child's parent – if they are separated.

Third is the damage that can be inflicted on the family by the perpetrators themselves, through threats of sexual violence to other siblings, physical and psychological threats to siblings and parents or the family home for example. These issues are discussed in more depth in Chapter 2.

Irene Ivison (1997) eloquently documents the pains of having a daughter who she felt unable to protect, and the impact on the rest of the family of Fiona being groomed, sexually exploited and pimped on the streets, shortly before she was murdered. Her account of trying to safeguard her child, limit the damaging effect on other family members and deal with the statutory authorities makes difficult reading. The consequences of what happened were so profound that it led her to want to use her experiences to support other parents who had a child who was being sexually exploited and abused; she founded the Coalition for the Removal of Pimps (CROP, now Parents Against Child Exploitation or PACE). Adele comments in the Introduction about the significant role Irene played in helping to secure the research bid for Rotherham that enabled her to work in the town, before Irene's untimely death in 2000.

Parents initially often believed, unsurprisingly, that they would get assistance from the police and children's social care in times of trouble, particularly in emergency situations such as when their child had gone missing from home. Unfortunately for some parents in Rotherham, that did not happen. The Jay report (2014) detailed a number of cases when the police response was quite the opposite of what the parent expected to happen. Two cases referenced related to fathers who – on separate occasions – found their daughters, who had gone missing, at particular properties where they were being abused. They tried to remove them from the houses, only for themselves to be arrested when the police were called to the disturbances; no action was taken against the perpetrators (Jay, 2014, p.36). The report noted another case where a child who was willing to give evidence against her perpetrators received a text saying her 11-year-old sister was with them and the choice of what happened next was hers. She withdrew her statement. Adele knows this case only too well, as she was sat with her at the police station ready to support her in meeting police officers to whom she could later give a statement, when the text arrived. The girl left, saying no one was able to protect them, and she did not return; her evidence was lost. Jay also cited the experiences of two other families who were terrorised by groups of perpetrators, which included often parking outside the family homes in a manner meant to intimidate all inside, smashing windows, and making threatening and abusive phone calls. She stated that sometimes children returned to the perpetrators as they believed this was the only way their family would not be harmed (Jay, 2014, p.36). One father summarised his thoughts:

'I think it's quite sad, not just what happened to my daughter but how the system has responded. I was brought up to believe that when something bad happened, you told the police or social services and they help you – something would be done about it – that isn't what happened.' A victim's father. (Casey, 2015, p.13)

In another case, Jay noted a mother who expressed concerns about her sexually active 14-year-old daughter going missing and repeated incidents of severe intoxication when she had been given alcohol by older men. She says the social worker's assessment was that the mother was not able to accept her child growing up, whereas she was in fact displaying key CSE and CSA indicators from the age of 11 (2014, p.39). Tanya's mother also did not receive any help when her daughter kept going missing:

Me mum begged 'em to take me away, that's how bad it were, she begged 'em to take me away from Rotherham and they were like 'no, she's fed, she comes home eventually', that sort of thing. Like, is that realistic? An 11-year-old going missing for two days and 'oh, she comes home eventually'?… Me mum was a single mum, so she was like struggling like to get to work, she were doing nights, she were coming looking for me all the time…school were reporting that I'd not turned into school. So it were like she were a yoyo, she weren't getting help from anyone. And I feel so bad for her now, cos I can't imagine going through that with my children, can't imagine it at all. (University of Sheffield Symposium, 2016)

Casey had similar findings:

It was clear from this victim's care files that there were repeated attempts by the family to get protection and support for their daughter. Yet the documentation shows that the social worker assessed that there was no statutory role for social services. Between September 2003 and May 2004 the social worker made five home visits. No support was offered. In the end her family ended up moving overseas to escape the perpetrators. (Casey, 2015, pp.57–58)

The vast majority of parents do their utmost to try to guide and protect their children, especially when they are growing up. If they feel their child is being threatened or is in any way unsafe, they will go to extremes to do whatever is required to remove them from harm, whatever or whoever the source. It is acknowledged that there are some very complex issues to consider. These will be discussed in Chapter 2 but include the rights of the child, patient/client confidentiality and Gillick competency and Fraser guidelines that direct health professionals to assess a child's maturity and ability to make their own decisions regarding their medical care and understand the implication of those decisions.

PACE understands very well the concerns of parents whose child is being sexually exploited, and their frustration at services which are either not able or not willing to share information with them. But common sense should prevail. When there is no evidence that a parent is abusing or neglecting their child, and their contact with authorities is in relation to their child who meets the indicators of involvement in CSE or CSA (see also Chapter 2), professionals should treat the parents as part of the solution – not part of the problem – and work with the family on this premise.

When practitioners and agencies fail to do so it is usually because they do not thoroughly understand the complex perpetrator behaviour in the grooming process and the impact on the victim (see Chapter 3). This is likely to exacerbate an already traumatic situation, which can eventually result in family breakdown and a child left isolated from the only people who genuinely love and care for them. This will be discussed further in Chapter 4.

The town and people of Rotherham

The consequences of agency failure to proactively address organised CSA have been immense and immeasurable for the people of Rotherham. Prior to the release of the Jay report on 26 August 2014, apart from some articles by Andrew Norfolk in *The Times*, there had been mostly piecemeal national and local media coverage of the issues in the town; certainly nothing that was a signal of things to come. Following the live television broadcast in August 2014 of Professor Jay giving a statement of her findings, a majority of the national news media arrived in the town centre along with local and regional reporters, closely followed by international news outlets. Whether or not they were on site, they all covered the story extensively. Understandably, all aspects of the coverage were very negative for Rotherham and its people, with no positive news stories emerging.

As the alleged perpetrators in the town were mainly of Pakistani origin, as is explored in more detail below, much of the media coverage initially centred on issues of race. This was particularly in relation to Rotherham Metropolitan Borough Council (RMBC) and South Yorkshire Police's (SYP) failure to respond effectively to this obviously sensitive matter, but also the role of the local Pakistani community itself. If all those whose heads were required to roll had resigned immediately it might have enabled the town to start the process of recovery more quickly, but the situation only deteriorated over a number of weeks. The Leader of RMBC, Roger Stone, resigned immediately, followed quite quickly by the Chief Executive Martin Kimber. But two other key individuals, Shaun Wright (former RMBC Councillor and Lead for Children and Families, then SYP Police and Crime Commissioner) and Joyce Thacker (Strategic Director Children and Families), refused to resign despite fierce public, press and political pressure. Even following difficult appearances at the Home Affairs Select Committee (HASC) (Commons Select Committee, 9 September 2014) and the Communities and Local Government Select Committee (Commons Select Committee, 10 September 2014) they still took some weeks to eventually go. Whatever their personal and professional reasons for refusing to step down, they appeared not to see the damage that continuing in their positions was doing to Rotherham's already devastated reputation. This was particularly pertinent as the HASC Chair asked them both to resign and, additionally, in the case of Shaun Wright, even the Prime Minister David Cameron became involved when he also called for him to step down (*Independent,* August 2014). They were portrayed as arrogant and uncaring of the victims, survivors and the people of Rotherham and seen as exemplifying the problematic attitude of RMBC.

The spotlight also fell on Rotherham councillors, as questions were being asked by the media about who knew what and for how long. As RMBC had been a Labour-run local authority for decades, the coverage took a political slant (The Guardian Online, 2014), particularly when the United Kingdom Independence Party (UKIP) became involved in the debate as the second biggest political party in Rotherham. Further revelations in *The Times* (February 2015) alleged that two Labour councillors and an SYP officer – PC Hassan Ali – were being investigated in relation to personal involvement in the abuse of some of the victims. To add yet another layer of complexity, in February 2015, PC Hassan Ali – having been notified of his referral to the Independent Complaints Commission (IPCC) for investigation – was hit by a car and killed. (At a trial in February 2017, a man was not found guilty of causing his death by careless driving.)

By October 2014, the initial media interest in Rotherham had finally started to recede. It was quickly reignited, however, in February 2015 following publication of the Casey report, which found RMBC not fit for purpose. It was a scathing account of a council still in denial of the extent of the abuse and more concerned with its own reputation than the plight of the numerous victims for whom it was responsible. It was consequently the first local authority to be placed under central government control by the Secretary of State for the Department for Communities and Local Government, who sent in five inspectors to run it for up to four years, replacing the RMBC Cabinet (RMBC, 2015a).

By October 2015, Rotherham had experienced one demonstration in the town centre each month for the past year in relation to the scandal. These were usually held by far-right groups such as the English Defence League, which were mostly coming to Rotherham from outside the local area to protest at the perceived involvement of Pakistani men in the sexual abuse of (white) British children. Some counter demonstrations also took place by left-wing organisations. All of these marches have in turn led to additional pressures for Rotherham. They have resulted in more negative media coverage, affected local businesses – some of whom have had to close on march days or seen their takings drop as shoppers have avoided the town centre – and the costs of policing the demonstrations were also significant for a police force already very financially stretched. One year on and the town had understandably lost patience with the continued stigmatisation and disruption and an online campaign 'Enough is Enough' was launched by RMBC Leader Chris Read (RMBC, 2015b). It aimed to highlight to central government the impact of the marches on Rotherham people and businesses, stating that such continued activity was preventing the town from moving on. The right-wing group Pegida was still able to protest in the town in June 2016, however.

All of the above circumstances have resulted in a town whose reputation has been devastated, by the actions of a relative few. This has led townspeople to feel angry, let down by the statutory bodies they pay to protect and serve them and stigmatised by the national and international media. As so much of the media focus was on the issues discussed here, it left the plight of victims and survivors, and the fact that for the most part perpetrators had not been investigated and therefore were carrying on the abuse largely unimpeded, mostly ignored.

The Pakistani community in Rotherham

> By failing to take action against the Pakistani heritage male perpetrators of CSE in the borough, the Council has inadvertently fuelled the far right and allowed racial tensions to grow. It has done a great disservice to the Pakistani heritage community and the good people of Rotherham as a result. (Casey, 2015, p.10)

The involvement of men of Pakistani heritage in the sexual exploitation of local children had been an open secret among professionals in Rotherham for many years. The Jay report covers a 16-year period commencing in 1997; her inquiry revealed that the perpetrators were described by victims as predominantly Asian. One worker reported that Asian men, particularly taxi drivers, had been involved in CSE in Rotherham for over 30 years, although then it was for personal gratification rather than organised abuse (Heal, 2006, p.11). In the quote above, Casey emphatically stated that Rotherham Council failed to take action against the perpetrators, but we believe this also applies to SYP. The Force had a unit dedicated to addressing issues of crime and crime prevention within different minority groups in the county; this included matters relating to specific black and minority ethnic (BME) communities. Two of Angie's reports made clear and specific references to the ethnicity of offenders in Rotherham (which differed from perpetrators in other areas, such as Sheffield):

> Ethnicity is becoming an increasing issue, which needs to be discussed in order to put it in perspective... In Rotherham, there has been concern about a number of brothers who are Asian, who are the main, but not sole, offenders... In Rotherham the local Asian community, from where the brothers come from, are reported to rarely speak about them. They are taboo and probably equally frightened of their violent tendencies as the young women they are involved with. These are the actions of a few unscrupulous career criminals, and whole communities should not be stereotyped on this basis. (Heal, 2003, pp.43–44)

> While the issue of ethnicity and sexual exploitation is one of great sensitivity, reports of such involvement should be thoroughly investigated by all agencies. Criminals in any environment can effectively dominate and intimidate people within their own community if they are left to act with seeming impunity. To commit such acts of sexual and physical violence will be an acute embarrassment to their family and friends, who probably feel unable

to speak out about such issues. When incidents come to light, it is the likes of the British National Party that seize the media headlines and do more damage than if the issue was tackled proactively. (Heal, 2006, pp.16–17)

While it is acknowledged that this would have been a most difficult and sensitive subject to broach, this was not a reason not to do so when children were being raped and abused. Issues of child protection are paramount, and no other concerns – including issues of ethnicity – should ever impede such investigations. Jay noted, 'Both the Council and the Police used traditional channels of communication with the Pakistani-heritage community for many years on general issues of child protection' (Jay, 2014, p.94). Yet despite SYP officers already having dialogue in relation to child protection issues and senior officers receiving Angie's reports – including those with responsibility for the Minorities Unit – no action appeared to have been taken to discuss this alleged criminality with the relevant imams and community leaders in Rotherham at that time. Jay made reference to two meetings in 2011 (Jay, 2014, p.91), but otherwise it is believed that no other attempts were made to discuss the concerns with the Pakistani community. Jay stated the inquiry did not find any evidence that social work staff were being inappropriately influenced by issues of ethnicity in relation to CSE perpetrators in child protection cases (Jay, 2014, p.91).

Within RMBC and SYP, however, there was a common belief that senior staff wanted such issues downplayed. Jay noted that this led to some confusion for frontline staff as to what their approach should be and concerns as to whether they would be perceived as being 'racist' in their practice (Jay, 2014, p.90). Despite law enforcement organisations such as the Metropolitan Police being found to be institutionally racist (MacPherson, 1999) and concerns repeatedly expressed about policing tactics such as 'stop and search' (Weber and Bowling, 2011, for example), UK police forces have not usually appeared unduly reticent to proactively target BME suspects. If Rotherham police were actively avoiding conducting investigations into crimes citing racial sensitivities as Jay and others state, this, Angie believes, was related to Rotherham only; it was not SYP policy.

Unsurprisingly, much of the initial media coverage focused on the racial element of the scandal and centred on the fact that most of the perpetrators were of Pakistani origin (The Telegraph Online, 2014; Mail Online, 2014). The media largely ignored the impact that such reporting would have on that particular community, as well as the plight of child sexual abuse victims of Pakistani origin. While we clearly understood the sensitivity of the racial aspect of this issue at that time, that did not prevent either of us from believing that it still should have been proactively addressed with local people, giving them the opportunity to work with the men involved and their families. Not doing so has resulted in a tragically missed opportunity to prevent the scale and extent of the abuse, and done a great disservice to the local Pakistani population in Rotherham. *The National* (Canadian Broadcasting Company, 2015), for example, interviewed young Asian men in the town centre as part of its coverage, who said that they had insults of 'Paki Paedo' shouted at them in the streets. As a result of the Rotherham disaster they have been traumatised and demonised, when they were already stigmatised as a result of Islamic extremism and religious terrorism. We acknowledge that community leaders either ignored the problem or were in denial about what some of their men were involved in and therefore did not proactively address the issue of CSE and organised CSA within their community. We also believe, however, that SYP and RMBC neglected their duties to take proactive steps to work with the Pakistani community, support them to investigate these violent and sexual crimes and undertake preventative work with them.

The situation continued to deteriorate. One year after the publication of the Jay report saw the British Muslim Youth group in Rotherham call for the Muslim community to cut all lines of engagement and communication with SYP. While the situation was remedied within a few days and the boycott was called off, they clearly felt very aggrieved at what they believed was them being scapegoated by the police, who were deflecting their own failures by targeting members of the Muslim community in the town (The Star Online, October 2015). In August 2015, Mushin Ahmed, an 81-year-old Pakistani man, was killed on his way to morning prayers at his mosque in Rotherham and two local white men were convicted of his murder and manslaughter (BBC Online News, 29 February 2016). One, a known racist, shouted 'groomer' at him before beating, punching and kicking him; Mr Ahmed died 11 days after the attack. In August 2016, a mosque in Rotherham received a bomb threat from a neo-Nazi group. It said, 'Next time it will be a bomb, you Muslim scum.' It was signed off with '1488', which is a Neo-Nazi code for the 14-word creed of white supremacists and 88, representing HH – Heil Hitler (The Star Online, August 2016).

So it goes on.

Rotherham Metropolitan Borough Council

> In the early years there seems to have been a prevalent denial of the existence of child sexual exploitation in the Borough, let alone its increasing incidence and dangers. By 2005, it is hard to believe that any senior officers or members, from the Leader and the Chief Executive downwards, were not aware of the issue. (Jay, 2014, p.101)

Much has been written about the failings of RMBC to adequately respond to the allegations of widespread organised child sexual abuse in the town. This concerned both local councillors and paid employees. As a result of the Casey report, which found that 'Rotherham Metropolitan Borough Council is not fit for purpose' (2015, p.9), the Secretary of State for Communities and Local Government ordered a central government takeover of the whole of the Council, rather than solely for children's social care as has been seen in other areas such as Birmingham and Slough. This demonstrates that the concerns highlighted in the Jay report (2014) were much wider than just one single department and that the whole Council needed systemic review and remedial action. Five commissioners were subsequently drafted in to begin the process of overhaul at RMBC.

Louise Casey had harsh words for RMBC officers and staff, and in essence was scathing about what she found in relation to the Council.

Our investigations revealed:

- a council in denial about serious and ongoing safeguarding failures

- an archaic culture of sexism, bullying and discomfort around race

- failure to address past weaknesses, in particular in children's social care

- weak and ineffective arrangements for taxi licensing, which leave the public at risk

- ineffective leadership and management, including political leadership

- no shared vision, a partial management team and ineffective liaisons with partners

- a culture of covering up uncomfortable truths, silencing whistle-blowers and paying off staff rather than dealing with difficult issues.

Despite Professor Jay's findings, which we fully endorse, and substantial quantities of information available within the Council, RMBC demonstrates a resolute denial of what has happened in the borough. This took several forms – notable in their recurrence – including dismissal of Professor Jay's findings, denial of knowledge of the 'scale and scope' of CSE, blaming others, and denial that CSE remains a serious problem in present day Rotherham. (Casey, 2015, pp.10–11)

There were three main groups within the Council that were deemed to be at fault. First were senior RMBC employees; as noted above, this led to the resignation of Martin Kimber, Chief Executive, fairly soon after the Jay report was published. Second were RMBC councillors, who were predominantly members of the Labour Party, which had been in power for the entire period covered by the report (1997–2013). Roger Stone, Labour Leader of RMBC, stepped down on the day the report was published; four Labour Party Councillors were subsequently suspended from the Party. This was followed by the whole of the RMBC Cabinet being forced to resign in February 2015, as a result of the Casey report's damning conclusion that the Council was not fit for purpose. The then Labour leader Ed Milliband acknowledged that the Rotherham abuse victims were 'terribly let down' by the party's representatives and had also let the Rotherham people down (The Star Online, January 2015). Jay stated:

> The Deputy Council Leader (2011–2014) from the Pakistani-heritage community was clear that he had not understood the scale of the CSE problem in Rotherham until 2013. He then disagreed with colleague elected members on the way to approach it. He had advocated taking the issue 'head on' but had been overruled. He was one of the elected members who said they thought the criminal convictions in 2010 were 'a one-off, isolated case', and not an example of a more deep-rooted problem of Pakistani-heritage perpetrators targeting young white girls. This was at best naive, and at worst ignoring a politically inconvenient truth. (Jay, 2014, pp.93–94)

The third group was social work staff in children's social care. Joyce Thacker had been Strategic Director of Children's Services since 2008, Deputy Director from 2006, and previously had been chair of the Risky Business Steering Group. Joyce Thacker, therefore, clearly understood the concerns of organised sexual abuse in the town and in her role as chair was in receipt of Risky Business reports to RMBC, including referral data. As the most senior manager in children's social care in Rotherham she refused to resign following the Jay report, repeatedly defending her position stating that she had made CSE an immediate priority on taking up her post in 2008, and was part of the senior management team that had transformed child protection services since 2010 (Jay, 2014). While this may have been true, and indeed the improvements were acknowledged in the Jay report, ultimately she could not continue to resist the very public calls by politicians in the Home Affairs Select Committee (Children and Young People Now, September 2014), the media and the public, and she eventually resigned on 19 September.

Overall the Jay and Casey reports make grim reading in relation to children's social care in Rotherham, although there were also references to good practice, particularly in later years. Specific issues of concern relate to social work practices such as assessments, chronologies, care plans and interventions, some of which are discussed in Chapter 4. Jay referenced particular concerns in relation to assessment and planning, risk assessment and management, looked-after children and care leavers (pp.47–53). She particularly noted that external inspections of children's social care – by Ofsted and others – commented negatively in relation to assessment and planning (p.46).

> There was evidence in many files that prior to 2007, child victims from around the age of eleven upwards were not seen to be the priority for children's social care, even when they were being sexually abused and exploited. (Jay, 2014, p.46)

Casey also noted the imbalance in the working relationship between RMBC and SYP. The inspection team expected to find a robust and equal partnership but instead concluded that the Council was excessively deferential towards SYP and consequently there was a lack of scrutiny in relation to police action against the perpetrators of CSE in the town (2015, p.10). One of the most disconcerting findings in relation to RMBC reported by Casey was:

> A report to the Audit Committee on 17th September 2014 identifies the Jay report as the second highest risk facing the Council. The risk is described as follows: 'Major reputation damage and loss of confidence in the Council; demoralising impact on employees; potential financial claims; potential impact on inward investment; short and medium term disruption/distraction from services; subsequent OFSTED and corporate governance inspections...

There is nothing about the risk to children. The risk of services continuing to fail children should have been the Council's highest priority. But it was not. This goes to the heart of the culture of the Council and what senior leaders think really matters. (Casey, 2015, p.84)

South Yorkshire Police

Prior to the Jay report being published, South Yorkshire Police were already under the media and public spotlight for their actions in relation to policing practices during the Hillsborough Disaster in 1989 (Hillsborough Independent Panel) where 96 Liverpool football fans died, and policing of the miners' strike at Orgreave Colliery in 1984. A dedicated team of over 130 staff was established for an independent investigation into the Force's actions regarding Hillsborough. 'The investigation is the biggest inquiry into alleged police criminality ever conducted in England and Wales' (IPCC, 2015b). Following an initial scoping exercise, the Independent Police Complaints Commission (IPCC) decided not to investigate the Force in relation to Orgreave (IPCC, June 2015a); the allegations related to assault, perjury, perverting the course of justice and misconduct in a public office. After some consideration the Home Secretary also rejected an independent inquiry.

The Jay report highlighted a number of serious concerns about the conduct of officers from SYP in relation to reports of the organised sexual abuse of children. While acknowledging examples of good practice, particularly in the latter part of the 16-year period that her report covered, she noted:

> While there was close liaison between the Police, Risky Business and children's social care from the early days of the Risky Business project, there were very many historic cases where the operational response of the Police fell far short of what could be expected. The reasons for this are not entirely clear. The Police had excellent procedures from 1998, but in practice these appear to have been widely disregarded. Certainly there is evidence that

> police officers on the ground in the 1990s and well beyond displayed attitudes that conveyed a lack of understanding of the problem of CSE and the nature of grooming. We have already seen that children as young as 11 were deemed to be having consensual sexual intercourse when in fact they were being raped and abused by adults. (Jay, 2014, p.69)

The Casey report quotes one officer as saying to a victim, 'Don't worry – you aren't the first girl to be raped by XX and you won't be the last' (Casey, 2015, p.56).

As a result of the Jay report, a number of complaints were made in relation to specific police officers from SYP. At this time, these complaints are being investigated by the IPCC in relation to child sexual exploitation in Rotherham (IPCC, 2015c) and Sheffield. The National Crime Agency (NCA) is also carrying out investigations into CSE inquiries conducted by SYP (NCA, April 2015; June 2015). The already damaged reputation of the Force was not further helped by the intransigence of the then Police and Crime Commissioner Shaun Wright, as referenced earlier. There was a collective sigh of relief when he finally stepped down, but yet more harm had been done to the standing of South Yorkshire Police.

The Police and Crime Commissioner Dr Alan Billings, who was elected to replace Shaun Wright, ordered an independent inquiry into SYP similar to the Casey review. Chaired and authored by Professor John Drew, the inquiry concurred with Jay (2014) and Casey (2015) that in the past the police response to safeguarding children and young people from CSE was inadequate, particularly in Rotherham (his review covered all of South Yorkshire). It found that some of the failures were associated with the lack of awareness of CSE at that time and that opportunities to examine the situation in more detail were not pursued. The Force had allocated some resources to CSE, but they were mostly in Sheffield. The inquiry report believed that SYP has made considerable progress in its response to CSE, which is monitored via a regularly reviewed action plan, and that its response was now adequate, although he made a number of recommendations (Drew, 2016, pp.4–8).

Professionals

Much focus of the public and media attention has rightly been on the well-paid senior police and council officers who had a duty to protect children; the police also oversee the investigation of reported crimes. There were, however, a number of workers who were trying to raise the issue of CSE and organised CSA as well as support the children involved and their families and who deserve recognition for the challenges they faced on a daily basis. In particular, Jayne Senior and the staff at Risky Business were very much at the coalface of such work, treading such a fine line when working with the children and young people who were in touch with their service and who unsurprisingly were quite emotionally volatile and unpredictable as a result of their experiences. Staff had to listen to stories told to them by abused and traumatised children which no one should ever have to tell. This was further compounded by being unable to prevent them associating with their 'intimate terrorists', as the fear of what would happen if they did not go with them was worse than what would happen if they did. Jayne Senior's book *Broken and Betrayed* is a testament to the difficult circumstances in which they worked, and the very complex lives of the children and young people whom they were supporting before RMBC closed the project down (Senior, 2016).

As well as Risky Business staff, other professionals in Rotherham such as youth workers, residential workers, teachers, nurses and some frontline social workers did their best to support the children in very difficult circumstances while struggling to understand the apparent senior management indifference for so long. Some professionals were also intimidated by the perpetrators themselves, particularly those working in residential children's homes, as noted by Casey: 'Fear was also evident at times among professionals, teachers, hostel workers and youth workers' (2015, p.17).

The damage to the reputation of SYP and RMBC has been significant, and the impact and consequences of the disaster have been phenomenal. Workloads and spending have increased dramatically as a result of the inquiries and inspections, in an environment where staff and resources are already reduced due to public sector austerity cuts. The combination of these factors is likely to have impacted greatly on the morale and stress levels of staff working in those organisations and elsewhere in the town. The majority of staff in all Rotherham agencies have been deeply affected by what has happened and are committed to improving the lives of the children and families with whom they work. However, they need sufficient resources, staffing levels and training in conjunction with effective management and supervision to enable them to work safely with children and young people at risk as well as those already embroiled in organised child sexual abuse.

Perpetrators

The first prosecutions for offences related to the organised sexual abuse of children in Rotherham – the result of Operation Central – did not occur until 2010, 13 years after Risky Business was first established and started highlighting the issue to SYP and RMBC. This trial resulted in the conviction of five men for sexual offences against children, who were sentenced to a total of 32 years (*Yorkshire Post*, November 2010). Unfortunately, two subsequent operations – Czar and Chard – failed to result in any prosecutions, although some men were arrested and some abduction notices served (Jay, 2014, p.4 and p.66). In 2012, Operations K-Alphabet, Kappa and Carrington began, and finally in 2013 an operation into historic CSE offences in Rotherham was announced (Jay, 2014, pp.4–5). As will be discussed in Chapter 5, the first Operation Clover trial resulted in five Rotherham offenders convicted for a total of 102 years; the second resulted in eight men convicted, including one who was convicted at both trials. At the time of writing those offenders are awaiting sentencing.

In light of the above, it is obvious that until 2014 when the first arrests under Operation Clover were finally made, perpetrators of organised child sexual abuse in Rotherham were largely untouched by law enforcement agencies. They were also mostly unhampered in their involvement in other crimes such as Class A drugs supply, violence and intimidation. This enabled them to continue to abuse and terrorise the victims and their families. The lack of disruptive action of any type, but particularly in relation to investigation and prosecution, meant that their criminal trajectories were allowed to proceed uninterrupted, drawing in other 'wanna-be' child sex abusers as it was unsurprisingly seen as low-risk/high-gain activity, commanding significant kudos among their peers.

> Perpetrators in Rotherham generated real fear. They were often perceived to be connected to other forms of criminality and violence and victims and their families were too frightened to speak and did not feel the police could protect them. They were threatened and intimidated into silence. Victims and their families speak of groups of men in cars waiting outside their house or outside children's homes, sometimes attempting to break in. Phone calls and texted threats, including threats to rape other members of the family, were described to us. (Casey, 2015, pp.17–18)

The ultimate consequence of agency failure was to render CSE and organised CSA as the gift that kept on giving to the abusers. For little effort and investment by the perpetrators, increasing numbers of young people were groomed and abused. The children of Rotherham were seen as easy targets, and there was no or little consequence for those perpetrating the abuse which they meted out to those children. It is, therefore, no wonder that the number of young people identified as being abused by Jay (2014) differed so significantly from that initially reported by Adele when working on the Home Office Pilot in 2001. What this means is that with the failure of statutory agencies in Rotherham to respond, increasing numbers of children were placed at risk and abused, when clearly their rape and torture could have been avoided, along with other serious forms of criminality which also damage local communities, such as the supply of Class A drugs.

It is pleasing to see that operations are now being conducted and offenders brought to justice (see Chapters 5 and 6) and it demonstrates exactly what can be achieved when erroneous attitudes and inaction by senior police and council officers are challenged by powers far mightier than the few of us who were working in Rotherham during the period covered by the Jay report. While we are very grateful for the tireless reporting by Andrew Norfolk from *The Times* into CSE and the statutory agencies in Rotherham, it leaves a bitter taste that so much effort has been expended on investigating perpetrators, essentially as a result of the damage inflicted by a national newspaper and the subsequent repercussions such as repeated appearances in front of the Home Affairs Select Committee. Operation Clover was first launched in the summer of 2013; this was within weeks of Arshid Hussain's name being printed in *The Times*, despite him not being convicted for CSA offences at that time. It seems that SYP and RMBC could risk ignoring reports from their own staff about the abuse and violence being meted out to children for whom they had a statutory duty to protect, but they could not risk ignoring negative media coverage and political criticism.

Financial costs

The economist Aliya Saied-Tessier, writing as part of an NSPCC report (2014), estimated that the cost of child sexual abuse in the UK was £3.2 billion in 2012. This includes intra-familial abuse as well as CSE and organised CSA, but comprises expenditure in relation to mental and physical health, children and adult's social care services, criminal justice services, children's services and the economic loss as a result of unemployment or reduced earnings.

The number of inspections and inquiries that have been ordered into Rotherham and South Yorkshire Police have been numerous. They include:

- Jay report (2014)

- Casey report (2015)

- Her Majesty's Inspectorate of Constabulary's *National Child Protection Inspection* (2014) and *Post Inspection Review* (2015)

- several internal audits (some conducted by external consultants)

- Ofsted inspections (2014 and 2016)

- SYP Police and Crime Commissioner's Inquiry (Drew, 2016) and an associated further review (forthcoming).

One way or another, the costs of these inquiries and inspections have come out of the national public purse, funded ultimately by tax payers. In addition, the local financial drain in terms of staff time and other resources for pre-inspection/inquiry preparations, and participation and follow-up work in relation to drawing up, implementing and monitoring action plans to address recommendations is immeasurable. And this is all on top of the day job for staff who are likely already to feel stressed and overworked, in services which are under-resourced.

In addition, there have been the costs attached to policing the far right and counter demonstrations in Rotherham, which initially took place on a monthly basis. There has been a wholesale training programme of police officers and other staff in relation to CSE awareness and understanding. There are also the costs of the major incident teams that have been established to investigate suspects with an aim of charging and bringing them to trial. The costs of the IPCC and NCA investigations are also significant, with many officers and staff working on operations related to SYP's handling of historic CSE and organised CSA cases. It is estimated that the NCA Rotherham inquiry alone will last for eight years (six years for investigations and a further two years for prosecutions), at a cost of over £30 million (*The Times,* June 2016). In June 2015 there were 32 officers working on the inquiry; 12 months on that number had doubled to 68, with funding for a further 48 posts agreed by the Home Office.

At the time of writing, approximately 40 victims and survivors are currently involved in bringing a class action against SYP for negligence and breaches under the Human Rights Act 1998, which protects against 'inhuman or degrading treatment'. In addition, approximately 55 victims and survivors are taking action against RMBC for these failures. While it may still be some time before these cases are heard in a court, they could result in these two organisations having to pay substantial damages to the women involved.

Summary

While this book is about learning the lessons for the victims and survivors of organised child sexual abuse in Rotherham, this opening chapter demonstrates there have been other very significant repercussions which have emerged as a consequence of the catastrophic statutory agency failings in the town. The public loss of confidence and the damage to the reputation of Rotherham by those employed and elected to serve the people of the town are immeasurable. It may have been inaction at its best, or wilful neglect and corruption at its worst. Only when all the inquiries and investigations are completed will we have any chance of really understanding what happened. The distress, anxiety, anger, frustration and damage to personal self-confidence and professional morale, which will have undoubtedly been suffered by victims, survivors, families, professionals, the Pakistani community and the people of Rotherham as a whole, are unfathomable.

In her 2003 report, Angie quoted from Lord Laming's report into the murder of Victoria Climbié, another pivotal moment in the history of child protection in England. In an effort to gird senior officers into action, she drew on the most important and influential report of the time:

> I strongly believe that in future those who occupy senior positions in the public sector must be responsible to account for any failure to protect vulnerable children from deliberate harm or exploitation. (Laming, 2003: 1.27, cited in Heal, 2003, p.54)

Unfortunately, in the case of Rotherham, it took another 11 years for senior officers and officials to be questioned about the failure to protect children from deliberate and organised child sexual abuse; some of whom were more than a little reluctant. This chapter evidences the mass fall-out from their woeful professional behaviour and touches on the impact this has had on so many lives.

It should not have occurred. It did not need to happen. It was all so unnecessary. If only people in senior positions had listened and acted.

Chapter 2

Defining and Identifying Child Sexual Exploitation and Organised Child Sexual Abuse

Introduction

The phrase child sexual exploitation (CSE) is a relatively new term for an established form of abuse. Public and professional recognition of CSE as child abuse had been slow to emerge until the shocking details of towns like Rotherham, Rochdale, Oxford and others appeared in the national and international media. The resulting dialogues have informed our understanding, so many of us now know it is abusive, traumatic, criminal and a child protection issue. In this chapter we explore some of the issues captured by the definition of CSE, including gender, age, the concept of reward and exchange, vulnerabilities, lack of recognition of abuse, online and mobile phone technology and violence and intimidation. We discuss different models adopted by perpetrators intent on initiating children and young people into organised child sexual abuse (CSA). We consider how professional assumptions can unwittingly facilitate the abuse, allowing the perpetrator to continue inflicting significant harm with impunity and the child to go unprotected and in turn increase their vulnerability. Finally, we discuss some of the indicators of involvement in CSE, both in relation to victims and their abusers.

This chapter is key for all practitioners working with children and young people, to facilitate understanding of the complex issues involved. It is illustrated with case studies or scenarios based on practice experiences. While there are specialist projects to which victims can be referred, CSE is a safeguarding issue to which all practitioners should be able to respond. Our intention here is to equip practitioners with sufficient knowledge to be able to recognise CSE and be able to respond more confidently, quickly, appropriately and with sensitivity, which will ultimately benefit the child and their family.

Defining child sexual exploitation

The term CSE is now recognised throughout the UK and beyond. When Barnardo's first published *Whose Daughter Next* (Van Meeuwen *et al.*, 1998), the term was 'abused through prostitution'. There were references in legislation such as the Sexual Offences Act 2003 to 'child prostitution'. Neither of these terms reflects the reality of this type of abuse, suggesting that somehow there is a transaction in it, an element of consent or reward, which in itself minimises the trauma experienced by the victim. It implies that they are somehow compensated, or responsible, for their abuse. It also proposes that the victim has a degree of control over their abuse. The reality is that victims of CSE are children, not consenting adults; such terms are therefore inappropriate and conceal the actuality of the harm inflicted. Often such children are extremely vulnerable, and are targeted, manipulated, controlled and abused without any real understanding of what is happening to them.

The term 'child sexual exploitation' first officially appeared in *Safeguarding Children and Young People from Sexual Exploitation: Supplementary Guidance* (Department for Education, 2009):

> The sexual exploitation of children and young people under 18 involves exploitative situations, contexts and relationships where young people (or a third person or persons) receive something (e.g. food accommodation, drugs, alcohol, cigarettes, affections, gifts, money) as a result of them performing, and/or another or others performing on them, sexual activities. Child sexual exploitation can occur through the use of technology without the child's immediate recognition; for example being persuaded to post sexual images on the internet/mobile phones without immediate payment or gain. In all cases those exploiting the child/young person have power over them by virtue of their age, gender, intellect, physical strength and/or economic or other resources. Violence, coercion and intimidations are common, involvement in exploitative relationships being characterised in the main by the child's or young person's limited availability of choice resulting from their social/economic and/or emotional vulnerability. (p.9)

This definition is probably the most comprehensive available and remains widely quoted. It is used, for example, by the National Society for the Prevention of Cruelty to Children (NSPCC) in guidance on its website and in statutory guidance such as the *Tackling Child Sexual Exploitation Action Plan* (Department for Education, 2011), as well as being used in safeguarding children policies and procedures written by Local Safeguarding Children Boards across the UK. In February 2016, the Department of Health launched a consultation on proposed changes to the current definition. While we are still awaiting the outcome of that consultation at the time of writing, we believe there are several points in the current definition worthy of further consideration.

Gender

When *Whose Daughter Next?* (Van Meeuwen *et al.*, 1998) was first published, it reflected a widespread belief that this form of abuse predominantly affected girls. As with other forms of sexual abuse, there was an unspoken assumption this was a type of abuse that did not affect boys; that boys could not be raped; that boys were able to look after themselves. Indeed, the majority of the specialist projects in the country only worked with young girls. It was not until the publication of *No Son of Mine!* three years later (Palmer, 2001), that there was an acknowledgement that CSE was also an issue for males in the UK. Although the legislation and guidance now makes gender-neutral references to children and young people, there is still a marked difference in service provision for boys and young men compared with girls and young women at risk of CSE, and those who are being groomed or being abused. The *Call to End Violence Against Women and Girls: Action Plan* (Home Office, 2011) did little to challenge such stereotypical views of boys. Publications such as *Research on the Sexual Exploitation of Boys and Young Men* (McNaughton Nicholls *et al.*, 2014) note how little is still known about their experiences and needs, despite them being a 'sizeable minority' of cases. The UK-wide work of the BLAST! Project in Yorkshire, which works with boys and young men at risk of CSE and high profile cases such as the murder of 14-year-old Breck Bednar (BBC Online News, January 2015), continue, however, to evidence the vulnerability of boys in relation to CSE.

The scoping study undertaken by McNaughton Nicholls *et al.* (2014), looking at young men in contact with Barnardo's projects across the UK, found that although there were commonalities in young girls and young boys' involvement in CSE, there were also some distinguishing factors. These included:

- Boys identified by services tended to be younger.

- More males than females were reported to have disabilities.

- The vast majority of young offenders identified as being at risk of CSE were male.

- Sexual orientation often resulted in different service responses to those who were heterosexual rather than gay.

Pathways to exploitation included the same models as for girls, but also some distinct ones: the trusted friend/shared interest model where someone befriends a young man, either directly or online, and establishes a friendship with them (often non-sexual and often building on a common interest such as gaming or a hobby). The sexual experimentation model is often hidden or covert and centres around a young man's exploration of his sexuality. Another identified model involves female perpetrators (often in a position of trust). The final model identified by the scoping exercise is one of institutional abuse. Additional enablers (which are discussed in more detail later in this chapter) were identified as trafficking, technology, online sexual content aimed at men, and professional responses, particularly those based on a belief that boys could not be sexually exploited.

Although awareness and understanding regarding the CSE of young girls has grown in the last few years, the same cannot be said of young men. Recent practice examples shared with the authors include professionals writing off abuse by older men as 'normal in gay relationships', assumptions that young men cannot be vulnerable and a misinterpretation of indicators that resulted in the young man concerned being labelled as being involved in anti-social behaviour. The following case study is reproduced with the permission of BLAST.

> Adam became mates with some of the men that he and his mate Declan met down the park. The men were in their early twenties, had alcohol with them, and gave some to Adam and Declan, and to other young people at the park. Once the young people had drunk a certain amount of alcohol, they would all start playing drinking games, which would include being dared to do sexual things. One night Adam was dared to have sex with a girl with everyone watching. He did this while the men in their early twenties recorded it on their mobile phones, who were laughing and joking.

In this case the grooming process involved normalising relationships with adult males, lowering inhibitions through the consumption of alcohol and gradually introducing sexual activity that appeared to be 'just a bit of fun'. In fact, both Adam and the girl concerned were incited to engage in sexual activity for the gratification of the older males. This, the recording of the abuse and the subsequent use of the material to ensure Adam's continuing engagement and compliance with the adult men were all crimes under the Sexual Offences Act 2003. Practitioners, however, did not initially recognise what had happened to him as being abusive or a cause for concern. Their responses were focused on the young woman, whom they had no difficulty as identifying as a victim of CSE.

As this illustrates, there can still be a significant difference in professional responses to CSE when young men are involved. Whereas professionals are often clear what action is needed regarding girls, boys are often seen in a different, less sympathetic light. Stereotypes around masculinity and vulnerability, along with assumptions made about female perpetrators, can often mean that young men do not get the appropriate response until they are high risk. This, along with public narratives concerning young men involved in sexual abuse always being perpetrators, acts as a further restraint to young men telling anyone about their abuse. The publicity of a 15-year-old boy groomed and abused by a male and female perpetrator (Daily Post Online, September 2014) attracted comments on a public news forum such as, 'Free sex and drugs at 15, he should be thanking his lucky stars.' Comments such as these, concerns about being labelled gay, indecent images of them being shared and feelings of shame that they could not protect themselves, all act to silence young men who consequently remain invisible to professionals and services. *The Office of the Children's Commissioner's Inquiry into Child Sexual Exploitation in Gangs and Groups Interim Report* (Berelowitz *et al.*, 2012) echoed these narratives in professional responses:

> the panel was concerned that some professionals did not view these relationships as exploitative. Boys were considered 'lucky' to be having sex with an older woman. This perception held, even when older men were implicated in setting up the exploitation. (p.89)

Berelowitz *et al.* also describe how 'gender sometimes influenced the decisions of professionals, with boys more likely to be perceived as perpetrators only' (p.85). They noted how professional awareness of young boys as potential victims of CSE was generally poor. Where it was good, there was a marked difference:

> Four out of the 14 sites failed to identify any boys and young men as victims, while girls and young women who were victims were identified at every site. Only one of the 23 young people interviewed by the Inquiry was a male victim. However, where agencies were looking out for boys and young men who were victims, the gender split, while still present, was less pronounced. (Berelowitz *et al.*, 2012, p.88)

The implications of this are that male victims of CSE are being missed by services. The Excellence for Boys project (E4B), funded by the Department for Education, ran from April 2013 to March 2015 and was delivered by BLAST in Yorkshire. The *Summary of Initial Findings* (BLAST, 2015) shows that at the start of the project, partners had cumulatively identified 91 boys and young men at risk of CSE. By the close of the project, this had increased to 249, an increase of 174 per cent. Contributing factors to this increase included practitioner awareness of boys as being potentially vulnerable to grooming and CSE, and improved confidence in practice responses. This suggests male victims definitely exist, but most practitioners are not looking for or recognising them. Practitioners and managers must also heed one of the key messages of the Equality Act 2010: service providers are acting unlawfully if they discriminate on the basis of a protected characteristic. This includes treating a person less favourably and/or discriminating against them as a result of their gender.

Age

As referenced in the Introduction, the legal definition of a child, as laid down in the Children Act 1989, includes those young people up to the age of 18. This distinguishes CSE as a child protection issue, not a consensual act. By including children up to their 18th birthday, the definition makes a distinction between those aged over 16 who are consenting to and engaging in healthy sexual relationships, and those who are children in need of protection, who are targeted and involved in predatory and abusive 'relationships'. In reality, however, this is not without its challenges. While the inclusion of 16–18-year-olds in the definition is compatible with the spirit and provision of the law, there has been a pervasive culture in the UK of regarding children in this age group as being different from those under 16. They are treated as already being adults, as less likely to engage in CSE and less in need of protection than younger children. This is illustrated by the following case study:

> Katie was nearly 16 when her mother noticed that she was bringing home expensive items such as clothing, handbags and jewellery that she had no means of purchasing. Concerned that her daughter may be involved in criminal activity such as shoplifting, her mother talked to Katie about how she had obtained these items. She told her mother that she had been given them by her boyfriend. Her mother became concerned as the value of the gifts was beyond the means of most young men Katie's age. She was also worried about the amount of time Katie was spending with him, and that she had begun staying out overnight and not attending school. She became even more concerned when she found out that her daughter's boyfriend was an adult male, several years older than Katie. When she tried to talk to Katie about this, there was a violent disagreement and Katie left the family home, saying that she was going to live with her boyfriend. Katie's mother reported her missing and also asked social care for help. She was told that as Katie was approaching 16, and that the relationship was clearly consensual, there was nothing anyone could do about it. The police took a similar view, saying that Katie did not tell them that she was being abused so there was no action they could take. In reality, the 'boyfriend' was 38 years old and a number of concerns about his relationships with young vulnerable girls had been shared with social care and the police in the past.

Katie's case demonstrates some of the challenges that may be encountered in cases involving children who are close to or over the age of 16. Although they are technically still a child under UK law, there can be professional confusion about the age a child becomes an adult and therefore is no longer entitled to safeguarding children interventions. Children aged between 16 and 18 have more rights and entitlement to independence. Katie, therefore, could consent to a sexual relationship and seek to live independently once she was 16. The significant issue here is to recognise the indicators of abuse that distinguish such relationships from healthy ones. In cases like Katie's, there can be a professional complacency concerning children of this age. There may be an assumption that because they are older they are less vulnerable and less in need than a younger child, that they are more capable of protecting themselves. As one practitioner stated to Adele, 'We are not interested in older children. They can look after themselves. We all know that it is the younger kids that die.' It is this type of professional response that permits children like Katie, still under the age of 16, to be abused without challenge and that incentivises abusers to target older children. Some professionals lack the skills to be able to distinguish between healthy relationships and those which may be abusive and criminal in nature. An additional complication is that as a result of grooming, dependency, isolation and trauma, many victims act in a way which suggests that they consent to their situation or that they do not need help. How enquiries are undertaken, how children are spoken to by professionals and how questions to them are framed are tremendously important. This is something we consider further in Chapter 3.

Reward and exchange

Also problematical is the perception that in cases of CSE an exchange takes place, that the perpetrator offers or gives the child a phone, jewellery or alcohol for example, in exchange for an act of a sexual nature. This suggests a transaction that is of mutual benefit; an agreed exchange which compensates or benefits the child. This is dangerous as it normalises an abusive situation and implies that this type of abuse is less significant than other forms of sexual abuse, such as intra-familial sexual abuse. In reality this is how a child is ensnared in such abusive situations. The so-called 'benefit' is the enticement to form a relationship with a predatory adult with abusive intent. We also need to consider the nature of the enticements. Often these are not 'rewards' but reflect the desperate circumstances of the child:

> Amanda had run away from home after an abusive relationship with her stepfather escalated. She arrived in a city without any idea of who she could go to for help, or what she would do when she got there. She quickly ran out of food and was sleeping rough, in parks, travel interchanges or on the street. She thought she must be invisible as no one stopped to ask her if she needed help. This reinforced to Amanda that there must be something wrong with her; that she was worthless and somehow to blame for everything that had gone wrong in her life. When she was sleeping rough one night, Graham offered her a bath and warm meal. It was several days since Amanda had eaten properly and she was hungry, thirsty, cold and tired. Graham told her she could sleep on his sofa and stay as long as she liked. After three days when Graham suggested how she might show her gratitude to him for helping her, Amanda felt unable to say no. She was exhausted, depressed and helpless and what Graham was proposing initially seemed better than returning to live on the streets. After the abuse Amanda had experienced from her stepfather she began to think that what Graham was proposing wasn't that unreasonable, that this was the normality of relationships between men and young women. Amanda was 14 years old.

In Amanda's case, the 'benefit' she received of being compliant in her abuse was a roof over her head, somewhere safe to sleep, food to eat, somewhere warm. These are the basic needs of any human being, let alone a child. By reframing Amanda's experiences in this way, it is clear that her basic needs were used and manipulated by an adult predator in order to groom and rape her, to make her believe her abuse was normal and that Graham was a generous benefactor to whom she should be grateful. The reality is that whatever the perceived benefit, this is something being used by an adult to groom and abuse a child. Often the 'benefit' is something derived from a child's vulnerability. There is no actual benefit for the child at all. Phones, clothes or pseudo-love do not compensate for the abuse they inevitably suffer.

Vulnerability

For most victims, they are often ensnared by an intense grooming process that focuses on their specific vulnerabilities and the opportunities that presents to their abusers. This is also an issue we consider further in Chapter 3. The child's vulnerability is identified by the perpetrator and becomes their direct focus during the grooming process. Often it directly feeds into something the child needs; this can be as simple as wanting love, affection and approval. Consider the following case study:

> Kirsty had experienced emotional, sexual abuse and neglect from a young age. She had been exposed to parental domestic violence, substance misuse, mental health issues and lack of supervision. By the age of six, Kirsty was a carer for her younger siblings, and by the age of nine was a carer for her mother who was experiencing bi-polar episodes. Her home environment was unstable, chaotic and there was a lack of nurture. When Kirsty was 11, she met Lee in the local park where she used to go to clear her head and escape from the noise and chaos of the family home. He was concerned for her welfare and over a period of weeks they met regularly, when Kirsty told Lee everything about her life. He was sympathetic and kind, and listened to her, while being critical of her parents. He paid Kirsty compliments, told her that she was beautiful, cuddled and kissed her. Kirsty had never felt so valued, loved and nurtured. When her abuse began, Kirsty saw it as a natural progress of her relationship with a man that by now she adored and relied on. When other adult males became involved, Kirsty was compliant as she would do anything for the man who made her feel so good about herself. Kirsty had no concept of what a normal or healthy

relationship was. She did not tell anyone about her abuse until she had been raped by a large number of adult men for over four years.

If food, safety and accommodation are considered as essential components in meeting the basic needs of a child, how do we rate the need to be recognised, valued, nurtured and loved? The need to be held, kissed and appreciated? The need to feel good about themselves? In this light, we can see that any perception of child sexual exploitation as a mutually beneficial transaction is distorted, ill-informed and erroneous. It is one that not only contributes to the continuing abuse of the child, but also can result in lifelong vulnerability as it establishes a pattern of them accepting abusive and degrading treatment as normal, and placing their needs and feelings below those of another person.

Victims' lack of recognition of their abuse

Some victims may already have 'distorted thinking' before their involvement in child sexual exploitation starts. This can manifest in a number of different cognitive misrepresentations that can skew someone's perception of themselves and their relationships with others. Usually this is the result of previous abuse, particularly sexual, which has become normalised, or is the result of the relationships around them, as with Chloe.

> Chloe was overheard telling another young woman that she had given ten men blow jobs in the park the previous night and received a pack of cigarettes in exchange. The context of the conversation was that she was boasting about how she had obtained the cigarettes 'for free' and how she could get more the next night. Chloe's perception was that she had obtained 'something for nothing'. When challenged by a project worker, Chloe responded that she was exploiting the adult males and would continue to do so. Prior to coming into care at the age of ten, Chloe had lived in a family home where her father was involved in a number of relationships and had been abusive to his partners. Chloe's mother had left when she was small and she had no subsequent contact from her. From a young

age she had been exposed to violent episodes in the family home and, as her father's alcohol and substance misuse increased, she had contact with adult men coming into the home to sell or take drugs with her father. Chloe was sexually abused by some of these men, and later used by her father as a method to procure substances. She had also suggested to professionals that her father had also sometimes abused her. When Chloe was abused by the men in the park and they gave her cigarettes, her perception of the abuse was at least this time she was getting some benefit from it.

As can be seen from this example, Chloe was preconditioned by her past experiences to accept that abuse was not only a normal part of her life, but also a reasonable demand in exchange for something that she wanted or needed. Sometimes, however, the distorted thinking is as a result of the grooming process, as this case study, reproduced with kind permission from BLAST, illustrates:

Joe was struggling to fit in at secondary school and was isolated with few friends. He was befriended by a local girl his own age and invited to a party. There were lots of young people his own age there and, encouraged by them, Joe drank heavily, took drugs and played games such as 'truth or dare' where he flashed in response to a dare. Joe was befriended by Mike, the adult male who owned the flat where the party took place and told he could go round any time he liked to hang out. He attended several more parties and stayed overnight on a few occasions. After a few weeks Mike told Joe that he owed him several hundred pounds towards the alcohol and drugs he had taken at the flat. Mike persuaded Joe to strip in front of some of his other mates while they masturbated. Although Joe felt unhappy with this, he accepted Mike's explanation that it was an easy way for him to make money, as he had not really had to do anything and none of the men had touched him. Joe later found that Mike had filmed him covertly. Mike said he would upload the video online if Joe didn't do what he wanted. Joe saw his continuing exploitation as the preferred option and did not initially recognise what was happening to him as being abusive or exploitative.

As can be seen from this case study, Joe's vulnerability was his isolation, and his lack of knowledge around warning signs of abuse. Joe did not perceive what Mike was asking of him as abuse, and this enabled Mike to normalise it and film Joe, gaining further ways to exploit him and keep him silent.

As will be discussed in detail in Chapter 3, the grooming process that precedes and accompanies organised CSA is intense and carried out by skilled perpetrators. Victims can be confused about what is happening to them, often believing that they are in a relationship with their abusers or that they care for them in some way. They frequently do not have any concept of healthy relationships and what is 'normal'. Their abuse can be so traumatic that they are in a state of shock or denial about what is happening to them. Some young people, in an effort to survive their ordeal, choose to believe they are in control of the abuse, or that they are responsible for it. Abusers often reinforce messages of guilt, confusion, blame and justification through exerting power and control over their victims. The CSE model shares similarities to models of domestic violence. We know through the work of organisations such as Women's Aid that adult females are often in denial about their abuse, that they are in 'survival mode', and that they find it difficult to leave abusive relationships with their 'intimate terrorists' (Johnson and Leone, 2005). The relevant question, therefore, is why should child victims, often vulnerable, traumatised, emotionally immature and with little or no life experience, be expected to make mature and intelligent assessments and decisions about their abuse? The reality is that they rarely do, nor should professionals expect such maturity.

Online and mobile phone technology

The definition of CSE includes online technology, which is a normal part of young people's lives. Children and young people are 'digital natives' (Prensky, 2001) and use technology to communicate regularly with friends and prospective friends. Part of current youth culture is the drive to share information about themselves and their lifestyles, and to collect 'friends'. Often these are people that they meet and know only in the digital world. In past years, the role of the internet and mobile technology to identify, groom and abuse children has significantly increased. Reports such as *Threat Assessment of Child Sexual Exploitation and Abuse* (Child Exploitation and Online Protection, 2013) detail this. There are a number of reasons given for this rise.

First is the motivation of the abuser for using the internet; it is their *modus operandi* for contacting children. This is because it provides an opportunity to access images of children, which cater for all tastes and perversions, and in the privacy of the abuser's own home. It offers opportunities to communicate with children and young people, but also exchange abusive images and messages with other abusers. It enables them to operate with relative anonymity. The internet also facilitates them to contact multiple children at the same time. It therefore provides limitless opportunities for abusers. Certain sites such as gaming sites can be targeted as they are places where children are part of an online community, where relationships are formed and children befriended. Often children accessing those sites are doing so away from the scrutiny and supervision of parents or carers, whose perception is likely to be that a child is safe, playing games in their bedroom. Parents and carers often feel overwhelmed by, or disinterested in, gaming or technology. They may have difficulty in having open and effective conversations with their children about online safety, and setting up robust parental controls on home computers, particularly for social media sites.

Social media sites are regularly used by abusers to seek out and form relationships with young people and children. Often young people post prolifically on social media: where they are, who they are with, what they are doing, often accompanied by photographs. Location settings are unlikely to be disabled as these restrict use of a smart phone in accessing and utilising popular applications (apps), enabling the perpetrator to know where the children are. Children often disclose personal information when using chatrooms, without being fully aware of who is seeing and using that information. Sometimes profile pictures or avatars attract attention to the young person, especially if they suggest that they may be sexually aware or rebellious. But any child can be vulnerable online. Using Facebook as an example, a young person may accept a friend request from someone they do not know and who they have no means of checking out. When the child accepts the request it means that the person now has access to all of the child's personal information and images, and potentially at least some of their friends'. That action opens up a world of opportunity and a new circle of children to the abuser. They can then begin to identify the interests of a child and any potential vulnerabilities, so they can befriend and skilfully groom them.

> Jonathan had been placed into care by his parents after he told them he was gay. He was groomed online by an adult male, posing as a young man of his age. He agreed to meet him. When he arrived he realised that his 'friend' was significantly older. The man said Jonathan should have sex with him because it was the only way to be sure whether he was gay or not. As an experienced older gay man, he would be able to tell, and if Jonathan wasn't gay, he could go home to his family. Jonathan was frightened that he had been lied to, but did not know how to say no. He described his mind 'going blank', as if it was all happening to someone else. He went with the male to a nearby hotel room, where he was raped.

Another advantage for abusers of the internet is the opportunity to persuade children and young people to make or distribute indecent images of themselves.

> Isobel was 12 years old when she was sent a friend request from a man online, which she accepted. 'James' told her that he was 17 years old and the exchanges between him and Isobel became increasingly flirtatious. James said that he wanted a 'nice picture' of Isobel and that she should use her imagination. Isobel sent a picture of herself in her underwear. James sent back an image of his genitals. He encouraged Isobel to take and share increasingly explicit images and videos of herself and share them with him.

Using instant messaging services and apps such as WhatsApp, the evidential trail can be controlled or eliminated by the abuser, particularly as some now have end-to-end encryption making data more difficult for law enforcement agencies to access. Using apps and websites favoured by young people is a successful method of identifying and contacting potential victims. The sheer number of cases and the complexity of tracing and capturing evidence also presents significant challenges for the police nationwide. It is no surprise that the profile of online and mobile technology has risen substantially in CSE cases in recent years. Two serious case reviews in 2016 highlighted the lack of professional understanding of online grooming, particularly in children's social care (Community Care, September 2016). From an abuser's perspective, using the internet to abuse young people lowers their risk of being apprehended either by the child's parents or the police. There is also a professional perception that online abuse is less significant than direct contact abuse. Where children have made and sent their own images, some professionals do not see this as abuse even when the children have done so as a result of being groomed by a predatory adult who has made contact with them for exactly that purpose.

Violence and intimidation

CSE and organised CSA are brutal forms of abuse. Children are often subjected to unbelievable and terrifying acts of violence in order to obtain and maintain their cooperation, compliance and silence. In *'I thought I was the only one. The only one in the world': The Office of the Children's Commissioner's Inquiry into Child Sexual Exploitation in Gangs and Group Interim Report*, Berelowitz *et al.* (2012) commented on the high levels of sadism and torture the team encountered while researching issues of child sexual exploitation. One quote illustrates how sexual abuse is used as a method to control and humiliate victims:

> In the call for evidence submissions, oral rape was reported most frequently, followed by anal rape... There was a consensus amongst experts that anal and oral rape could be viewed as more humiliating and controlling than vaginal rape and, as such, may be favoured by those who are sexually exploiting children. (p.11)

The following case studies from Adele's private practice are examples of such:

> Ellie said she didn't want to go to a hotel because she knew from previous experience that she would be forced to have sex with a number of men. She was punched repeatedly in the face and taken to an industrial estate. An adult male held her arms behind her back while a petrol can was taken from the back of the car. One of her abusers then produced a lighter. Ellie was told that she would be set on fire unless she agreed to go to the hotel and do what she was told without complaint.

> Kaye had the end of her finger amputated by her abuser while other males held her down. The assault was filmed using a mobile phone and used to intimidate and ensure the compliance of other children.

> Jo was forced to witness a severe physical and sexual assault on another girl and was told that the same would happen to her if she did not agree to the demands of her abusers.

The examples above detail how threats against others are used to intimidate young people. Often this involves someone whom the young person cares about, such as a parent or younger sibling, as the following cases illustrate:

> Jenny was told that evening that a group of men would abduct her mother walking home from work, rape and torture her to death.

> When Jay tried to avoid his abusers, a lighted bottle containing flammable substances was pushed through the letterbox of his family home during the early hours of the morning.

> Louisa was telephoned by her abuser, using her young sister's mobile phone. He told her that failure to comply with his requests would have immediate and severe consequences for her sister.

Sometimes the threats are made to 'expose' the young person. This can involve distributing via group contacts on phones, posting images online or telling others what the young person has been doing. *Hunting the Paedophiles – Inside the National Crime Agency* (Channel 4,

December 2015) showed how online grooming was an effective tool to abuse children (again online) and then force the child to abuse their younger siblings and friends.

In examining the definition of CSE, therefore, there are several key components to note:

- the vulnerability of the child

- the resulting opportunities to groom and abuse

- the identification and use of things that the young person needs or wants

- the intensity of the grooming process

- the use of violence and threats to control.

CSE and CSA are complex forms of significant harm that involve emotional, physical and sexual abuse and the targeting of vulnerable children by groomers who turn into abusers. It never involves a consensual exchange or activity in which the child has any control.

Models of child sexual exploitation

There are a number of different ways in which children become involved in CSE and organised CSA, and throughout the UK there are several prevalent paradigms. Some perpetrators act opportunistically as individuals, for example by identifying a vulnerable young person who is missing from home or school, or targeting them online. Others act in groups, in which the abuse is more organised. It can be a one-off act, or a series of abusive incidents over a period of time. It often involves groups of abusers acting together.

The 'boyfriend' model

This model was originally developed by Barnardo's in 1998. Although it has been adapted several times since, the core principle remains the same. This is where a process of grooming makes the victim believe they are in a relationship with the perpetrator. The process focuses on making the abuser seem like the solution to any issues the young person has, for example making them feel attractive and valued, persuading them that there are more fun places to be than school or home, criticising the treatment of the young person by carers or professionals such as teachers – all of which serve to increase the young person's dependency on the abuser. In a relatively short period of time, the perpetrator can make the young person believe that they are the only person who understands them and their issues, and who can be relied on to respond to their needs. The process creates a total dependence on the perpetrator and a willingness to do anything to both please and appease them. Often the use of drugs or alcohol by the young person is encouraged or facilitated by the abuser to create an additional dependency. This model closely echoes the Duluth (Home of the Duluth Model, undated) domestic violence paradigms of power and control where the victim becomes isolated, intimidated, coerced, abused and controlled. The reinforcement of the grooming process becomes intertwined with acts of physical, emotional and sexual violence and abuse which are minimised by the abuser, who often places the blame on the victim. It takes advantage of the intensity of adolescent relationships; first relationships as teenagers or young adults often involve powerful emotions of being in love, and feeling valued and appreciated as an individual for the first time. Any child can be vulnerable to this *modus operandi*. The term 'boyfriend' model, however, is misleading as both boys and girls can be abused in this way and by male and female perpetrators.

Groomers often target their victims in places where they naturally congregate – places of apparent safety such as parks, leisure multiplexes and shopping centres. This makes their initial advance seem more normal and less threatening. Often victims are with their friends when they are initially approached by a group of people around their own age. That this happens in an everyday place and that no one objects or seeks to prevent it reinforces to the young person that any misgivings they have are misplaced or wrong. Often they want to fit in with their peer group, or impress someone older or adult; this further suppresses any anxieties they may have. Abusers often manipulate children's lack of experience or knowledge to make them feel that what is happening is normal. Professional responses can also reinforce a young person's perception of normality, if the relationship is not seen as a cause for concern.

At the core of this model is a process of ensnaring, creating dependency and gaining control. The young person's compliance is driven by feelings of love for their abuser, of not wanting to lose them, not wanting to displease them and the certainty that the abuse must in some way be normal or acceptable because they believe their abuser loves them and would not intentionally hurt them. Like victims of domestic violence, when the abuse escalates victims often blame themselves for their abuser's behaviour, certain that it must be something that they have done because things used to be good. They are driven by a need for the situation to return to how it was in the grooming and ensnaring period, without recognising that the abuse is the true basis of the relationship. They are victims, not only of CSE, but also emotional manipulation and psychological abuse. This model fits with Johnson and Leone's theory of the 'intimate terrorist' (2005) as discussed in the Introduction. The following quotes from Adele's private practice show the hold that some abusers had over young people that she worked with:

> I loved him so much and when I couldn't see him any more I felt like I was dying, like my heart had been ripped out from my chest and I had nothing left to live for.

> All I wanted was to see him. All I could think about was when I was going to see him next.

> I thought to myself 'How lucky am I, to have a boyfriend like this?'

Party house model

Another paradigm is the 'party house' model; also colloquially known in some parts of the country as the 'fag house' model. Sometimes young people are invited to a party or just to 'chill' at a house, owned or occupied by an adult, sometimes a couple, where there is a relaxed, welcoming or exciting atmosphere. Young people can spend time with other young people, and also with adults who provide them with alcohol and drugs (including 'new psychoactive substances' formerly known as 'legal highs'), and give them access to gaming consoles as well as pornography and, perhaps most attractively, impose no boundaries or rules on them at all. In such houses there is no challenge to any behaviour or language; these adults encourage young people to go missing from home, to visit them and bring other young people with them. They are good listeners, sympathising with the young people's problems and grievances and reinforcing the belief that parents and professionals working with them do not understand them nor have their best interests at heart. They encourage young people to phone or text their parents and carers so that they are regarded as 'unauthorised absences' rather than 'missing' from home or care, which has implications for safeguarding and police responses (as discussed in Chapter 4). These adults also help to conceal the young person if the police visit the property in response to a missing person's report, which gives an added feeling of collusion and protection. Over time, the grooming process leads to abuse, either by the adults themselves or by other associates visiting the house who are introduced to the young people.

There are several elements to this model. Young people abused after visiting a party house often blame themselves for their abuse, as these quotes from Adele's private practice demonstrate:

> I knew I shouldn't have been there. I mean, we were drinking, smoking stuff and hiding from the police. Lying to parents and stuff. I knew it was dodgy but it just seemed like a bit of fun at the time.

> The police must've thought that I was a right pain in the arse, they were always there looking for me. They told me they were going to charge me with wasting police time.

As a result, young people involved in this model can feel disconnected, isolated and misunderstood by parents, carers or professionals. The 'party house' initially offers something attractive and fun, that initially meets their needs. There is also the perception that risks are diluted when young people are part of a group, and that they will be safer. In reality, however, any misgivings or doubts they express are often minimised or dismissed by their peers, as well as their abusers. The process of isolation and dependency on their abusers increases as they gain a reputation both in the local community and with professionals as being 'trouble'; engaging in anti-social behaviour, low-level offending and misusing substances. In this way, young people targeted by this model of exploitation are even less likely to be seen as victims of abuse or as children in need of protection.

Peer-on-peer exploitation

Peer-on-peer exploitation is a difficult model for many professionals to identify, perhaps because it is often misinterpreted as 'normal' childhood relationships or because there is a common misconception that CSE is only perpetrated by adults. It can involve a child being abused by a child who is the same age, older or, in a few cases, younger than them. The abuse can take place at school, in their local area and online. The abusing child may be the opposite gender or the same sex as the victim. As with the other models, it often involves a power imbalance between the abuser and their victim. This can be the abusing child taking advantage of the other child to explore their sexuality, or the abused child feeling isolated because of bullying or because they are from a different cultural or religious background to the majority of their peers. A child may befriend a vulnerable child who is unhappy because of problems at home. A child may persuade another to engage in sexual acts because 'everyone else is doing it'. An abusing child may give another child alcohol or drugs, with the purpose of disinhibiting them so that they can more easily persuade them to engage in sexual activity.

There are several patterns associated with this model. Older children may take an interest in younger children, befriending them both in the real world and online. Sometimes an older child has a history of having 'relationships' with younger children. Children of any age can be groomed by older children on social media. Often they are encouraged to 'sext' – exchange provocative or indecent images or videos of themselves which are then used to blackmail them into providing more explicit images or to engage in a sexual activity with the older child. This type of abuse is also employed by older perpetrators, as discussed above. Peer-on-peer CSE and abuse are common as part of a gang culture. Children can be recruited, 'claimed' or targeted by gang members, either as rivals or even within their own gang, as discussed in more detail below. Often they are identified and targeted in the community or through social media. With gangs, sometimes the initiation into the gang involves acts of abuse and sexual exploitation. Children already involved with abusive adults can also groom and exploit other children, often introducing them to the perpetrators. As with all forms of CSE, one or even both of the children (if the 'abusing' child has been groomed and abused themselves) may be unaware that they are involved in abuse. Also, as with other models of CSE, there are likely to be feelings of confusion, doubt and self-blame which prevent them from identifying or telling anyone about the abuse.

Online abuse

As discussed above, the rise of online abuse is causing concern. In its publication, *Threat Assessment of Child Sexual Exploitation and Abuse*, CEOP notes:

> the most common offending environment was social networking (SN) at 48.5%, with instant messaging and chat accounting for another 31%. OCSE (online child sexual exploitation) on gaming sites and mobile phones featured in a total of 10% of reports. Of interest is that 16% of reports received during 2012 involved multiple online environments. (2013, p.11)

Inevitably, sites commonly used by children and young people are most likely to be targeted by abusers. This includes Facebook, Instagram, Snapchat, Tumblr and YouTube, as well as gaming and websites aimed at children with blogging or chat facilities. Children and young people who use attractive photos of themselves or suggestive names or avatars are most likely to be approached by predatory adults scouting for potential opportunities. Skype is also a site used by potential abusers, with speculative requests to chat being linked to attractive profile pictures, names and avatars that suggest that someone might be approachable.

The model of online abuse differs from direct abuse not just in the different levels of risks and potential availability of numerous victims, but also in the reduced length of time required in the grooming process:

> the period of time between initial engagement with a child and an offending outcome is often extremely short... A key departure from traditional ideas of online grooming is that offenders focus on quickly gaining leverage over a victim rather than first establishing a trusting relationship. A common feature of OCSE in 2012 was the investment of small amounts of time by perpetrators in a large number of potential victims. (CEOP, 2013, p.10)

What this tells us is that online abuse has quickly become established as a very efficient model for abusers to identify, target, groom and abuse children and young people. There are also perceived additional advantages against the backdrop of police nationally struggling to respond effectively (Daily Mail Online, October 2014).

Gangs

Phase two of the Children's Commissioner's inquiry published two further reports: *'If only someone had listened'* (Berelowitz *et al.*, 2013) and *'It's wrong...but you get used to it'* (Beckett *et al.*, 2013). The research team identified several key features of gang-associated sexual violence and exploitation that were unique to, or exacerbated by, a gang environment. These included using sex as a means of initiating young people into a gang; sexual activity in return for (perceived) status or protection; young women 'setting up' people in other gangs; establishing a relationship with or feigning sexual interest in a rival gang member as a means of entrapment; and sexual assault as a weapon in conflict. In gang situations, young women are thought to be more vulnerable to sexual violence and sexual exploitation than young men. Young women who have already been exploited in gangs are also said to be more likely to experience repeat victimisation as they are seen to have lost rights to refuse or have been conditioned to comply. Also at risk are female members of a gang member's family – either from a member of their own gang or from a rival gang.

Group-orientated CSE is often mixed in with gang-related CSE, but the two are very different. Group-related CSE tends to occur where a number of abusers act in a coordinated way for mutual sexual gratification, as the following news story from Rochdale shows:

> Nine men who ran a child sexual exploitation ring in Greater Manchester have been jailed. The men from Rochdale and Oldham, who exploited girls as young as 13 were given sentences ranging from four to 19 years. They were found guilty of offences including rape and conspiracy to engage in sexual activity with a child. Liverpool Crown Court heard the group plied five victims with drink and drugs and 'passed them around' for sex. (BBC Online News, May 2012)

One of the abusers arranged for a 15-year-old girl to have sex with a group member, as a birthday treat for him. Other members of the group groomed individual young women with the intention of sharing them with group members. As can be seen from this example, while there is some crossover with the gang-related model of CSE, including misogyny, power and control, group-related CSE is a distinct and separate model.

While this chapter has provided a summary of the most prevalent models of CSE and organised abuse in the UK, there are other models in existence. These are worthy of mention as the complex nature of CSE means that the prevalence and types of models change over time. As professionals gain knowledge and confidence in responding to models of CSE-related offending behaviour, perpetrators shift their tactics in order to reduce associated risks. As technology changes, so will opportunities for abusers to target young people.

As young people's behaviours change, so will that of their potential abusers. Some other current models of CSE are outlined below.

Trafficking

While the issue of international trafficking has been in the public and professional domain for some years now, less recognised is the concept of domestic trafficking, where children are moved from one location to another within the same country, city, town or community for the purposes of sexual exploitation. The advantages for an abuser is that the child is more likely to be disorientated, isolated, more dependent on the abuser and therefore more compliant if they are in an unfamiliar place. The child is less likely to know where to go for help and less likely to be seen by those who know and can help them. While long distances are not necessary for it to be classed as trafficking, there is an advantage for abusers in travelling to another local authority or police area, where professionals are less likely to be aware of them and their involvement in CSE, and therefore there is less scrutiny of their abusive activities.

Families

A hidden model of exploitation, already referenced above, involves the abuse of a child in the family home, by family members or by multiple adult visitors. The child may be used by the adults (usually parents) as a method of procurement for drugs, alcohol, payment of debts or in exchange for money. In some cases, a parent is already involved in adult sex work and their children subsequently become involved either at the request of an abuser or because the children are following a familiar and recognised pattern of behaviour established by their parent. This is not to suggest that the children of sex workers regularly become involved in child abuse, but it is a model that needs to be recognised. What also needs to be acknowledged is that often the parents are victims themselves, targeted by perpetrators as a result of their own vulnerabilities, as well as the possibility of abusing their children.

Targeting groups in the community

Some models are purely opportunistic. As already noted, perpetrators will often target or visit places where young people congregate such as leisure complexes, shopping centres and parks, public places as well as those places associated with anti-social behaviour. There are opportunities within those settings to identify individual vulnerabilities, target, groom and abuse. Legitimate businesses may be used by perpetrators to lure young people into direct contact. Takeaways, clubs and taxis premises have featured in several reviews such as Jay (2014) and Griffiths (2013), and are discussed in Chapter 7. In the cases identified, young people were enticed to these places with the promise of free taxi rides, food, alcohol, cigarettes and drugs, as well as a place to 'chill' and hang out with older children and adults, before the grooming and abuse starts. As they visit, either the children are introduced to abusers and groomed or a demand is made for payment in kind: sexual favours in exchange for the items that they have been given. Children are encouraged to bring friends with them or tell other children about the benefits of visiting certain individuals at the business. Anecdotal information given to Adele suggests a similar use of other legitimate businesses, such as car washes, restaurants, nail bars and beauty salons. The latter two examples have an additional feature – they are often run by female proprietors who befriend young women and then introduce them to male friends or partners, who go on to abuse them. Child sexual abusers are highly skilled at creating and exploiting opportunities.

Survival and independent involvement

A final model involves young people who are involved in child sexual exploitation as a method of survival. This includes young people who are missing from home or are homeless, or those with a dependency on drugs and/or alcohol. There may be an element of independent action on the part of the young person involved, in that they seek out sexual contact as a means of obtaining what they need or want. As considered earlier in this chapter, this also applies to those who have previously been abused and view sexual exploitation as a continuation of that abuse, with a perception that they are getting something in exchange. The 'reward', however, often highlights the exploitative nature of the exchange – food, money or shelter for example. There is also a group of young people who believe that their involvement in CSE will be lucrative and 'easy money'. Yet these young people are as vulnerable as others who are also involved, as they have no understanding of the abuse they will experience and with whom they will have contact. The reality is that whatever young people's reasons for their involvement, they are children. The responsibility for the exploitation rests entirely with the adult abusing them.

Indicators of child sexual exploitation

Although CSE is complex and often covert, there will usually be some sign that a young person is involved or at high risk. In Pearce, Williams and Galvin's study (2002), the majority of the 55 young women interviewed had 20 or more indicators. Indicators can often seem related to generic adolescent behaviour or another safeguarding issue and may not initially be questioned by professionals; sometimes they are the result of other issues – such as mental ill health or problems at home – and should not automatically be assumed to be indicators of involvement in CSE. Often it is only when they are considered in a risk assessment or when information is shared between different services that a child's involvement in CSE begins to emerge. It is important to acknowledge that some of the initial indicators may – on the surface – look positive for the young person. In the early stages of the grooming process they may feel personally validated and that their needs are being met. It is possible to see them becoming increasingly happy and confident, taking a pride in their appearance and talking animatedly about new friends or relationships. It is only by considering a full range of information can informed risk assessments be made and the risk of CSE identified. Across the UK, risk assessment tools such as Barnardo's Sexual Exploitation Risk Assessment Framework (SERAF) toolkit (Clutton and Coles 2007) are used to assess whether a child is low risk, medium risk or high risk. Although all levels of risk require a response, different levels of risk require different interventions. It should be remembered, however, that low risk does not mean no risk. A lack of intervention is likely to result in the risk increasing and the young person being abused. Vulnerability, unless addressed, may lead to a young person becoming at risk of being targeted by perpetrators.

Some have expressed concern about the application of CSE indicators within some toolkits, which may be too prescriptive and do not allow room for practitioner judgement (for example, Eaton and Dalby, 2016). Brown *et al.* (2016) also note:

> there is a lack of good quality research on the indicators of risk of, and protection from, child sexual abuse and child sexual exploitation to identify either victims or perpetrators... Many risk assessment tools exist in the UK, but the majority are based on a limited evidence base and have not been evaluated or tested using large-scale, methodologically rigorous research. (p.4)

While bearing such reservations in mind and while we await more evidence-based information about indicators, practitioners should consider the following categories when they are concerned about potential warning signs that a child is involved in CSE or organised CSA. These should be considered as part of their overall assessment and in partnership with the child, their family and other colleagues.

Physical symptoms

There may be obvious signs of physical abuse such as bruising, welts, signs of restraint and other evidence of physical assault. There can be physical indicators of sexual abuse, particularly where the child is abused by a number of perpetrators, such as recurring or multiple sexually transmitted infections, repeated pregnancy tests, pregnancy or termination of pregnancy and multiple urinary tract infections. Additionally, the young person may request more condoms than would normally be expected by dispensing health services. Often their physical health is neglected and there may be indicators of such, including repeated illnesses or increasing susceptibility to illness.

Often victims can start to look unwell or in poor health, and changes in skin and hair condition are sometimes evident. As the abuse progresses, there may also be a decline in their personal hygiene, but as responses to abuse are very individual, other victims can become obsessive about their hygiene and appearance.

Other physical changes in a young person's appearance include rapid weight loss or, less commonly, weight gain. They may start changing their appearance, where there is a sudden interest or decline in their self-presentation or they adopt a different style of clothing that they wear or are interested in buying. There can also be physical indicators relating to the emotional trauma. This can include chronic fatigue, low motivation or aspiration, poor sleeping patterns (in addition to being kept out late or all night), self-harming (including eating disorders and cutting) as well as evidence of drug or alcohol misuse. Psychosomatic indicators such as headaches, migraines, stomach pains, compulsive vomiting and other similar symptoms can occur. Often indicators relate to physical possessions as well, such as money that has no identifiable source, the acquisition of clothes, mobile phones, credit on mobile phones, a number of SIM cards, and other possessions without plausible explanation. Often young people will give accounts of social activities or going somewhere, but the means by which this is funded is in question.

Emotional and behavioural indicators

These indicators are individual to the victim. They can range from volatile and unpredictable behaviour, suffering an extreme array of mood swings, or alternatively becoming extremely passive and compliant. CSE victims can become antagonistic to practitioner engagement or increasingly distrustful of professionals. They can exhibit extreme hostility, use abusive or sexualised language and engage in anti-social or offending behaviour, often as a result of continuing significant abuse combined with underlying feelings of fear and a complete lack of control. Victims often become extremely secretive about their lives and their involvement with perpetrators or other young people. They may use the internet excessively and display anxiety about having their mobile phone with them at all times (in case their abuser wants to contact them). Sometimes this can involve hiding it on their person or having several mobiles or SIM cards.

There can be notable indicators associated with education: unauthorised absences; disordered or aggressive behaviour; loss of concentration or fatigue during lessons; decline in attainment; changes in friendships and leaving school premises to meet or be collected by adults in cars. One issue practitioners may find particularly challenging is an increase in sexualised behaviour where the young person seeks out or engages in multiple and repeated sexual experiences. The reasons for this are debatable. One possibility is that it is a young person's way of proving that they are not damaged by their abuse, that they are no different to any other young person. Another is that they have become conditioned by their abuse so they seek out intimate contact that, however fleeting, makes them feel cared for, as this quote from Adele's private practice suggests: 'When I was having sex I would feel good, loved. Afterwards I felt shit. So I would try again to find someone to make me feel good about myself.'

As referenced above and discussed in more detail in Chapter 4, a key indicator is where a young person is persistently missing or absent from home or care. It is often significant when they are found in places previously identified as being associated with CSE – CSE 'hotspots' – or with adults or children who have been likewise linked. Where the 'boyfriend model' is employed, for example, young people may form associations with peers or adults already identified as possible CSE perpetrators. Another indicator can be a young person's self-perception. They can develop a low self-image as a result of mixed messages from their abusers, and begin to talk about themselves in an extremely negative way. They can display low self-esteem, and express negative expectations of both themselves and others. Depending on the level of trauma and the individual resilience of the young person, symptoms may indicate mental health problems such as profound depression, and self-harming and personality disorders may also emerge. Often these issues can be accompanied and compounded by the misuse of drugs and alcohol.

As the grooming process progresses, an abuser isolates their victim from any person who may either identify what is happening or recognise warning indicators of the abuse. They also make it more difficult for young people to share concerns about what is happening to them with anyone, particularly practitioners. Grooming often involves subtle criticism of key people in the child's life, as well as encouraging behaviour that makes it more likely that the child will be identified as a 'problem' in practitioners' eyes, such as repeatedly going missing from home, low-level offending and unacceptable behaviour at school or home. Often an abuser will manipulate arguments between young people and their parents or carers, and may encourage allegations of abuse against them. As a result, hostility in relationships with parents, carers and other family members often emerges, often accompanied by physical and verbal aggression. This can be targeted at parents, carers, practitioners, siblings, pets, peers and property. Consequently, there may be a placement breakdown if the young person is in care. There may be family breakdown where they are still living at home, and a voluntary decision may be made by the parents for their child to go into care as they feel they can no longer cope with or protect them.

As the young person's isolation increases, they are also likely to become detached from age-appropriate activities and there are changes in their friendship groups. It is likely that they will associate with other young people who are known to be sexually exploited, or they may form a relationship with an older person with no explanation regarding how they met them. Activities and interests also decrease as the victim's world shrinks to include only their abuser, their abuser's friends and associates and their needs. It can be difficult to differentiate between a healthy relationship and an abusive one, especially if the victim and abuser are of a similar age. The distinction can become clear when the young person does not know simple facts such as the abuser's full name, home address, details about their work, school and interests, or know any of their family. These are facts that in a healthy relationship a young person would ordinarily know.

Environmental indicators

This third set of indicators relates to factors external to the young person. Often practitioners focus on indicators around young people's behaviour, and indeed the emotional, behavioural and physical indicators should alert practitioners that the abuse has likely already occurred and requires an effective multi-agency response where the young person consents. Yet the most telling indicators are where information is received in relation to victims visiting CSE hotspots – flats, houses, budget hotels, nightclubs, shopping centres and parks – where previous concerns have been identified or going to adult venues where children would not normally visit. It is often emerging environmental indicators that alert us that a young person is being groomed or is at risk of becoming involved in CSE, before they are abused. Environmental indicators therefore have great significance, particularly regarding early identification and prevention. They often link to specific models of CSE, such as the party house paradigm, the use of legitimate businesses and online environments.

Indicators relating to perpetrators

While the above indicators relate to the behaviour and environments of young people, there are also some specific indicators regarding the behaviour of possible perpetrators. These include:

- online behaviour – sending friend requests and seeking contact with children online and visiting sites popular with children and teenagers such as Teen Chat, Snapchat, Facebook and Instagram; having contact with a number of children online; seeking, viewing or sending indecent images of children, including communications to children

- being frequently seen, alone or with others, in places where young people congregate, but not engaging in any activities other than observing and befriending young people

- making sexualised comments or expressing views about sexual relationships, including normalising contact and sexual relationships with young people or making derogatory comments about younger people that suggest a distorted view

- having friendships with a large number of, or different, young people

- encouraging and facilitating visits by young people to their home or their business premises.

In Brown and colleagues' (2016) rapid evidence assessment, they noted there were a small number of indicators of increased risk of becoming a perpetrator of CSA, which included:

- sexual abuse victimisation

- other forms of abuse and neglect victimisation

- atypical sexual interests/fantasies.

In relation to peer-on-peer abuse, the following indicators can also be relevant:

- having friendships with older people and introducing their peers to them

- having repeated relationships with different younger children

- associating with younger age groups

- exhibiting behaviour and expressing views regarding children which suggest a sexual interest, distorted thinking or a lack of empathy

- showing anti-social behaviour targeting younger people

- mentoring younger people, especially those who are isolated or considered to be vulnerable

- being a member of a gang

- bullying and domineering behaviour towards young people either online or in the real world.

Sometimes there is an overlap of models and indicators. While some indicators relate to a variety of safeguarding or generic adolescent issues, it is vital that we all have professional curiosity and satisfy ourselves that we understand what the issues are for the child or young person. The more indicators there are, the less likely there is to be another explanation; some can only be signs of abuse.

Indicators relating to the behaviour of potential abusers can be just as significant as those relating to young people who may be at risk of CSE. What needs to be remembered is that abuse is associated with a number of indicators, and they all tell a story. It should also not be forgotten, however, that indicators are what they say they are: they signify possible involvement in CSE and organised CSA. They should be used as a part of overall practitioner judgement and not employed in isolation. There is some concern that CSE toolkits, developed and used by many LSCBs and including indicators, as well as being too prescriptive are also too female centric, and where some indicators do not apply to boys and young men (pregnancies, terminations, sexualised clothing, for example) this could result in them being assessed as lower risk when the opposite may in fact be true (Eaton and Dalby, 2016).

The consequences of not recognising indicators are clearly demonstrated by Tanya's account below:

> There'd be occasions we'd be parked up and police would come straight there, and they'd just leave it and go…do you know, like that sort of thing. It were just weird like… They were older, it were always forced upon me…and police couldn't do anything, social services wouldn't do anything. Me mum begged 'em to take me away, that's how bad it were, she begged 'em to take me away from Rotherham and they were like 'no, she's fed, she comes home eventually', that sort of thing. Like, is that realistic? An 11-year-old going missing for two days, 'oh, she comes home eventually'. Do you know what I mean? I mean my mum found me locked inside somewhere and there were a police officer present and he never even did anything. Well, we're still trying to find out if he did ever report it into office. It were just like…'how can you do that?' A 12-year-old

locked in a room, like a metre, a metre-sized room, all damp and disgusting, nowhere to go to toilet, nowhere to get a drink of water, DNA all over place and he were just like 'Do you want dropping off at home or...' and Mum was like 'we'll make us own way'. And it was just left at that. 'Oh I'll come and visit ya in a couple of days to take a statement' and he never turned up and so it were just like... Me mum was a single mum, so she was like struggling like to get to work, she were doing nights, she were coming looking for me all the time...school were reporting that I'd not turned into school. (University of Sheffield Symposium, July 2016)

Tanya's situation demonstrates some of the key learning points from this chapter, and how they were missed in her case. There were a number of very clear indicators that she was being sexually abused. The failure of the professionals who had contact with Tanya and her mother to recognise these as signs of abuse allowed her to continue to be abused. The lack of action taken by professionals – combined with the language used, assumptions made and the lack of support for her family – reinforced the abusers' power and control over her. This is an illustration of how poor professional practice can enable abuse by empowering perpetrators, making victims even more vulnerable and contaminating professional discussions with false assumptions and denial of the facts.

Summary

This chapter highlights a number of key issues of which everyone working with children and young people need to be aware. Children who are being exploited and abused are likely to only disclose their experiences to people they trust; their trust is more likely to be gained when staff can respond confidently and knowledgeably to the details they divulge. While it is the legal responsibility of the police and children's social care to take action in relation to CSA, it is the duty of all practitioners to share information and make referrals to the statutory agencies when they have concerns about a child, as is discussed in Chapter 4.

This chapter has examined some of the specific issues that lie within the statutory definition of CSE, such as gender, age and online and mobile phone technology. Practitioners must be alert to the fact that boys and young men are victims of grooming, sexual exploitation and abuse by child abusers in either the same or a similar way to girls and young women. In comparison with the number of services for girls, there are fewer services working with boys, but that should not be taken as an indication of the prevalence of male child victims. The inclusion of children up to the age of 18 in the definition of CSE presents some challenges to some practitioners. We must remember, however, that vulnerability is not something that dissipates at 16, nor indeed 18. This chapter has also discussed why perpetrators are attracted to online technology, its allure becoming obvious. The perpetrator can be anonymous, have ongoing contact with numerous young people and with relatively little risk. While the internet is of benefit to most, it has a hidden, dark side where its qualities are manipulated for perverted and criminal motivation.

This chapter has also discussed some of the different models of CSE that exist, so that practitioners can understand how perpetrators are able to make contact with victims. This is usually done in such a subtle, skilled way that their relationships with children may go unquestioned by practitioners who do not practise with professional curiosity. Finally, we discussed indicators of CSE, in relation to both victims and perpetrators. There are a number of clear signals that a child is being targeted or is already being sexually abused. The sooner these are identified by practitioners, the quicker appropriate interventions can be offered with the agreement of the young person. Even if the young person does not feel able to participate initially, knowing what is on offer and how to make contact with practitioners when they are ready can reduce their level of risk and increase their protective factors.

As is clear from this chapter, perpetrators are very skilled at grooming and abusing children. They are also highly likely to share information with other abusers; such communications will be concerned with how they can reduce the risk of arrest and investigation and how best to target children for the purposes of their paedophilic and criminal activities. They adapt their *modus operandi* when necessary, in relation to both reducing their risk and targeting children. It is essential that all relevant agencies, therefore, work together using best practice methods in an attempt to keep up with such changes and challenges. In the next chapter, we build on these discussions and consider issues of vulnerability, grooming and trauma.

Chapter 3

Understanding the Impact of Grooming and Organised Child Sexual Abuse

Introduction

The trauma of CSE and CSA should never be underestimated. There is the impact of the emotional abuse, of being betrayed by someone whom the child thought they could trust and whom they thought cared about them. There is the impact of being raped or sexually assaulted, often by multiple perpetrators. There may be the trauma of being trafficked to a location that is unfamiliar, so that they do not know where they are or how to keep themselves safe. They may be in situations where the only way to get out is to comply with the demands of their intimate terrorists, or other abusers. There will be additional threats against them but also against those they love or care about to ensure that they do not tell anyone about the abuse, ever. CSE is a true horror in every sense of the word – sadistic, cruel, depraved, unrelenting and without pity or mercy.

Without doubt, being groomed and abused impacts on all victims. The extent of the impact often depends on the severity of the abuse, the resilience of the individual victim and the vulnerabilities that led to them being targeted in the first instance. This chapter explores issues of vulnerability and grooming, which were introduced in Chapter 2. It also considers the effect being groomed and the subsequent abuse has on victims and their families, and the consequential influence on behaviours and future vulnerability. This chapter is written in two parts: the first details the effect of grooming and abuse on the child and their family; the second discusses practitioner responses, including the impact of poor practice and how it can exacerbate existing trauma.

What makes children and young people vulnerable to child sexual exploitation?

In order to understand the impact of grooming and CSE, we need to understand the reasons why young people become involved in the first place – because grooming frequently targets and exploits an unmet need or existing vulnerability.

There has been a commonly held belief within local authorities and services working with children that those involved in CSE are troubled young women, in the care of the local authority and from broken, dysfunctional or abusive families. In fact, while children in the care of the local authority are particularly vulnerable, there is a range of vulnerabilities that may result in any young person – male or female – being targeted and involved in CSE. Some of these vulnerabilities are well documented and recognised, such as:

- already being in the social care system for reasons such as neglect, emotional and physical abuse

- having parents with issues such as mental health, domestic violence and alcohol and substance misuse

- having a disability – children with a disability are particularly vulnerable as they often have (especially in the cases of cognitive disability) a restricted ability to recognise grooming and unhealthy relationships, to understand the motivations and intentions of those grooming them, or to see their abuse as such (see also Brown *et al.*, 2016)

- having previous experiences of being abused, particularly sexual abuse
- having associations with others already involved in or at risk of CSE
- being homeless
- being accommodated by the local authority
- having a dependency on substances
- missing from education or home
- living in poverty
- being isolated for reasons such as sexual orientation, cultural or religious reasons.

There are, however, other less obvious but perhaps more common vulnerabilities which may result in a young person becoming involved in CSE. All of the following have been present in case audits and reviews that Adele has undertaken in recent years:

- problems at home including significant bereavement and traumatic family breakdown
- an older sibling leaving home or having problems which impact on the family
- unsupervised access to the internet and social media without a good understanding of how to stay safe on the internet
- low self-esteem and confidence, concern about their social interactions and peer integration
- experiences of rejection (particularly parental rejection)
- poor self-image, low aspirations, low expectations

- anxiety about academic attainment and difficulties with transitioning from primary to secondary school

- bullying and poor experiences with peers

- adolescence generally, including imperatives to take risks and reject authority and control

- lack of knowledge and skills regarding healthy relationships and risk.

This wider range of vulnerabilities suggests that any child has the potential to be vulnerable. Even children who are well supported and resilient can become vulnerable. At a trial of eight defendants in October 2016, the prosecution barrister said:

> 'In the space of months, she [the victim] had gone from being a normal happy child from a stable supportive family to one who was secretive and distant... Her mother watched her daughter change from a loving, lovely girl to one she describes as horrible and she was powerless to control it.' (The Star Online, October 2016)

A common period of initial risk is puberty. The 'push' and 'pull' factors associated with adolescence – boundary testing, excitement, approval of peers, self-image and emerging sexuality, as well as rejection of authority and control – can be a time of significant risk. What can add to their initial vulnerability are the attitudes and beliefs of those around them. Views such as 'young gay men often experiment with older men'; 'boys are not as vulnerable as girls'; 'boys should be responsible for what happens to them' or holding the young person accountable for their behaviour and consequent abuse create additional barriers to young people being able to recognise what is happening to them as abuse, and be able to speak about it. This is an issue we consider later in this chapter.

The common denominator in the above examples is the child's unmet needs. They may need validation as a person, advice, companionship, self-worth and to feel wanted, desired, understood, valued and loved. An additional factor that is often overlooked is that the attention of the perpetrator during the initial grooming process is exciting and fun, and is something that the young person often knows a parent or carer would not approve of. In cases where there is no apparent vulnerability, adolescence and its imperatives to seek out excitement, in conjunction with a poor ability to assess levels of risk, create vulnerability. What can also increase their vulnerability is a lack of knowledge about healthy relationships, grooming and risk. We should acknowledge that for some young people their involvement in the grooming process can make them feel real, alive, visible and relevant. The excitement of running away, being where they should not be, with people they should not be with, must not be underestimated. But when this starts to become full-scale abuse and trauma, it can have the opposite effect – they feel dead, invisible and irrelevant.

Disability and vulnerability

As outlined above, there are some immediately obvious vulnerable groups, including children with a disability. Franklin, Raws and Smeaton (2015) summarise this vulnerability:

> A small number of research studies carried out in the UK report that young people with learning disabilities or difficulties constitute a significant minority of sexually exploited young people…and that young people with learning disabilities or difficulties are at increased risk of CSE. (p.27)

They also reference Berelowitz *et al.* (2013), who state how learning disabilities are a 'typical vulnerability' in a child prior to abuse. Franklin *et al.* cite evidence from studies on the abuse of disabled children which suggest that the increased vulnerability of disabled children is attributable to a number of factors, including the lack of recognition that children with disabilities are sexual beings, as well as a lack of sex and relationships education, although this is a risk factor for all children. Often young people with disabilities do not or cannot disclose their abuse, or are not understood when they try to tell someone. A final significant factor is the poor reaction of professionals to the child if they do disclose, for example disbelief or normalisation.

Franklin *et al.* (2015) also identify further vulnerabilities:

- impairment factors such as impulsive behaviours and needs associated with a different understanding of social cues, interaction and communication

- societal treatment including over protection, disempowerment and isolation

- a lack of parental and professional knowledge regarding CSE and children with disabilities

- focus being placed on behavioural issues without recognising signs of CSE

- a lack of understanding concerning the ability to consent.

Adele has noted additional factors during her practice relating to children with disabilities. These include communication difficulties inhibit disclosure; enhanced feelings of dependency on the abuser; fear of the abuser; and the challenges that exist in any criminal investigation and court case where the victim is a disabled child and where they may not be able to communicate or give evidence in a sequential manner. In particular, children with a learning disability are an attractive target for perpetrators, as they are easier to groom, manipulate, control and are less likely to disclose. There is, therefore, a reduced chance of charges being brought against them. As one practitioner stated in Franklin *et al.*'s research, 'Young people with learning disabilities are a perpetrator's dream' (p.46).

Looked-after children

Young people accommodated by the local authority ('looked-after children') are another particularly vulnerable group. They have often had significant previous experiences of abuse, neglect and trauma. Historically, few have been routinely referred for therapeutic intervention until effects of the trauma begin to emerge through mental health issues, extreme behaviour and identification of issues impacting on their health and development. Behaviours that they have already been involved in – such as going missing, being absent from education and seeking out relationships online – make them even more vulnerable to being targeted by predatory adults and peers. They are additionally exposed by the reduced power of children's residential workers or foster carers to prevent young people leaving their care, of which perpetrators seem very aware. This has been exacerbated, historically, by poor relationships that often existed – across the country – between police and children's residential workers, which often impacted on outcomes for the child.

There is evidence from Adele's private practice to suggest that some perpetrators are well versed in some local safeguarding policies and procedures, including the distinction between the police categorisation of a child who is 'missing' or an 'unauthorised absence' (which is discussed in Chapter 4). A final risk factor is where a young person is accommodated in a placement where other young people are already involved in CSE or are being encouraged by abusers to recruit other young people. This increases their vulnerability to also being groomed by the perpetrators.

In Rotherham, there were cases where the relationship between a child and a parent or carer – which was previously positive and with good attachment – broke down, often accompanied by an allegation of abuse (usually physical) made by the child. They would then request to be placed into care. In more than one case, practitioners were later told by the young person that it was their abuser who had made this suggestion. Practitioners believed this was to get them away from protective carers and parents and into a setting where the perpetrator believed the young person would be more accessible to them. In her book *Broken and Betrayed,* Jayne Senior gives such an example:

> Charlie had previously made an allegation against her stepfather, which was found to be untrue…it was her perpetrators who put her up to it in the first place…when Charlie's troubles were beginning and she started to go missing for hours at an end, her mother spent

ages scouring the streets looking for her, not understanding that she was being groomed by her new friends, Charlie was angry at these apparent restrictions. So her abusers told her to accuse her stepdad so that she could go into a kid's home and come out whenever she wanted. And that's what she did. (2016, p.226)

Current practice reviews conducted by Adele, however, suggest that as awareness among practitioners and other protective factors develops (including the use of closed-circuit TV (CCTV) and improved multi-agency responses), it is children living at home who may now present an easier target. The lack of knowledge and understanding among parents and families may present additional risk factors in these cases.

A lack of knowledge of CSE and grooming

In this chapter we have considered several different types of vulnerability that could be a contributing factor to a young person becoming involved in CSE. Another significant factor is a lack of knowledge of CSE and grooming. In *Violated*, Sarah Wilson (2015) describes how her lack of knowledge about sex resulted in her abuser being able to use that as part of a grooming process, to persuade her that there was no harm in her performing sexual acts with adult men. The 'test' that Sarah was subjected to involved one of her abusers asking her to close her legs and then feeling for a gap at the top. Her account eloquently shows how her lack of sexual knowledge was used by the men to confuse her and make her believe what they said:

> I was way too young to know what was going on. He rested his hands near my crotch once more. 'I told you to relax,' he said. I sensed a hint of aggression in his voice and it scared me. 'Now, you see this little gap between your thighs?' I nodded meekly, not wanting to make him angry. 'That means you're not a virgin. If you close your legs and your thighs are touching, you're a virgin,' Sarif said. 'If they're not, you've had sex before.' ...I was sure I was a virgin, but what if I wasn't? If I'd never had sex before, why didn't my thighs touch like they should?... I was confused, full of self-doubt and

beginning to believe these men who were much older and more experienced than me. (pp.53–54)

The lack of sexual knowledge and experience was used differently with another young woman, one of the Rochdale victims; described in her book *Girl A: My Story*. In this passage, she describes how the perpetrator rationalises his abuse of her as something he is entitled to, that she owes him:

And that's when he started to talk about all the things he'd given me for free at Tasty Bites: the vodka, the cigarettes, the chicken tikkas, the kebabs...and how I should repay him. 'It's part of the deal, Hannah,' he said as he smiled at me. I suddenly realised that he sounded sinister, like someone I didn't know: had never known. And he went on. 'I buy you things, you give me things,' he said. 'I've bought you vodka. Now it's your turn to give something to me.'... He just kept telling me I had to pay him back, and all the time he was coming closer. 'We're friends,' he was saying, 'and friends do things for each other.' (Anonymous (Girl A), 2013, p.59)

Increasing vulnerabilities

In the first part of this chapter we have explored how all children may be at risk. Some children have had experiences which have resulted in a vulnerability, others may be seeking excitement and fun but have not got the life experience and knowledge that equip them to recognise grooming and predatory behaviour, or know how to respond. Whatever the cause of the child's initial vulnerability, perpetrators who are skilled in the grooming process recognise, exploit and increase it.

For all children involved in CSE, their relationship with their abuser and the grooming process increases their vulnerability. Grooming is a manipulative process, which conditions a young person into a passive state where they accept abuse as the norm or believe that they cannot avoid it, and that somehow they are also responsible for it. The abuser seeks to isolate the young person from those who may be able to protect them or recognise there is something amiss.

The perpetrator seeks to make the young person dependent on them. They distort their thinking and make them start to believe that their abuser is the only person who treats them with respect, who listens to them and who understands them. The abuser skilfully tightens their control over the young person by meeting their needs and increasing the false emotional attachment between them. Over time this changes how they view their family, their friends, their ties and themselves, as this quote from a survivor illustrates:

> The only thing I saw was him. I did anything for him. I believed every word he said. So it got to the point where I actually started to hate my own family. (Coming Out of the Darkness, March 2016)

Groomers target the most intimate and sensitive issues for the child in their life, and then exploit them. It is little wonder that children who have been abused describe their abuse as a total betrayal. The abuse is as much emotional as sexual, and the impact is devastating, as we discuss later on in this chapter.

Understanding the impact of trauma

Any trauma has an impact. As Dr van der Kolk states, 'Trauma, by definition, is unbearable and intolerable' (2014, p.1). When considering the impact grooming has on victims, there can be a tendency to assume that the trauma suffered is not significant, that the victim has had a 'lucky escape'. The reality is that even where grooming does not result in direct abuse, the child has been targeted, manipulated and a vulnerability has been created by the process of being conditioned to meet someone else's needs and desires. Acts of abuse where there is no direct contact can still result in trauma, as the following case example from the Taking Stock project in Sheffield shows:

> Lucy was too young to have a Facebook profile but had joined because her older sister was on Facebook and she wanted to impress her friends. She did not disclose her true age and did not enable any of the security settings. Within a short time she received numerous

friend requests from unknown adults, one of whom was able to persuade her over the course of an evening to send indecent images of herself to him. He did not tell Lucy his real name or age. Those images have been shared across the UK and beyond. Lucy has no control over who sees those images, what they do with them, whether she will be recognised in the future and whether later those images will ever come back to haunt her. Lucy also has had to come to terms with the fact that she was manipulated and deceived into sharing those images, and that several adults including teaching staff at school and her parents know that she made and shared the images. The impact on Lucy has been significant. 'I thought we'd be together forever...the only thing that's forever is my picture on the internet.' (McDonald *et al.*, undated, p.5)

Grooming and 'no contact' acts of abuse still create trauma to which there needs to be a response. Failure to do so leaves a future vulnerability, which may result in the child having further abusive experiences, either while still young or as an adult.

Direct abuse causes trauma, especially where it is perpetrated by someone whom the victim knows, trusts, has confided in and perhaps loved. It can be devastating. A trauma perpetrated by someone to whom they opened up when they were already vulnerable can cause lifelong trauma, as does repeated and extreme abuse. While child sexual exploitation is manipulative and traumatic, once it progresses to child sexual abuse it is often deeply sadistic on a number of levels. An abuser meets a child, builds trust, creates hope and dependency, takes advantage of them and then exposes them to multiple abusers, repeatedly, often over long periods of time, and forces them into acts of a particularly violent nature.

There is also the trauma of how the child's body and brain respond to the harm they are experiencing. We reference 'fight or flight' as common responses to sudden trauma. In reality, the most common responses are 'freeze', 'friend' and 'flop'. Victims of sexual assault often describe out-of-body experiences, extreme states of passivity and not being able to think logically or clearly. Van der Kolk (2014) describes three distinct stages that the human brain experiences when responding to trauma. The first is social engagement – trying to engage the abuser or find help from around us. Anonymous (Girl A)'s account of her first rape shows this first stage:

> Even now Daddy was still looking happy. 'When are you going to let me have sex with you?' he asked merrily, a big cheeky smile on his face. I tried to answer in the same way, laughing. I thought he was joking, that I could handle it. 'I'm not, Daddy,' I giggled. (Anonymous (Girl A), 2013, p.58)

The second stage is 'flight or fight', where the victim will contemplate trying to escape or fight off the danger if possible:

> I knew then, knew without a shred of doubt, that he was more dangerous than anyone I had ever met; I knew that he meant to hurt me…I didn't know what to do. I didn't think to beat him off because he was so big compared to me, and I had no idea what he would do. Would he beat me up? Kill me? (Anonymous (Girl A), 2013, p.59)

The final stage is 'freeze or collapse', where the mind is trying to preserve itself and the body by shutting down. Van der Kolk (2014) notes:

> Finally, if there is no way out, and there's nothing we can do to stave off the inevitable, we will activate the ultimate emergency system… this is the stage where we disengage, collapse and freeze. (p.82)

This is exemplified by Anonymous (Girl A):

> My heart froze…in the midst of the urge of my rising panic and the fear freezing my veins… I couldn't move, I couldn't breathe… I couldn't scream because my throat had closed up so tight with fear. Instead I screamed the sort of scream that could find no release but reverberated around my brain. (Anonymous (Girl A), 2013, pp.60–61)

For some children involved in organised CSA, there can be some significant elements which in turn deepen the existing trauma. First, victims often feel betrayed by their own responses to the event, and ask themselves, 'Why didn't I just…?' Logical answers always appear after an event and contribute to a feeling that it is somehow the victim's fault – if only they had acted differently maybe the abuse would not have happened. Second, as referenced earlier, is where victims are engaged in activities or relationships which they know are risky, and of which parents and carers do not approve. This results in self-blame: 'If only I had listened...' The abuser will often tighten their control over a victim at this stage. They can do so in a number of ways: suggesting the abuse was the child's fault, that they owed the abuser for something which needed to be repaid, that the abuse was 'normal', that they participated in the sexual act without protest, that as they were not a virgin so what was the problem? In addition, victims often feel betrayed by their own bodies. The sense of helplessness that comes from not being able to scream for help, run away or fight back – as described above – results in a pervading sense that nowhere is safe any more.

The third factor is the professional responses to the trauma. When a child discloses abuse to a professional, if their experiences are minimised, ignored or dismissed as commonplace, that reinforces to the child that it is their perspective that is skewed. This has the effect of further normalising the abuse. In Operation Bullfinch in Oxford, the trial judge described 'sexual crimes of the utmost gravity' (Crown Prosecution Service, 2013). Yet in the subsequent serious case review, a young person told the author that 'social services had washed their hands – "It's your choice," I was told' (Bedford, 2015, p.14). We discuss professional responses in more detail later in this chapter.

When victims can no longer trust their minds, their bodies or the people around them, the world becomes a terrifying, unsafe place where everything is uncertain. This has severe consequences for the psychological wellbeing of the young person, both at that time and in the future. For those children have been psychologically manipulated into the abuse (as opposed to being physically threatened and violently raped, for example), there is likely to be a heightened sense of self-blame and self-loathing. Pearce (2009) discusses the identification of symptoms of post-traumatic stress syndrome in some young people involved in CSE. Given the nature and extent of the abuse, this is hardly surprising. In cases of severe and sustained trauma, even an emotionally balanced, intelligent and mature adult would struggle to function effectively, engage with services and make good decisions. Children who are already often damaged and vulnerable, emotionally and psychologically immature and then become the victims of severe abuse are unlikely to behave differently. Envisage yourself as a vulnerable child and consider how you would react in the following real events.

- Your younger sister was enticed into a car with an abuser when you were trying to disengage from your abusers. You were told you had to make a choice, that you had to make it there and then, and the wrong choice would have severe and immediate consequences for your sister.

- You knew that your abusers had raped and brutally harmed a number of young women. You were taken upstairs in a building where there were a number of adult males. You were told to have sex with a number of them. You could hear a young woman screaming in apparent agony in the room next to you. You were told that a broken bottle was being forced into the young woman's vagina. You were told that the same would happen to you if you did not do what you were told.

- You were told that your rape had been filmed and photo-graphed and if you told anyone, it would be posted onto Facebook and YouTube.

We doubt that many of us would make a choice which did not involve compliance in order to avoid harm or exposure.

The way many children deal with such trauma is two-fold. The first is denial that they are being abused, and compliance with their intimate terrorist or abuser. At the University of Sheffield Symposium, Stephens (2016) outlined betrayal trauma theory – that victims of CSE can become 'consciously unaware that the abuse is happening'. It is easier to tell themselves that the abuse is acceptable and normal, than to acknowledge the reality. Consider the following case study, which we also featured in the previous chapter:

> Jonathan had been placed into care by his parents after he told them he was gay. He was groomed online by an adult male, posing as a young man of his age. He agreed to meet him. When he arrived he realised that his 'friend' was significantly older. The man said Jonathan should have sex with him because it was the only way to be sure whether he was gay or not. As an experienced older gay man, he would be able to tell, and if Jonathan wasn't gay, he could go home to his family. Jonathan was frightened that he had been lied to, but did not know how to say no. He described his mind 'going blank', as if it was all happening to someone else. He went with the male to a nearby hotel room, where he was raped.

Jonathan had experienced a significant rejection from his parents at a vulnerable time of his life and emotional and physical development. It was easier for him to reframe his abusive experience as something that he chose to allow, rather than accepting that he had been rejected again. In believing he had consensual sex with the male concerned and that it was his choice, Jonathan could normalise his abuse and avoid the fact that in reality he had been targeted, manipulated, groomed, lied to and raped. He could also ignore that he had been unable to act to protect himself when he was in danger.

The second way that children often react to trauma is through behaviours they exhibit. Their struggle to process the continuing or significant abuse is often reflected in their relationships with family, friends and practitioners, as well as educational attendance and attainment, personal presentation, general demeanour and attitude. The trauma of the abuse can emerge through behaviours such as eating disorders, mental ill health, chronic fatigue, problems sleeping, mood swings, hypersensitivity, poor physical health, growing dependency on alcohol or drugs. They may exhibit low self-expectation and motivation and unpredictable behaviour, including aggression. Van der Kolk, noted for his research in the area of post-traumatic stress since the 1970s, offers a simple starting point to understanding these responses: 'It needs tremendous energy to keep functioning while carrying the memory of terror and the shame of utter weakness and vulnerability' (2014, p.2).

The trauma can also result in self-harming, risky sexual behaviour, intolerance towards others, withdrawal from social situations and relationships, and disinhibited and anti-social behaviour. Often with encouragement from the abuser, the young person may become engaged in minor offending such as shoplifting, or more serious crimes such as carrying Class A drugs. The Rochdale Serious Case Review (Griffiths, 2013) provides details of problematical and rebellious behaviour, where young people were described as 'hard to reach' or exhibiting challenging behaviour. All of the behaviours described were symptoms of maladaptive coping strategies to deal with the level of abuse they experienced.

Trauma literally changes the way the mind thinks – the victim may struggle to remember exact details of their abuse or that they were abused at all. Van der Kolk offers some explanations for these self-destructive responses to trauma, using one of his patients to illustrate: 'His molestation had scared her beyond her capacity to endure, so she had needed to push it out of her memory bank' (2014, p.131). Trauma is often not stored in an orderly and normal way in the mind, leaving memories to often return as flashbacks, isolated images, sounds and sensations of terror for no logical reason. This can result in the victim feeling that there is something wrong with them, that they are mentally ill. What is happening to them is a normal response to trauma. If the child's internal sense of security is broken, as a result of parental breakup or bereavement for example, van der Kolk suggests that potentially dangerous situations will appeal to them as they can make them feel alive. Constantly seeking relationships, however fleeting, is driven by a continual need for attachment. He also discusses how the presence of stress hormones in the body will continue so long as the trauma remains unresolved:

If elements of trauma are replayed again and again, the accompanying stress hormones engrave those memories ever more deeply in the mind. Ordinary, day-to-day events become less compelling.

Not being able to deeply take in what is going on around them makes it impossible to feel fully alive. It becomes harder to feel the joys and aggravations of ordinary life, harder to concentrate on the tasks at hand. Not being fully alive in the present keeps them more firmly imprisoned in the past. (van der Kolk, 2014, p.67)

This is illustrated by the mother of one of the Rotherham victims:

It totally destroyed my daughter's childhood. Instead of being happy and at home playing with dolls, which she should have been at her age, it were just living a nightmare of abuse. (Coming Out of the Darkness, 2016)

The impact of child sexual exploitation and organised child sexual abuse on families

In drawing up and implementing child in need or child protection plans, professionals have tended to focus on the child and not considered the impact that the exploitation and abuse has on the family. The trauma of organised CSA impacts on all members, particularly parents as this quote from Adele's private practice shows:

I went out looking for her. I was out for hours. When I found her, I saw her with a group of men. She was 13. I screamed abuse at them and ran to get my daughter. The memory of seeing that will haunt me for the rest of my life.

In this harrowing case example, the mother concerned was a protective factor. She went to extreme lengths to try to protect her daughter: staying out until the early hours of the morning looking for her, constantly ringing the police, gathering information such as telephone numbers and car registration numbers. Despite this, she and other family members were regarded by practitioners involved as part of their child's problem.

If a plan does not consider the impact of CSE and CSA on the family as whole, it can have significant consequences, as it:

- fails to take advantage of the protective factors that may exist in a family environment

- ignores the needs and issues of those who are caring for the child in extremely challenging circumstances

- fails to consider the needs of other children who may be living in the household and their future vulnerability

- reduces a parent's ability to parent effectively.

Consequently, plans which aim to be protective and reduce the child's vulnerability may in fact increase the risk to them and other children because parents and carers are stressed, exhausted, demoralised, depressed and disillusioned, as well as traumatised themselves. The following quotes demonstrate the reality of being a parent of a victim (from the Coming Out of the Darkness Conference, 2016):

> She became quite dark and deep and really, really violent.

> I felt suicidal myself. I thought I'd hit rock bottom with it all, depressed and not knowing which way to turn, who you could trust as well.

> It's so scary having to watch your little girl go through stuff like that and nobody'll listen to you.

> It ripped me family apart.

Plans and assessments that recognise the horror of the abuse, the impact it has on whole families and the need for support and specific interventions are key to responding effectively to CSE and CSA. This is something we consider further in the next chapter.

Understanding non-engagement

As a result of the issues discussed above, unsurprisingly, children often feel unable to disclose their abuse. They often feel confused and hopeless, not knowing what to do, and operate in a 'survival' mode of just getting through one day at a time alive. They will also be afraid of the consequences of disclosure, concerned that they will be disbelieved or judged, as well as still having confused feelings of love and loyalty for the abuser. The key to successful engagement with young people who are victims of CSE and CSA is recognising that, initially, not only will they keep their abuse to themselves, but also they will probably perceive anything that requires them to talk as stressful and without merit, regardless of how close a relationship they have with their parents or professionals.

In the past, failure to engage has been seen as a justification for withdrawing services or closing cases, particularly where young people were perceived as being 'difficult'. This is also true of cases where families were perceived as being hard to engage, or where the children were close to the age of 18. In such cases there were perceptions, some of which we explored earlier, that responsibility for addressing the abuse lay with the family or the young person. Opinions were that such young people had 'voted with their feet' so it was pointless if they did not cooperate and were not involved in the service, and that younger children were more in need (and perceived as being more deserving) of often hard-stretched resources. The reality is that failure to engage is an additional risk factor. Where it is not addressed this increases the risk to the child and others, by:

- reinforcing to the young person that they have no value and that no one can help them

- increasing their dependency on their abuser

- increasing their abuser's control and power over them

- increasing risk to other children, including siblings, who will be affected by what is happening to the child

- disempowering families and carers and placing them under unbearable stress which will, more likely than not, impact on their long-term mental and physical wellbeing

- resulting in future abuse

- significantly increasing the young person's chances of developing mental health problems and becoming an adult with long-term care and support needs.

Phrases such as 'will not engage' need to be re-examined in light of this. The reality is that, as professionals, we cannot engage them. They may be 'out of control', or out of our control, but unfortunately not the control of others – their abusers (Firmin, 2016). The challenge for practitioners is to reflect on how we try to engage them, and what we need to do differently. Many of the potential reasons for non-engagement and some of the behaviours discussed above are predictable and reasonable responses to unimaginable abuse. As practitioners, once we discover and acknowledge the horror of their daily existence, the question regarding non-engagement changes from 'Why won't they?' to 'Why would they?'

There are several contributing factors to non-engagement, although this is not an exhaustive consideration. Engagement requires motivation and trust, but when most young people are in survival mode, getting through each day is their priority. Engagement with agencies and professionals is often a huge step for them and they may have anxieties as a result. These may include information being shared about them with people they do not know; no longer having choice about where they live, go to school and how they live their daily life; being asked constantly about the abuse, which will force them to acknowledge what has happened; being expected to reveal information about their abuser and being concerned about such consequences; and being held responsible for protecting themselves and making major life changes for which they often do not feel ready. As observed earlier in this chapter, we also should acknowledge that for some young people their involvement in child sexual exploitation (which they do not recognise as such) serves a purpose. It can make them feel alive and desirable. And the excitement of running away, of being where they should not be and with people they should not be with, must not be underestimated. This does not, however, make them complicit in any abuse or trauma that is inflicted on them, which has been an erroneous view of some practitioners in the past. For children and families, the result of their involvement in CSE and CSA is chaos and crisis. As one young person from Adele's private practice put it: 'It's like having a head full of white noise.' Asking children in crisis to take responsibility for addressing their own risks, changing their behaviour, altering their coping strategies and remembering their appointments and detailed plans, is clearly unrealistic.

Involvement in CSE and CSA can cause deep-rooted trauma in most victims, which will be lifelong and debilitating if not addressed. Not all victims, however, want to engage in therapy; it is not appropriate for all. The most important contribution that professionals can make in challenging abuse, therefore, is in establishing positive relationships with children and their families – relationships which have the needs of the young person and family at their core. Practitioners need to recognise and appreciate that establishing those relationships with young people involved in CSE and CSA takes time. Effective interventions take patience, imagination, persistence, commitment and contingency planning, This is an issue we consider in the next chapter.

Consequences of professionals and agencies' failure to act

As the effects of grooming on the child have been detailed above, this section addresses professional responses. Chapter 1 discussed the different groups of people living and working in Rotherham who suffered as a result of the lack of action from statutory agencies to tackle organised CSA in the town. Those most affected by such failings are, of course, the victims and their families. The process of grooming and the types and extent of the abuse they suffered have been outlined above. The abuse was horrific enough in itself, but the children and their families were further traumatised where agencies failed to respond adequately to such reports and did not protect them from continuing significant harm. Tanya exemplifies this in the Foreword:

> Before all this came out nationally I felt alone, ashamed of myself, degraded and hurt. I thought I was the only person in Rotherham who had gone through such horrific things. And all this was made more believable because the people who you are supposed to put your trust in are the very people that allowed me to feel it was my fault and that I didn't need to pursue – what would have been – the right course or action.

It was Rotherham Council and South Yorkshire Police of whom Jay (2014) was most critical in her report. The role of both agencies in relation to the protection of children is laid down in the Children Act 1989. The statutory guidance *Working Together to Safeguard Children* clearly spells out the processes for all agencies involved in the protection of children. The 1999 edition – which became operational soon after the beginning of the period covered by the Jay inquiry – noted 'the police have a duty and responsibility to investigate crimes against children' (Department of Health, Home Office and Department for Education and Employment, 1999, p.23) and 'a key objective for social services departments is to ensure that children are protected from significant harm' (Department of Health, Home Office and Department for Education and Employment, 1999, p.13). As the statutory agency failings in Rotherham were so catastrophic, it is essential to understand how this could have happened in order to prevent it from ever occurring again.

The impact of professional responses

If children are seen as victims of abuse, and the motivations of the perpetrators questioned, it is highly unlikely that children would be exposed to continuing abuse. In cases where abuse is not recognised or is minimised, children take professionals' appraisals of their abusive relationships and conclude that any doubts or fears they have must be misplaced. A young person from Adele's private practice recounted how one professional's response stopped her telling anyone else about her abuse:

We'd had a proper row. I was really scared. He really hurt me. I mentioned it to my worker and she told me that all couples fight. He'd bought me a necklace to say sorry, and she said that proved how nice he was and how she wished she had a partner like that. I thought 'What do I know? I've never had a boyfriend before.'

In other cases, abusers have erroneously been seen by practitioners as people with whom the child would be safe. In a case reviewed by Adele, a professional suggested to a parent that their child should remain with a suspected abuser because 'at least you know where she is; she isn't wandering the streets'. The reality, in her case, was that 'wandering the streets' might have been a far safer option.

Other examples of poor professional responses concern how victims of CSE and CSA have been regarded and their conduct judged. Over our years in practice we know that practitioners have referred to children – some as young as 12 – as 'promiscuous', 'fully consenting', 'a drama queen', 'a prostitute', 'attention seeking', 'streetwise', 'a fantasist' and 'troubled'. In another case from Adele's private practice, a young man abused by a large number of adult males was described as a facilitator, someone who had encouraged the abuse. This use of language demonstrates who those professionals felt were responsible for the abuse: that the children concerned were either in some way contributing to the abuse or lying about it to gain attention. Added to the self-blame that many victims already feel, professional responses such as these serve only to strengthen the abusive relationship and discourage future engagement of the young person to work with them.

The following case studies illustrate the consequences of such professional attitudes and responses:

Kayla was visited by the police at her 'boyfriend's' flat after concerns about possible abuse had been reported to the police. She was asked if she was safe and well – in the presence of the adult suspected of abusing her. Her affirmative answer was accepted without challenge, because in the view of the police officers Kayla had been given an opportunity to tell them if she was worried or if anyone was abusing her (even if this was in the presence of her abuser). Kayla continued to be abused by multiple adult males for over a year afterwards.

Tessa's mother, grandmother and younger sister were threatened with rape when Tessa started attending a specialist project. Tessa told a practitioner about this, who sought advice from social care and the police. She was told not to worry; it was 'probably just empty threats'. Consequently, Tessa refused to attend the project or engage with any professionals.

Macie's house was subject to criminal damage. The family was offered a panic button and extra door locks. The person who the family thought was responsible for this and for abusing their daughter was not questioned by police. The family stopped reporting their daughter as missing from home and Macie refused to engage with any professionals.

Professionals must recognise that sexually exploited and abused young people often do not act like victims. They can be hostile, aggressive, verbally abusive, involved in low-level criminality such as criminal damage, be under the influence of drugs or be drunk and disorderly. Professionals may receive information about them being excluded from school, causing damage and repeatedly placing themselves at risk. These children require significant input in terms of time and resources, but they need such a response because they are either suffering or likely to suffer significant harm. The focus of overworked and stressed professionals often shifts to younger children who are perceived as more deserving of professional help, and where results are easier to achieve. As one professional once said to Adele, 'If they won't help themselves, what are we expected to do about it?' As discussed above, failure to engage is an additional risk factor and should be recognised as such. We should never lose sight of the fact that these are children who have been severely abused and traumatised. Practice issues in relation to applying thresholds will be discussed in Chapter 4.

Statutory agency failure: what goes wrong?

The report of the Office of the Children's Commissioner's Inquiry into CSE in gangs and groups (Berelowitz *et al.*, 2013) identified nine significant failings in common agency responses. While it is acknowledged that these findings predate the Jay report (2014), they remain relevant and should be considered regularly and repeatedly during strategic and operational audits, as stressed in the Children's Commissioner's follow-up report (Berelowitz *et al.*, 2015). The Inquiry found the following issues affected the reaction of agencies:

1. *Forgetting the child:* Children at high risk of becoming involved in CSE or who were already victims were often ignored; the child became invisible to agencies.

2. *Failing to engage with children and young people:* There was a lack of understanding from professionals and agencies on how to engage with children and young people in relation to issues of CSE. Specialist organisations stated that statutory services often did not have a good understanding of the children they were working with and their specific needs. There was a significant difference between children's and professionals' views of the children's needs and what would help; this disconnect contributed to children disappearing from agency contact.

3. *Lack of leadership:* Some senior local decision makers did not understand the seriousness of CSE, and therefore failed in their leadership roles in relation to this issue. This resulted in a lack of commitment to essential resources and no coordinated multi-agency response. At both a national and local level, it was unclear whether CSE was seen as predominantly a child protection issue or a crime and disorder issue.

4. *Limited or no strategic planning:* Almost half of all LSCBs did not have a strategy in place to tackle CSE. An absence of strategy could result in differing approaches and an uncoordinated response across agencies.

5. *In denial:* Too many people who should have been protecting children were in denial about the realities of CSE and therefore did not believe what children told them.

6. *Failing to recognise victims:* Damaging and persuasive myths still existed about the profiles of both victims and perpetrators. This resulted in different patterns of sexual exploitation being ignored and victims left unprotected, for example those in gangs.

7. *Working in isolation:* Nearly a third of LSCBs had no plans to appoint a CSE coordinator. Information sharing remained an issue; some agencies held information that they did not share with the police, children's services and others.

8. *Delayed response:* This hampered practice development and improvement. Only two police forces had sought to locate and log the connections of girls and young women associated with street gangs, despite recommendations made in the Office of the Children's Commissioner's interim report.

9. *Results not monitored:* Statutory agencies were failing to check whether actions were working and there was no common agreement as to what they were trying to achieve.

Assessing strategic and operational practice in relation to these nine factors are key to the success of any local CSE action plan and interventions (see also Chapter 7).

The role of agencies and professionals

As can be seen from the discussions above, the role professionals and organisations play in the lives of children and young people involved in CSE and CSA is vital. This is not just about practitioners identifying exploitation and abuse, sharing information and taking action; it is about the quality of the relationship practitioners have with that child. It takes great courage for anyone – a child or an adult in later years – to tell anyone about the abuse they are suffering at the hands and minds of their abusers. It must be particularly difficult to share their trauma with a professional. The child has to put their trust in someone who may be not much more than a stranger, but who they know has to follow an unfamiliar set of rules or procedures which will take their experience out of their control. Their decision to tell the professional may either be spontaneous as a result of an event, or considered at length beforehand. Whichever it is they will have shared for a reason; that they can no longer keep it to themselves. Considering the threats and intimidation they will have undoubtedly already received to deter them from telling anyone, it is a brave act to share current or historical abuse.

Supporting victims and survivors of CSE and CSA may present practitioners with significant challenges, whatever their discipline and however experienced they are in their field. The psychological damage that has likely been inflicted on the young person – in conjunction with threats, intimidation and actual physical harm – often results in them finding it difficult to trust anyone, either personally or professionally. Working relationships, therefore, must be built slowly, patiently and at a pace the young person dictates and controls (Cooper, 2012). The practitioner must be clear at the first meeting about the ground rules for professional working and discuss with the young person what will and will not be shared with partner agency colleagues and the process that will take place in such circumstances. Where possible, a consent form should be signed at the outset to confirm that the young person has understood the issues discussed and agrees to this. 'The first meeting is a chance for the worker to get to know the client, create expectations and to lay out what you have to offer' (Cooper, 2012, p.88). The ability of the professional to confidently manage the relationship is key to its success. This is discussed in more detail in Chapter 4. At this stage the professional may also informally or formally assess the young person's Fraser competence (or Gillick competence as it was previously known). It should be remembered, however, that this guidance was issued with the purpose of helping health professionals and other practitioners assess a young person's understanding of an issue and their ability to give instructions or consent. A young person may be Fraser competent, but that does not mean that they have the ability to make decisions that protect them from harm, nor should they be expected to.

As also noted by Cooper (2012), the professional may informally have to undergo 'tests' set by the child before they know whether they feel they can trust the worker. This may include, for example, trying professional boundaries – such as missing repeated appointments – to see how the professional reacts, and checking with whom and when they would share information about them. The practitioner should not mistakenly view such tests as game playing, or an indication that they do not really want professional support. These behaviours are far more likely to be a result of the impact of exploitation or abuse. While it may, at times, be a source of frustration for a practitioner who probably has a number of external pressures in relation to competing work demands, it is imperative for the child's psychological wellbeing and the fledgling relationship that they resist any temptation to try and move things along more quickly. That would likely be viewed by the child as the professional having failed the test, and will purely confirm for them that they were right to be wary, that the professional did not have their best interests at heart and reaffirms their instinct not to trust them in the first instance. When the child feels that they are starting to trust the worker, they may often begin to reveal incidents of abuse. This may start with less traumatic events; these again may be a test to see how the practitioner responds to such disclosures. They may want to see how they react, including facial expressions, what they say and what they do – both immediately in the session and after they have left the meeting. The child may be concerned that the worker may not return again. Their fear will be that their disclosures will drive them away either because they are horrified by what they have heard or that the professional does not believe them.

Once the child does start to disclose, they may reveal even more abusive sexual and physical violence, and psychological abuse. The practitioner must be trained and experienced in order to be able to cope emotionally with such traumatic personal accounts. Supervision, peer support and additional professional support when required, such as counselling, are vital for the emotional health and wellbeing of staff working with such issues, and are discussed in more detail in Chapter 7. Managers and employers must prioritise support structures for staff in order for them to work effectively with the victims and survivors. This may otherwise result in poor work practice leading to errors and/or long-term sickness as a result of being so traumatised. This impacts on the practitioner, their team and their colleagues, but most of all it affects the child.

Disclosures may include reference to other victims of CSE and CSA, but also other crimes, including those of close friends, acquaintances and family members. The child's disclosure may also include what they had to do to limit the harm done to them or others. Strategies should be agreed between agencies as to what action may need to be taken if victims or survivors reveal their own involvement in crimes, which may range from shoplifting and petty theft to violence or their own involvement in grooming other children. While overall policy may be agreed in relation to such offences, such cases will need to be decided on an individual basis.

As will be discussed in more detail in Chapter 7, while convictions against perpetrators should always be sought wherever possible, the first concern must be the emotional and psychological health and wellbeing of the child. If they feel able to report such crimes to the police, while officers will be keen to take a statement and commence an investigation, all interactions with the child should be at their own pace with the practitioner constantly checking with them as to what they feel able to provide and achieve. It must also be respected that some victims decide not to report the crimes to the police and may choose never to do so. The victim's safety and wellbeing take precedence, although there are clear expectations regarding information sharing if the abuser is still a risk to children or other vulnerable people. Staff who demonstrate patience and overriding concern for the young person are, however, more likely to be able to build good working relationships with them. This may lead to them agreeing to provide a statement, which can be used to start building the police investigation into the perpetrators.

Finally, when a child shares such intimate and horrific details, they will expect something 'positive' to happen as a result. They will believe that other agencies – such as the police – will become involved as a result. While they will probably be very scared at what action will be taken as a consequence of their disclosure, particularly by the police in relation to their abusers, they will expect them and their family finally to be able to feel safe. What they do not expect is that nothing will happen, that nothing will improve or that the authorities unintentionally make the situation worse. If the perpetrators of the abuse become aware of the allegations, which is very likely if they are questioned by the police, unless substantial efforts are made to protect the victim, the abuse will continue and probably escalate as a result. It is up to all professionals involved to ensure their safety.

This chapter has detailed that the emotional cost of professionals not acting effectively in safeguarding children involved in CSE and CSA is immense, for both them and their families. Poor practice results in more abuse and trauma, as well as risks to other children who are vulnerable. As discussed in Chapter 1, failing to offer good support also results in a financial cost. Saied-Tessier (2014) estimated that child sexual abuse cost the UK £3.2 billion in 2012, including the impact on health services, criminal justice services, children's services, adult services and the loss of productivity to society through unemployment or reduced earnings. For those victims involved and their families, of course, the cost is far greater; as Jayne Senior notes, 'The ripple effect of CSE tears into families like the aftershock of a bomb going off' (2016, p.227).

Having a child as the result of organised child sexual abuse

Many CSA victims become mothers themselves. While parenthood inevitably brings a number of challenges for any mother, their relationships with their children can be incredibly complex in a number of different ways. Some children are born as a result of rape or gang rape, which was also accompanied by intimidation, physical assaults and threats. Sometimes the mother may not know who the father is, either because of the number of men she was forced to have sex with or because of the effects of drugs or alcohol that she was given, or took in an effort to block out what was happening. Often the young person believes she is in a true relationship with her intimate terrorist 'boyfriend', that they are going to be a family together, that she is his one and only. When the truth emerges she is devastated and her hopes of family life are shattered, particularly if she discovers he has a wife and children.

Once the child is born, a number of issues may emerge. There are accommodation issues, as to where the victim is going to live and who is going to support her, particularly if she is young. If she is still at school, there is the issue of her education while she is pregnant and once the baby is born. The mother may suffer from postnatal depression or other mental health problems exacerbated by the stress of the pregnancy and birth. She may have already become dependent on drugs or alcohol; the baby will need additional monitoring throughout the pregnancy and after birth to treat any withdrawal symptoms or other health issues. She may need referral to drug or alcohol treatment agencies. In such circumstances and where there are other concerns about the mother's ability to safeguard her child, the baby will need a pre-birth assessment to ascertain if the multi-agency child in need or child protection procedures need to be followed, including putting in place a child in need or child protection plan. The victim may still be a child herself when she becomes pregnant and will have to make a decision at a very young age as to whether to give birth to a child or have a termination. If she decides to give birth, she then has to decide whether to keep the baby and, if so, how she will be able to raise the child.

Once she has given birth to the baby, she may have to maintain some contact with the father, who is the perpetrator of her abuse. There are a number of possible scenarios. She may want to keep him in their lives, believing that ultimately they all have a future together.

She may not want him in their lives, due to the violence and abuse he has meted out to her, but she is too frightened and intimidated by him to refuse him access to his child. He may threaten to take the child from her, to live with him or relatives. He may make such threats to ensure her compliance. The abuse to which she has long been subject may continue, but now she is more concerned for the safety of her child than she is for herself. The psychological abuse, of which she has always been a victim, may indeed now escalate as she is even more vulnerable with a child to protect.

Once the child is older, and where the mother is now estranged from the father, he or she may start to ask questions about who the father is, where he is and why they are not together. Mothers and other family members will have to be prepared for such occasions, and know what they are going to say. In small communities, it may be common knowledge as to who the father is, however much the mother tries to keep it secret. This may be particularly so if the mother had thought she was in a genuine relationship with her abuser. Some police officers raised the issue of the child of the victim and abuser attending the same school as the child or children of the abuser and his wife, both sets of children unaware of the existence of their half-siblings, in another class. This is the perpetrator's public image as a father, belying the fact that he is in fact an intimate terrorist of teenage girls. These exceptionally complex situations need to involve specialist workers, who can offer counselling to such mothers in order to help them prepare for what they are going to say and when to their child. While any such proactive conversation will be immensely difficult, the alternative – of the child finding out through other people in an uncontrolled and potentially very damaging way – is beyond imagination. An additional complication is mothers giving evidence against the child's father in criminal court cases in relation to the organised child sexual abuse in which they were involved. Again, in small communities it may be known who is giving evidence against whom, and this also needs to be taken into consideration when giving explanations to those children about their father. Some practice issues in relation to the children of victims and survivors will be discussed in Chapter 4.

Summary

In this chapter, we have identified groups of children who may be particularly at risk, but the reality is that any young person can become vulnerable as a result of events that have happened in their lives. Given particular circumstances, any young person can be vulnerable to being targeted and groomed. The key factor for perpetrators, in all cases, is opportunity. We have also considered the consequential trauma that children who are targeted are likely to experience and the psychological impact, as well as its effect on behaviour and engagement with services and professionals. Good practice responses by professionals can decrease children's risk factors and limit opportunities for abusers to exploit them. Poor practice, however, can increase risk by normalising and validating abusive relationships; by focusing on the child's behaviours and choices and not the crimes of their abuser; by failing to see CSE and CSA as abuse and therefore a child protection issue and not considering the issues for the child and family as a whole. In the next chapter we consider these issues further and examine what good practice responses to CSE and CSA look like and how we can assess their effectiveness.

Chapter 4

Taking Effective Safeguarding Action within a Safeguarding Framework

Introduction

National guidance such as *What to Do if You Suspect a Child Is Being Sexually Exploited* (Department for Education, 2012) and policies developed by Local Safeguarding Children Boards (LSCBs) state that when a young person is identified as at risk of child sexual exploitation or organised child sexual abuse, there should be a swift response from professionals that addresses and reduces the likelihood of such harm. Recognising the indicators, as discussed in Chapter 3, and being able to distinguish them from generic and less risky adolescent issues is a key factor in managing resources and ensuring appropriate professional responses at this stage. Early intervention is key in CSE cases, as once young people have become entrenched in CSA, not only is the abuse horrific but interventions and plans are less likely to be effective in the short to medium term. Additionally, the young person's needs will increase as their abuse continues, resulting in more services being involved and for longer.

As seen in the preceding chapter, professional responses can either reduce or increase the vulnerability of the young people they are working with. In this chapter, we explore what good practice looks like and reflect on some of the challenges that CSE and CSA present for practitioners and how different local authority areas have responded. We will also consider risk assessment tools and different approaches within a safeguarding framework, from both a single and a multi-agency perspective. Tanya's harrowing narrative – cited previously – reflects many of the issues we consider in this chapter, including the impact on the family and the child when abuse is not recognised or responded to by key safeguarding practitioners.

I think my main issue is trying to get over fact that like when my mum took me to police and social services when I were 11 and 12 years old and they basically ignored her and shunned her off all time. It were just like we were alone and like there were nothing else to do, so it were like the more they did that the more it allowed the perpetrators to do what they wanted to do and it made me feel like, where…how can I ever get away from it? They knew that, they had somebody on their side and they knew they could get away with it, they knew… It would never change like, there'd be occasions we'd be parked up and police would come straight there, and they'd just leave it and go…do you know, like that sort of thing. It were just weird like. For an 11- or 12-year-old, that just proved to me, that police had got no power. The police had no power whatsoever. I were brought up to know that the police were the ultimate, the ultimate service that can help you like, get out of things and help you out of things like that. But it were like…they didn't care. And it put me in a position where I couldn't change what were happening, I were only young. They were older, it were always forced upon me…and police couldn't do anything, social services wouldn't do anything. Me mum begged 'em to take me away, that's how bad it were, she begged 'em to take me away from Rotherham and they were like, 'no, she's fed, she comes home eventually', that sort of thing. Like, is that realistic? An 11-year-old going missing for two days, 'oh, she comes home eventually'. Do you know what I mean?

> I mean my mum found me locked inside somewhere and there were a police officer present and he never even did anything. Well, we're still trying to find out if he did ever report it into office. It were just like…'how can you do that?' A 12-year-old locked in a room, like a metre, a metre-sized room, all damp and disgusting, nowhere to go to toilet, nowhere to get a drink of water, DNA all over place and he were just like, 'Do you want dropping off at home or…' and mum was like 'we'll make us own way'. And it was just left at that. 'Oh I'll come and visit ya in a couple of days to take a statement' and he never turned up… (University of Sheffield Symposium, 2016)

It is to be hoped that cases like Tanya's will become less likely, as knowledge of how to respond effectively to CSE and CSA with a safeguarding children framework develops. This is precisely why we have written this book – to help challenge poor practice and develop better professional responses. In Adele's practice she has seen evidence of practitioners avoiding addressing issues of CSE and CSA as a result of perceptions that it is too complex, too specialist an area for some practitioners to respond. The reality is that these are safeguarding children and child protection issues, and all those working with children and their families need to be able to properly respond.

Understanding and applying thresholds

Most LSCB procedures contain a risk assessment tool with identifiable levels of risk and prescribed levels of response. These toolkits can often be invaluable to practitioners in helping them to determine when a case may have elements of CSE and CSA and what action they need to take. There is currently some debate in the UK as to whether having different thresholds according to levels of risk is helpful when working with such issues. On one hand, it is possible that practitioners feel uncertain that the case has reached a certain threshold and this may delay them taking action. On the other, there has to be acknowledgement that a low-risk case requires a very different response to that which is high risk. In addition, the numbers of cases being referred to social care are overwhelming, which requires, therefore, a screening process in order to prioritise need. Having a staggered response to different levels of risk allows cases to be managed so that those requiring an immediate, multi-agency response are not lost or delayed. What is important, however, is that an assessment of low or medium risk is never used to justify taking no action or solely to be a measure of reassurance.

Often the issue is not the existence of thresholds, but the way in which they are applied and how risk assessment tools are used. There are several factors that influence their application in CSE and CSA cases. One is how victims are regarded, and their behaviour judged. As seen in the previous two chapters, victims are also often treated as adults or as being more mature than other victims of child sexual abuse, and therefore perceived as being able to make decisions about their lives. In some cases, young people are allowed to dictate the terms of their care. In one case Adele worked with, a vulnerable 16-year-old young woman – living in residential care and with previous involvement in CSE – was regularly allowed to stay out 'with friends' without any attempt being made to determine who these friends were and whether they presented a risk to her. In reality, police systems recorded her being linked to a large number of men across different parts of the UK, but this had never been discussed within a multi-agency setting, despite her having been in care for a number of years. In this case, the professionals involved lost sight of the fact that she was a vulnerable child, probably experiencing abuse on a regular basis.

It is hoped that practice has now moved on sufficiently for practitioners both to recognise indicators of abuse and question the reason that the child may be behaving in a certain way. Case audits, effective training, team-meeting discussions and staff supervision should assist in helping practitioners to continue to develop their knowledge, skills and practice, and for their managers to be able to identify any practice issues that require improvement. Procedures and risk assessment tools will only have appropriate uses and outcomes if staff who use them are clear that all issues involving CSE and CSA require a safeguarding response.

Risk assessment tools

One of the first CSE risk assessment tools was developed by Derby Safeguarding Children Board and the National Working Group. Over recent years other LSCBs and CSE teams have developed risk assessment toolkits specific to the profiles and characteristics of their local area. The BLAST! Project in Yorkshire has also developed a guide for professionals working with boys and young men at risk of CSE (Michell and Dye, 2014).

As noted in Chapter 2, concerns have been expressed by some about the use of CSE risk assessment tools. In their rapid evidence assessment, Brown *et al.* (2016), for example, raise a number of questions about the basis on which indicators in the tools have been developed and whether some of them are indicators of abuse rather than of risk, with which we concur. They observe that the tools are reliant on practitioners having the knowledge and skills to complete them properly and whether they actually exclude professional judgement and analysis, which can result in young people being left at risk. They also question the lack of consistency in the tools which may mean that a young person may be assessed as high risk in one region, but not in a neighbouring one. Eaton and Dalby (2016) also discuss the lack of evidence base in response to Brown *et al.*'s report:

> The reality is that we continue to use diagnostic toolkits under the presumption that there is proven causal relationship between the risk indicators and the risk of CSE. Rigorous study is the only way to validate and test whether risk indicator toolkits are doing what they say on the tin and we welcome this recommendation from the authors.

While all of these concerns are valid and need to be debated, researched and a solid, evidence-based toolkit subsequently developed, current risk assessment tools should not be condemned absolutely. In terms of evaluating an individual young person's level of potential risk, it can be argued that such tools can be an effective starting point in helping practitioners achieve consistent standards of practice in their own locality. Risk assessment tools can assist them to identify CSE and CSA indicators and build a picture of what is happening in the young person's life, triggering conversations with other practitioners and services working with their family. They can assist practitioners in analysing what they know about a case and deciding what action to take. Some local authority areas have started to develop cross-regional tools (for example, Merseyside, Greater Manchester and West Yorkshire). Some LSCBs such as Derbyshire have audited practitioner responses to CSE and within this explored the role of risk assessment tools. Others have moved away from traditional risk assessment tool indicators. In Rotherham, for example, the CSE screening tool subdivides indicators into different categories:

- identification of vulnerability factors

- early indicators of CSE

- strong indicators of CSE

- significant risk factors.

This use of terminology is arguably more helpful to practitioners than the standard 'low', 'medium' and 'high' risk categories, and possibly reflects the local area's practice redevelopment since the publication of the Jay report (2014). The grouping of indicators in this way should leave any practitioner in no doubt that they may be considering indicators of abuse.

Some of the risk assessment tools reviewed by Brown *et al.* (2016) contain a very narrow view of a complex and difficult subject, which could mean that some victims are not likely to be identified if the indicators contained within the risk assessment tools are the only method of identification. Each local authority area must ensure that tools are used in appropriate ways and that practitioners do not exclude their own professional judgements. Some risk assessment tools contain specific prompts for practitioners to do this.

The debate following the publication of Brown *et al.*'s work has also revealed a concern that risk assessment tools can be seen to be more about managing resources and workloads than responding swiftly and effectively to CSE. Indeed, this is something noted by Brown *et al.* themselves (2016, p.24). There has to be a realistic and pragmatic approach to this. No local authority has the resources to immediately respond to all cases involving CSE and CSA. An assessment of risk and priority is therefore needed. While this may be unpalatable, in reality this is no different to established safeguarding practice. The key question is the effectiveness of local knowledge and procedures in guiding practitioners in making such assessments, so that all children whether vulnerable, at risk or abused through exploitation receive the appropriate response in a timely manner. Risk assessments are one part of a safeguarding structure in which all services have a role to play. Assessments are only effective when accompanied by action. In Wakefield, for example, risk assessments conducted by practitioners go to the CSE team where they are recorded centrally, which then triggers a multi-agency response. Cases assessed as high risk are considered at a regular multi-agency CSE (MACSE) meeting, which assesses information on a county-wide scale and identifies emerging patterns and trends.

We would suggest that the way forward is not to condemn risk assessment tools absolutely but to acknowledge the validity of the points that Brown *et al.* (2016) raise. While we await publication of evidence-based research in relation to risk indicators and guidance tools, all LSCBs should consider the appropriateness of the content of their current risk assessment tools (including the indicators, language and prompts for practitioners to analyse and use professional judgement), and the effectiveness of their implementation in practice.

Current Local Safeguarding Children's Board guidance

Guidance produced by each LSCB should be available alongside related procedures and training programmes, which are discussed in

Chapter 7. LSCB guidance should direct practitioners to identify the following categories, although it is acknowledged that terminology differs from county to county.

Identification of vulnerability factors

As discussed in Chapter 3, some young people have identifiable vulnerabilities which may lead them to becoming involved in CSE, or experiencing other safeguarding issues. While identification of such vulnerabilities is more likely to result in an early help assessment than trigger children's social care involvement, it is a vital intervention as it may prevent such abuse from ever occurring. Some of the factors identified by the Rotherham CSE screening tool include:

- lack of protective factors with a family unit

- migrant, refugee or asylum seeker

- living in a residential or foster care or unstable adoptive placement

- previous victim of CSE.

The last point is particularly important. Often following professional interventions, risk factors decrease but the original vulnerability is more than likely still present, along with the additional vulnerability that arises from being a victim of abuse. Any effective plan needs to address these issues with the young person.

Children who are missing or absent from home or care

Concerns have regularly been raised about the response of some statutory agencies when young people go missing. There was previously a more 'relaxed' attitude to those who repeatedly went missing, but who always eventually returned. What happened to them during that time was usually of little interest. The response to missing children is discussed by both Jay (2014) and Casey (2015). It is now appreciated that the more frequently a child goes missing, the more they are at risk of significant harm. These children are not 'streetwise'; they are extremely vulnerable. All agencies should abide by the Department for Education's statutory guidance in relation to children who go missing from home or care (2014).

Since April 2013 police forces have worked to the following definitions of 'missing' and 'absent' in relation to both children and adults reported to them as missing:

> missing: anyone whose whereabouts cannot be established and where the circumstances are out of character, or the context suggests the person may be a subject of crime or at risk of harm to themselves or another; and absent: a person not at a place where they are expected or required to be. (Department for Education, 2014, p.7)

Whether someone is classified as missing or absent is based on the ongoing police risk assessment, which is regularly reviewed until they have been found or return home.

There are consequences of erroneously labelling a young person involved in CSE as absent without authorisation as opposed to being missing. These include:

- the risks are minimised or not recognised

- there is no coordinated police search for them

- potential opportunities for intelligence gathering are lost

- parents and carers feel unable to protect them

- the child is more dependent on the abuser, because of their role in facilitating the child's absence and returning them home

- criminal acts committed go unchallenged

- patterns of repeated episodes are not tracked or identified

- potential people and locations of interest are not identified.

Many police forces have a policy that a young person at significant risk of or involved in CSE should never be regarded as absent, even when their whereabouts are known. In Derbyshire, a missing person's liaison worker reviews missing episodes involving young people known to the CSE team in order to identify any emerging pattern and assess whether a strategy meeting is required. In cases considered low risk, a professional should still review absent episodes and speak to the young person; low risk still means that there is some risk, including the risk of CSE. The ethos of the constabulary is that a response to a missing person report is not just concerned with returning them home safely, but also with investigation: why did the young person go missing; what happened while they were missing; who were they with; where did they go? This approach actively seeks to identify possible offending, and potential sources of time-limited evidence – such as CCTV and DNA – can be captured and used.

Low-risk/early indicators of CSE or CSA

In cases where the risk assessment suggests a young person is low risk, this should never be seen as a term of reassurance. Low risk does not mean no risk, and requires a professional response. The Rotherham screening tool describes this category more accurately as 'early indicators of CSE'. These include:

- becoming estranged from the family

- detachment from age-related activities

- returning home late

- hostility towards other family members.

In such cases, any intervention with the young person should involve consultation with children's social care and continuing involvement from an early help, intervention or multi-agency preventative team. A plan should be developed with the young person. This should have the aim of identifying and addressing the 'push and pull' factors that have enabled their involvement with their abuser, address any unmet needs they have and provide an alternative to whatever they feel the relationship with their abuser offers. Practitioners involved with the family or carers should provide them with specific information about CSE and CSA. Issues the practitioner should discuss with the young person include risk, healthy relationships and keeping safe. Wherever possible, information about the abuser should be gathered and shared with the multi-agency team, but particularly with the police, who should commence a plan of disruption and deterrence wherever possible. Often this can take the form of a Harbourer's Warning, which is a formal letter issued by the police advising a suspected abuser that a young person is under age and that the person with parental responsibility does not consent to the young person being with them. This is considered in the next chapter.

Medium-risk/strong indicators of CSE

This category reflects cases where indicators suggest that the child is involved in CSE, or that their involvement is imminent. The Rotherham LSCB screening tool uses the term 'strong indicators of CSE'. Some local authorities have historically treated medium-risk cases as 'child in need' cases. The risk indicators, however, show that this is an inappropriate and inadequate response to the risks identified, which include:

- considerable change in school performance/attendance/behaviour

- association with other victims of CSE or CSA

- found in areas with no known connection

- missing or absent from home

- unexplained relationships with adults

- changes in physical appearance, including a change in dress, weight loss, looking unwell.

Some of these factors are, unarguably, indicators of child sexual abuse. In these cases, there should be a targeted and specialist response to the identified risk factors for that young person, including a police response to any criminality identified and linked to the perpetrator. As with the low-risk/early indicators category, there should be a multi-agency plan of disruption in relation to the abuser, and active gathering and analysing of information to evaluate whether any police investigations can be initiated based on the intelligence assessments (this is discussed further in Chapter 5). In relation to the young person's risk assessment, the multi-agency team should actively share information, plan interventions and regularly review progress. Parents and carers should be supported in knowing what action they should take and when, particularly if they are tasked as witnesses to collect evidence from their child of grooming and abuse. Practitioners should undertake intensive and targeted work with the young person, including attempts to engage them in discussions about sexual abuse and healthy relationships. The role that education, health and residential care services play here is considerable as they can incorporate such work into natural settings and environments and deliver key messages without obviously targeting the young person.

High-risk/significant risk factors

The indicators here suggest that there is little doubt that the child is being sexually abused. These include:

- information about involvement in CSE/CSA from reliable sources

- inappropriately meeting known or unknown adults

- visiting hotels or other premises with adults

- associating with known CSE/CSA perpetrators or victims

- presence at 'hotspots'.

In these cases, there must be a child protection response, with strong, effective multi-agency partnerships making and reviewing decisions that actively protect the young person and result in action taken against the suspected abusers. This is likely to include helping young people recognise their own abuse and start to be able to talk about their experiences. It should also include identifying a geographically and psychologically safe place where they can have space to enable them to recognise that there is an alternative to their relationship with the abuser. It may involve a local authority considering legal measures to protect them, such as the use of injunctions and asking the court to use its inherent jurisdiction powers to restrain a person who may be a risk to young people from having contact with them (as seen in Birmingham City Council v Sarfraz Riaz and Others, 2014). Most LSCBs now have thresholds documents and accompanying guidance and procedures that follow the above structure. This assists in ensuring that children who are high risk are not lost in the overwhelming number of cases classified as CSE. Issues pertinent to LSCB policies and procedures are discussed in more detail in Chapter 7.

Components of effective practice

What is clear from both local and national guidance (for example, HM Government, 2015) is that the most essential element of good practice is effective multi-agency partnerships. Key practice points in relation to good partnership working are outlined below.

All practitioners have relevant knowledge and skills to recognise early indicators of CSE

CSE training should not solely be delivered to key professionals. As with any safeguarding issue, it is often staff in a prime position to recognise CSE indicators who are least likely to receive the necessary training. This includes school lunchtime supervisors, community support workers, park wardens, security staff, hotel reception staff and support staff such as administration staff. While there is a place for online learning, there is value in bringing staff together to explore and debunk some of the myths and stereotypes associated with CSE and CSA and the behaviour of the young people involved.

Such information can be met with disbelief and mistrust, so where there is no trainer on hand to discuss issues that may emerge in online learning environments, for example, this may limit the learning value.

There should not be just one level of awareness raising and professional development. Practitioners working with complex cases require far more detailed and specialist training than those who essentially need to know risk factors and indicators, how to make a referral and to whom. CSE and organised CSA are complex and evolving areas of safeguarding; knowledge surrounding them does not remain static. Practitioners find value in participating in a learning environment where they can reflect on their own cases, consider and discuss obstacles and challenges, as well as understand lessons learned from reviews and practice audits. A learning environment which facilitates sharing of ideas, experiences and innovative practice from different services or areas of the country helps practitioners recognise best practice and review their own and that of their team.

Questioning young people's behaviour and interrogating 'facts'

Behavioural indicators are often the first warning signs that a child may be involved in, or is at risk of, CSE or CSA. Yet all too often it is the behaviour, not the cause, that is identified as the problem. As discussed in previous chapters, the child's behaviour is the symptom of the abuse and the method by which they may be processing or communicating the trauma. If it is not questioned why the child's behaviour has changed, it is more likely that no one will recognise that they are being abused, thus allowing the abuse to continue. As discussed in Chapter 3, it also makes it less likely that the child will make a disclosure, as they will likely feel that no one cares about them and that there is nothing they can do to stop the abuse. Practitioners must recognise that abuse is never the child's fault and not something to which they have contributed; it is also essential they communicate this to the child. As discussed in earlier chapters, children often blame themselves for the abuse. They may also blame themselves – and are blamed by the perpetrator – for any professional action that is taken as a result of their disclosure, especially if there are consequences for them or their family. The following case example illustrates the importance of close questioning of behaviour:

> The police found Terri with three of her abusers when she was reported missing from care. When she was abusive to the police officers, they told her that she was not helping herself. She was given an option to cooperate with the police in front of her abusers and responded by running away from the officers. The officers did not pursue her, and recorded on police systems that Terri was not a 'real' victim of crime. She returned to care the following day. She refused to engage with any professionals. It was several months before she disclosed prolific and repeated abuse involving the three men that the police had found her with, but had not questioned.

This can be contrasted to another case example:

> A police community support officer identified that Lisa was demonstrating indicators of CSE. She was immediately given targeted and intensive support that was empathic, understanding and nurturing. She began talking about her experiences and the conversations she had with her workers enabled her to understand that she had been groomed and exploited. Lisa was able to make a full disclosure about her abuse, including talking about other young people who were also involved, and felt confident to agree to make a statement to the police.

In the first case example, the police should have questioned the actions and motives of the three adult men found with Terri. If they had done so, their responses to her and her behaviour would have been very different. She may have found the confidence to tell the police what was happening to her, rather than endure further abuse for several more months. In the second case, indicators of CSE were promptly recognised and Lisa was immediately seen as a victim of abuse. The consequent supportive environment and responses facilitated Lisa's disclosures about the abuse and her cooperation with a police investigation.

The second practice point that emerges from this is about interrogating the facts of a case. Often when conducting case reviews, it is possible to see comments in case records such as 'Jason is said to have a new mobile phone'. What becomes clear when speaking to the practitioner who made the record, is that no thought had been given to the following issues:

- Does Jason actually have a new phone?

- If so, where did he get it from?

- If Jason says it was bought, from where and does he have the funds to buy a phone?

- Has the phone been given as a gift, and if so, who from? What is known about this person? What is their motive in giving Jason a phone?

- Did Jason need a new phone or has this appeared without explanation in addition to another existing phone? If so, why does Jason need another phone?

And finally…

- Is the phone an indicator that Jason is involved in CSE or CSA?

The fact that Jason has a new mobile phone should be recorded in his case notes; exploration of the implications of the new phone should also be included. Case reviews conducted by Adele have often identified similar records which, if analysed by the practitioner or their manager, should have led them to identify issues of risk and indicators of CSE or CSA. Instead, the children's abuse continued for several more months until it was finally recognised. Another instance is where there is a query regarding an entry in the young person's case notes, but the practitioner assumes the answer. For example, one young woman was said to be regularly collecting a lot of condoms from a local sexual health service. The practitioner made, and subsequently recorded, a number of assumptions including:

- she was exaggerating the number

- it was good that she was practising 'safe sex'

- she was probably giving out condoms to other young people

- if there was a problem, the sexual health service would inform the practitioner.

In reality, the sexual health service was making their own assumptions that if there were concerns about the young person, social care would contact them. A key opportunity to find out why she was requesting so many condoms was, therefore, lost. This was a key indicator of abuse that was missed by the practitioners involved and was not actually picked up until a case review was held.

Preventative work with children and families

In previous chapters we have considered how a lack of knowledge and understanding of relationships has often made young people vulnerable to CSE and organised CSA, and yet we can only expect them to know what a healthy relationship is if we give them that information. In assisting them to have a healthy lifestyle, we might give them information on diet, exercise, road safety, alcohol consumption, protection against sexually transmitted infections and unwanted pregnancies. In such instances, we guide them to recognise what is healthy and what is risky. But when it comes to relationships, we expect young people instinctively to know what is good or what is not. A young person might say the key ingredients of a good relationship are:

- an attractive partner

- excitement

- fun

- someone who is nice to them

- someone who is generous

- someone who pays them compliments.

We can forget that without similar life experiences and knowledge of older adults, young people often have a different view of healthy relationships. In reality, their perceptions may be naive, but they tend to focus on what feels good and what is fun. This, of course, also reflects the grooming process as discussed in Chapter 3. Initially, therefore, it can be difficult to distinguish a CSE 'relationship' from other teenage relationships where young people are learning how to be emotionally, physically and sexually intimate with another person. Prevention is key in safeguarding young people and enabling them to protect themselves. This includes supporting them to be able to recognise:

- an unhealthy relationship

- people who may pose a risk to them

- signs of grooming

- how some behaviours may make them more vulnerable.

The role that the personal, social, health and economic education (PSHE) curriculum in schools can play in this is significant. Good quality awareness raising that supports young people to make informed and safe decisions is essential. Schools, colleges, academies and other places where young people socialise should also look at innovative ways to raise awareness and start discussions. This can involve the use of posters, social media, educational topics and projects and assemblies.

Independent Training Services in Barnsley, for example, is an educational establishment that works with young people who cannot or do not want to access mainstream further education; it offers education and development opportunities, including apprenticeships. CSE and safeguarding issues are embedded in the curriculum from the point of induction, when the students are introduced to their tutors and learning environments. The curriculum includes 'hot topics', of which CSE is one, and further learning is continued through lesson plans and one-to-one reviews with learners. This proactive approach has resulted in staff being able to identify and respond to issues of CSE which have been raised.

Several external organisations also deliver specialist awareness raising programmes in schools. One example of this is the Alter Ego Theatre Group. Their production, *Chelsea's Choice*, has been delivered to over 410,000 young people in schools throughout the UK and has prompted a significant number of disclosures (Alter Ego Theatre Company, undated). In 2015 BLAST in Leeds, which works with young men affected by issues of CSE, delivered group work in educational and youth settings to 3,565 children and young people (mostly boys) on how to recognise the signs of grooming and where to get information, help and support. Of the young people who gave feedback, 92 per cent talked about what they would do differently because of the session, and a number of disclosures were made.

While we have considered the role of education here, this is by no means the only service that can and should raise the awareness of young people. Residential services such as children's care homes have an important role to play in this and in giving positive adult role models to children. In Jonathan's case, which we discussed in Chapter 3, it was the good quality work delivered by residential staff that enabled him to recognise and talk about his abuse. In other cases it has been intensive youth or family support or MATs (multi-agency teams) which have been able to deliver this. Derbyshire County Council is currently producing an education resource, *Dani's Story*, for use with young people, schools and professionals. This is based on the experiences of one young woman, her family and the professionals working with them. In that case, the work of the MAT was of consistent and exceptional quality and helped Dani and her family considerably. Any service which has contact with young people should consider what they can do that might make a difference to a young person, or a setting, especially when they have established a good relationship with one young person, or a group of young people.

The need to educate and inform is also very relevant for parents and carers. One observation from parent support organisations, such as PACE in Leeds, has been that parents have been at a loss to understand their child's change in behaviour. Most initially decided that it was just typical teenage behaviour. The impact of finding out that what they assumed was adolescence was in fact the warning signs of abuse is considerable. Working with and supporting families who may be a protective factor can play a significant part in safeguarding plans, which are more likely to be effective than without the families' input and involvement. Additionally, empowering parents to have a role in protecting their children and enabling investigations to commence against their abusers is a powerful component in their ability to cope with what has happened to their child. One parent from Adele's private practice visited the PACE website and downloaded its Advice to Parents guidance. Following the information, she was able to gather evidence against her daughter's abuser; that evidence led to his subsequent conviction and imprisonment and marked the start of the family's recovery. PACE has supported many parents across the UK. It uses a range of methods to share experiences and advice with parents, including:

- national parent network days

- an online parent forum for 24/7 peer support

- one-to-one peer matches and befriending to provide additional emotional support to complement support given by the national parent support team

- local parent groups for low-level risk cases in areas where they have co-located parent liaison officers (currently in Yorkshire, Lancashire and Greater Manchester) to talk about prevention and managing low-level risk situations. Families experiencing high risk have intensive one-to-one support.

Safeguarding strategic overviews

These are considered in more depth in later chapters, but here we acknowledge developments that have impacted on improving local safeguarding practice. CSE and organised CSA are too complex for a response by one service in isolation. Some areas, therefore, have created CSE coordinator or lead posts which act as single points of contact in local authority areas and with whom concerns about practice and advice on complex cases can be sought and shared. This is a similar concept to multi-agency hubs or teams, which operate as a partnership service with co-located practitioners. Best practice often results when cases are shared with partners, and where there is a multi-agency response that addresses issues of protection, prevention and investigation and offers targeted support for the young person and their family. A strategic overview is essential to ensure that local data is interrogated in order to facilitate the recognition of profiles and patterns that exist in the area. Where CSE and CSA is only responded to on a case-by-case basis, the ability to recognise perpetrators, offending patterns and locations is lost, as is the capability to act in order to prevent the abuse of another child. We consider this further in Chapters 5 and 7.

Derbyshire County Council, for example, has amended its internal case management system to place a flag on a young person's record to alert staff that they are considered to be at risk of CSE or CSA. To ensure consistent practice, standard forms – such as the looked-after child statutory review forms and return from missing forms – have boxes which are ticked where the relevant indicators are identified. This assists the locality staff to identify children and young people who are involved, as well as identifying further issues for exploration. As will also be discussed in later chapters, some local authorities have started public awareness campaigns aimed at both equipping local communities to identify concerns and increasing the flow of information shared with the police. These approaches are examples of strategic approaches that address issues of CSE and organised CSA and aim to create communities that are safe havens for vulnerable young people, not places where perpetrators can hide and take advantage of opportunities.

Information sharing

Information sharing will be discussed in more detail in Chapter 5, but it is pertinent to reference here Operation Retriever, in Derby in 2010, which resulted in the first police investigation in the UK to bring about convictions of perpetrators of organised CSA. The intelligence that led to the investigation and subsequent prosecutions in Derby came from information being shared by services in the area, predominantly by a third-sector organisation, Safe and Sound. In any local area, practitioners and services have information regarding young people and possible perpetrators. Some of this may seem irrelevant or insignificant and not appropriate to share with the police, but sharing it with the police will enable them to build the bigger picture, investigate possible criminality, map and profile local activity and identify potential suspects. The value of such information cannot be understated and should not be underestimated by those in partner agencies.

Operation Retriever led to police forces across the UK investing in intelligence systems, and information-sharing protocols being designed with LSCBs. In some areas there have been jointly launched operations designed at prompting the sharing of information with the police. Operation Liberty in Derbyshire is one such example, where practitioners share CSE and organised CSA information with Derbyshire Constabulary, whether it is known fact or information that has been passed to them by a third party. The Operation is referenced in the LSCB policies and procedures and multi-agency training; it has also been accompanied by a high-profile publicity campaign encouraging members of the public and local businesses to identify CSE and share information.

Robust multi-agency partnerships

As is also discussed in Chapter 7, where practice is most effective is where there are strong multi-agency partnerships with common goals and each plays an active role in ensuring that the strategy and practice are evaluated, reviewed and scrutinised. It is where honest dialogue takes place regarding challenges and partners' experiences and when practice does not meet expected standards. Robust and transparent review should also ensure that plans or action points of individual cases are not being delivered by one lone practitioner or a service acting in isolation. Difficult and informed decisions about cases where the risk is not reducing can – and should – be made together. Gaps in local resources and services can be identified and senior managers informed as part of the strategic response.

Although which service is involved will vary depending on the needs of the child, broadly speaking the types of services that should be considered when developing plans to respond to CSE are social care, the police, health (this could be number of different services. including therapeutic provision), education, family support and specialist CSE services. The success of the partnership lies in having a clear vision of risk, effective working thresholds guidance and actions taken which encompass a holistic approach to the needs of the child and their family. Successful partnership action is more likely to result in improved outcomes for the child and their family.

Creative engagement with the child and dealing with non-engagement

As acknowledged earlier in this book, engaging with children involved in CSE and organised CSA is often a challenge, which requires persistence, imagination and patience. Being able to withstand tests set by the young person is part of the process of engagement. In her autobiography, Jayne Senior, former manager of the Risky Business Project in Rotherham, recollects an incident where she collected a young person to take her shopping:

> I sat in my car outside the broken and peeling front door... As she walked down the scruffy, can-strewn path, I examined the outfit she'd chosen for the trip – a black baby-doll nightie, completely see through, with feather trim. She had nothing on underneath but a G-string and on her feet a pair of tottering high heels... 'Fuck off,' she said. 'Good morning to you too. Debbie,' I said brightly. 'You look nice...' 'Fuck off.' 'Just the thing for going bed shopping,' I said. 'You couldn't have chosen better.' The night before, we'd had some trivial argument over the phone that ended with her telling me where to go and that she never wanted to see me again. This was normal. Of course, I never did what she wanted, which is why she

was trying so hard to shock me with her appearance…her looking like something from a trucker's dirty magazine and me trying to keep my cool. I never mentioned the outfit again, which infuriated her even more. Finally, we got to the bed store at the edge of town. 'Right,' I said. 'Let's go and have a look. You coming?' She looked at me, then pulled her nightie around her… 'Oh fuck off,' she replied before pulling a top and a pair of jeans from her carrier bag. Then she smiled at me. 'I'm sorry, Jayne,' she said. (Senior, 2016, pp.1–2)

Engagement with young people involved in CSE and CSA usually offers countless challenges such as the example above. Others include unpredictable behaviour, irregular contact, hostility, changing their minds about decisions already made, testing practitioners out and pushing them away. Engagement needs dedication and understanding. It also has to offer the young person something that counterbalances the excitement of having contact with the abuser, or that meets their needs. Offering young people a safe place to talk is not enough; quite often talking is the last thing they want to do.

Creative approaches to engagement, developed in recent years, have included a 'mindfulness' approach – contacting a young person by text or a messaging service to remind them that they are not alone, that there are places they can go to for support, that they do have value and choices and that there are places that can help them. Websites such as It's not OKAY help young people find out more about issues of CSE and know what to do to report abuse. It lets them know that there are people who care about them and who can help them. An online app, due for release in 2017, has been developed by the Children's Commissioner in partnership with Dame Esther Rantzen and practitioners, including Adele, around the UK. Aimed at teenagers who may not recognise they are being groomed or abused, it can answer their questions about their experiences or about what is happening in their lives and give them access to a confidential advice service that may result in them being able to identify they may be at risk and act to prevent abuse.

Ultimately, the key to engagement is seeing the child, not simply their behaviour, and understanding why engagement may be so terrifying when for practitioners it is the obvious and only choice the child should make. Practitioners should ensure that attempts to facilitate engagement are balanced. They should not increase the risk to young people by overlooking or not addressing risky behaviour, or allowing children to dictate circumstances which ultimately facilitate abuse. This is often a difficult balancing act and one that differs with each individual child. Good line management support, supervision and effective multi-agency scrutiny, as discussed in Chapter 7, are key to ensuring that this balance is achieved and that there is a collective responsibility for addressing failure to engage.

Addressing a child's failure to engage

The preceding chapter considered why a child may not engage with services. Here we discuss how this may be achieved. There is no easy answer or quick fix to lack of engagement but a good starting point is to consider why there is no engagement. The following should be considered:

- What does engagement offer the child?

- What might they think it will cost them?

- What are their presenting issues?

- What might be an effective trigger to starting a working relationship? Who is best placed to do this? Are they able to give the time and commitment necessary?

- Who is going to be there for the young person out of hours?

- Who is going to support the practitioner or organisation that is trying to engage the child?

Failure to engage is not an issue for just one organisation; it is a problem which needs to be reviewed, discussed and addressed by all the services involved. It includes monitoring the child's risk while exploring different ideas and approaches. In some cases, it has to be acknowledged that the young person might never engage.

These are perhaps the hardest cases for practitioners; where there are no positive outcomes, no reduction of risk and a young person repeatedly experiences abuse. Such cases can feel hopeless, but continuing attempts by practitioners to engage can give the victim hope and make a difference; small affirmations of self-worth which result from such contact can mean long-term survival, as historical survivors acknowledge. No case is without hope, and practitioners, therefore, should never give up on a child or stop considering with partner services what to offer and how to protect them.

Engagement with families and carers

Principles of engagement also extend to families. Where they are a protective factor in their child's life, working in partnership with them strengthens that protection and supports them in addressing issues for both the child and themselves. Sometimes their family is the key to their survival, as Tanya clearly believes:

> My family's the main thing. My mum, my uncles, my close uncles – they're the only thing that has shown me the way. (University of Sheffield Symposium, 2016)

Tanya's mother went to extraordinary lengths to try to safeguard her child. She was so desperate to protect her child that she wanted to place her in local authority care, only they failed to see the obvious risk to the child and would not help.

> Me mum was a single mum, so she was like struggling like to get to work, she were doing nights, she were coming looking for me all the time… school were reporting that I'd not turned into school. So it were like she were a yoyo, she weren't getting help from anyone… I remember one specific occasion, she come and when we went down [to children's social care], literally, about a month before finding out I were pregnant, and she said to them, 'If you don't take her now, something mad's gonna happen to her.' And they said, 'No, we can't, there's nothing…she comes home, you're feeding

her, she's not neglected, what do you want us to do?' (University of Sheffield Symposium, 2016)

When parents try to protect their children, it makes them part of the solution rather than the problem. Practitioners should consider what they would want services to do if it was their child being harmed or abused; what would be their needs? Where parents are actively involved in strategies regarding their children, the family becomes stronger. The following case studies illustrate this:

In Case A the parents of a 14-year-old girl had been raising concerns for a number of months about their daughter. They had raised concerns when she was missing from home, only to be disillusioned by the response of the police which included reprimanding the young woman for wasting police time when she was found. Their attempts to gain support and guidance from the local authority were equally frustrating. There were a number of incidents where the response they received left them feeling stressed, anxious and helpless in the fight to protect their daughter. Eventually, the case became a safeguarding referral and after a case conference the young woman was placed on the list of children subject to a child protection plan. The plan contained strategies that the parents had tried and knew would not work but they were not consulted. The plan also contained a proposal that the parents attend a parenting course. Not understanding that this was something that could help them, but instead seeing this as a direct criticism of their parenting skills, the parents refused to engage further with the plan. The plan had an overwhelming number of objectives, over half of which related to the actions of a family which was no longer engaging.

In Case B, the circumstances of the case are broadly similar. In this case, however, the family was involved in discussions around strategies and invited to comment on proposals as the experts on their daughter. The plan was formulated which included serving a Harbourer's Warning on the offenders and tasking the parents with gathering evidence, including keeping a log, details of phone calls, messages, computer screen shots and details of cars collecting Emily from home. It also involved a prioritised police response when she was reported missing, and tasking her parents with collecting her underwear and giving it to the police for forensic testing. The actions of her parents enabled a case to be brought against the offender, who pleaded guilty to child sexual offences in the face of overwhelming evidence. Emily's parents felt empowered by the role they had played to protect their child.

In some case reviews conducted by Adele there was a misidentification of parents as positive factors, and assessments were made that they could effectively protect their children. In some of these cases, however, the parent had initially sought help because they felt unable to adequately protect their child. In other cases, some of the families were identified as protective factors when previous or even recent social care involvement showed that they were anything but. This included cases where parents had consistently been unable to meet their children's needs or put them first, and where they had failed to act to protect their children in the past (for example, by not reporting them missing to the police or actively questioning where they were, who they were with and whether they were safe). In some cases there appeared to be an assumption that if a child was living at home, then their parents were protective factors.

Equally, accurately identifying parents as protective factors should mean working in partnership and using extra resources to assist and support the family. Professional support and intervention should not be withdrawn on the assumption that the family can adequately protect their child and professional involvement is, therefore, not needed. Practitioners should consider how – if the parents were unable to stop the child being targeted in the first instance – they will realistically respond to issues of trauma, chaotic behaviour, ongoing and increasing risk and abuse without support. Withdrawal of services in such cases should be decided on evidence-based assessments and multi-agency discussions, which do not result in the child being placed at further risk.

Therapeutic responses

As discussed in the previous chapter, CSE and CSA cause extensive trauma to the victim. Even with the most effective plans and interventions, such trauma will not disappear without specialist provision. Yet while not all abused children want to access therapy, many not only want to but also vitally need such interventions. Family members, including parents and siblings, may also need their own therapy in order to try and process what has happened, or is happening. They may also be included in the therapeutic response for their child, such as family therapy sessions.

Enabling a child to access therapy may:

- help them understand and cope with their experiences
- help them develop coping strategies in dealing with the effects of trauma and possibly preventing future abuse
- address previous and future vulnerability factors (including those for siblings)
- assist parents in repairing the damage to the family
- assist carers in forming loving relationships with children whom they care for
- assist professionals in forming positive relationships with abused children
- enable children to form positive relationships of their own
- increase positive outcomes for the child and enable them to become survivors of their abuse
- improve outcomes for other children in the family, by helping them address the trauma that they have witnessed and of which they may have been a part.

Incorporating therapy into plans is likely to make professional interventions more effective and shorten the timescales that services need to be involved with the family. It can avoid the need for future professional involvement and it can also assist with staff welfare – being involved in a case where a young person is able to move past the abuse is rewarding and motivating for the practitioners involved.

Effective planning and review

Cases involving CSE and organised CSA often result in the involvement of a large number of services in order to address the child's different risk factors. As noted previously, these cases can feel overwhelming to the professionals involved, let alone the family. A way forward is for a smaller dedicated group to look at the issues identified by the proposed plan, whether it is a strategy plan, CSE plan, child in need plan or child protection plan. The risks and issues that require immediate responses should be identified; those remaining should be divided into medium- and long-term aims. Where possible, the issues and needs of both the young person and family should be incorporated into the short-, medium- and long-term planning. Approaching the plan in this way immediately makes it appear more achievable. As the desired outcomes of the child and their family are included, they are more likely to engage and maintain participation. There will also be fewer practitioners working with the child and their family, but undertaking very targeted work. By starting to work on medium-term aims once short-term goals have been achieved, the plan can build on early successful outcomes, which is positive for all involved.

We have discussed how CSE can result in unpredictable behaviour from the young person. Change, even that which is positive, can lead to a sense of panic, loss or confusion. Additionally, abusers may have invested a lot of time, effort and risk in a young person and will not want to lose power or control over them. We see breaking away from perpetrators as positive but, as with domestic violence relationships, it often represents the time of greatest risk to the young person. Contingency planning is, therefore, an important element of effective plans. Plans are often based on the 'what needs to happen' approach; effective plans should also have a 'what if they don't' element of planning. Given that most crises occur out of hours or unexpectedly, it is important that consideration is also given to what can and should happen in such circumstances to support and protect the child, what services are available out of hours and whether they will be able to accurately understand their needs and the risks facing them and be able to safeguard them.

An essential element of effective planning is review. The aims of a plan – whatever type – need to be SMART (specific, measurable, achievable, realistic, time measurable). If a plan is not reviewed how do the child, their family and practitioners know if it is being effective? How can they assess whether the risks are changing and new ones emerging? No effective plan remains static; it should develop, evolve and reflect the child's current situation. However good a plan is 'on paper', it is meaningless without an evaluation of its effectiveness. Plans need to have multiple foci: on the needs of the young person, the risks to them, the family or carers and tackling the abuser/s. They should also feed into wider CSE and organised CSA profiling and strategies in the locality, contributing to analysis that identifies patterns, locations and persons of interest, as well as other young people who – currently – may be low risk.

Finally, before plans are de-escalated or concluded, final questions should be asked:

- Have the practitioner responses to the risk presented by the abuser been responded to in a way that is likely to protect other young people?

- Have the original vulnerabilities that led to the young person being involved been addressed?

- Has there been a response to the trauma which, if otherwise left unaddressed, would have resulted in future vulnerability leading to further abuse?

- Have the difficulties and challenges identified in the child's case been reflected on in individual supervisions?

- Have those same difficulties and challenges been communicated to senior manager's level so that they can be addressed strategically?

Staff supervision and support

In the UK, we seem to increasingly view practitioners as automatically having personal and professional resilience, able to appropriately respond to cases involving horrific abuse and carry on with their day-to-day lives and practice unaffected. This perception loses sight of the practitioner as an individual and the recognition that they are human and as such are often personally impacted on by the children with whom they work. This is certainly likely to be true of CSE and organised CSA cases, where children suffer appalling levels of sexual and psychological abuse. Staff more likely to be impacted by such work are those who:

- are new to practice, inexperienced or unconfident

- have never previously worked with a child involved in CSE or CSA

- are working with a child who is suffering particularly sadistic or extreme abuse or the victim is particularly vulnerable

- are working with a child whose risk factors are increasing and they and their family will not engage

- are poorly supported, with ineffective supervision or none at all

- have been allocated the majority responsibility for achieving the aims of the child's strategy or plan

- have engaged with the young person or family in a way which has blurred professional boundaries or roles

- have a number of traumatic or difficult cases in their caseloads

- do not have access to any kind of professional support

- have recently returned from maternity leave or extended leave due to ill health, particularly mental ill health

- are experiencing difficulties in their personal lives

- have their own experiences of abuse.

The serious case review into Operation Brooke (Myers and Carmi, 2013) found that the service model in operation in one of the authorities involved was particularly demanding for the staff who were trying to safeguard the children:

> Such a model of service delivery was at immense personal and emotional cost to staff. One of the team managers in the case group reported that she felt totally responsible for the young person's missing episodes and impact it was having on police time. The social worker and team manager gave vivid examples where they were out at night and weekends looking for the young person or bringing them back to a safe place. (p.27)

The model was subsequently discontinued, and redeveloped to one that provided increased supervisory support to its staff.

In the same way that young people often do not talk about their abuse, professionals such as those above may be reluctant to approach a manager or supervisor. This can be out of personal or professional embarrassment or fear of being regarded as inadequate or weak, or may be due to their inability to recognise that they need support and assistance. Where practitioners are working with children involved in CSE and organised CSA, welfare and wellbeing checks should be built into regular supervision. Additionally, the supervisor should make regular, informal checks on their staff, have an 'open door' policy for unscheduled discussions and ensure that there is access to independent support if required. These types of support help to ensure a consistent quality to the work of the practitioner with children and their families. It also impacts positively on the contribution that they make to their service and with colleagues working with other such cases. It also helps safeguard their own generic health and wellbeing.

Group supervision may also be of value in teams where a number of practitioners are involved and is useful in multi-agency teams where there are different roles and responsibilities. This type of supervision helps colleagues learn from one another's practice, as well as share feelings related to both the difficulties and successes of their work. Group sessions may be conducted without managers present, or with external facilitators, to enable practitioners to feel they can speak more freely about some of the issues they are experiencing. Ground rules for such sessions are as crucial for group work as for individual supervision, so that everyone knows what is permissible and what might ultimately have to be shared with managers. Group supervision can also be used in the evaluation of service responses to CSE and CSA, to gather staff opinions about what is working well and what improvements need to be made both within organisations and externally. Chapter 7 discusses management and organisational responsibilities in relation to staff support and supervision.

Practice issues for staff working with adults

Although much of the focus in relation to organised sexual abuse is rightly on child victims and children's services, there are different but related and equally complex issues for adult services. Once a young person turns 18 years old, they usually – unless the local authority is the corporate parent – transition into adult services. Adult services need to be able to respond effectively to issues of organised sexual abuse.

There are different groups of adult victims and survivors. There are adults who were groomed and abused as children, and this continues once they turn 18. Where they disclose abuse or it otherwise comes to light, with their consent and presuming they have mental capacity, they should subsequently become the subject of a safeguarding adult enquiry with an associated police investigation. There are also adults who are no longer being abused but disclose historic organised CSA to which the statutory adult agencies have a duty to respond, including a police investigation. There are also those who may become victims as young adults, particularly those who are vulnerable due to having learning or physical disabilities. As discussed in Chapter 3, young adults with learning disabilities can be particularly vulnerable. Much of the information in preceding chapters is relevant and useful for staff working with adults who have been, or are, victims of organised sexual abuse.

Even when the sexual, physical and psychological abuse has ended, the majority of survivors will require some type of care and support as adults, due to significant and complex personal issues as a consequence of their experiences. These include mental ill health, self-harm, pregnancy, termination, motherhood and raising a child who was the result of rape or other abuse with the father, problematic use of illicit drugs or alcohol, interrupted education resulting in unemployment or low-paid jobs with subsequent economic insecurity. The main principles of the Care Act 2014 include promoting wellbeing and preventing, reducing or delaying care and support needs. Local authorities must apply these principles when working with adults with care and support needs (Department of Health, 2016), including undertaking assessments and safeguarding enquiries. As adults, their care and support needs must be assessed and plans developed with them and actioned in order to be able to offer them the most appropriate support and promote their wellbeing.

Under the Care Act 2014 the local authority has a duty to make enquiries if there are concerns that an adult with care and support needs is experiencing, or is at risk of, abuse or neglect and as a result of those needs is unable to protect themselves. This applies, for example, where an adult with care and support needs discloses sexual exploitation or organised abuse, or if a family member or member of the public expresses concerns about such an adult. Staff should follow their own organisation's procedures in conjunction with their Local Safeguarding Adults Board (SAB) procedures, in order to take the correct course of action. Where a referral is received by adult social care, it may be decided that a discussion or meeting should be held to plan who takes what action. This must include the police, whose role is to investigate any crimes that may have been committed, collect evidence and – where they believe there is a case – present to the Crown Prosecution Service to decide whether it is appropriate to charge suspects.

Undertaking assessments can be a key point for victims and survivors. They may disclose distressing, intimate information as well as taking initial steps to form trusting relationships with the professionals tasked with protecting them. Relationships of trust need to be built over time and staff need to be appropriately skilled in active listening to pick up on small clues or unexplained changes in behaviour which may arise during an assessment with adults who are experiencing or have experienced sexual abuse. Where adults do disclose concerns about sexual abuse, these must be heard, taken seriously and acted on. Where care staff suspect that adults living in their organisation's residential homes or supported living arrangements are being targeted by perpetrators, they should undertake an assessment in relation to this specific risk. Where assessments identify specific issues related to organised sexual abuse, whether it be current or historic, the practitioner should discuss with their line manager and, where the adult gives their consent, refer to relevant specialist services. Transition assessments, required under the Care Act, should also be conducted with young people who will be in the process of transitioning from children's services to adult care and support. For young people who have been subject to child sexual exploitation, it is crucial that their needs are clearly identified through assessment and action taken to ensure ongoing support and protection. The local authority should ensure that the support needs of their parents or carers are also identified through assessment and a plan developed with them.

It is recognised that organised sexual abuse is very likely to have long-lasting effects for victims, survivors and their families. These may range from psychological and emotional issues requiring counselling services, to entrenched mental ill health and substance misuse. These, in turn, place further stress on them and their families and require intervention from health and social care services in order to reduce or delay a deterioration in their health. The provision of appropriate post-abuse support to those who have suffered trauma can significantly improve their lives in terms of health and family relationships. Survivors are likely to require support and therapeutic intervention for an extended period of time. Local SABs should work with partners to ensure the delivery of post-abuse support, and that staff, frontline managers and victims and their families know how to refer adults to such support.

Children of adult victims and survivors

In Chapter 3 we discussed some of the issues for girls and young women who become pregnant as a result of organised CSA, a significant number whom in the past would have been failed by children's social care when they became pregnant or mothers. We have received some reports in the course of writing this book that mothers who have been victims of CSA and had children with their intimate terrorists are being treated differently because of their past abuse. The concerns relate to:

- children removed from the care of mothers who asked for, but did not receive, help to protect them from their abusive ex-partners. They were removed on the grounds they failed to protect them

- perpetrators of CSA being asked if they want to adopt their children

- children being removed rather than offering the mother the support she requires in order to be able to stay with her children, safeguard them and promote their welfare

- social workers not adhering to court orders in relation to contact between mother and children, so contact has failed to take place on a significant number of occasions

- out-of-date information in relation to the mother being included in court reports, with her significant progress being omitted

- parents of victims looking after their grandchildren as they have been removed from their daughter, having to facilitate contact and access visits for the perpetrator fathers.

These are a small number of cases, some of which are the subject of local authority complaints and ongoing court cases. Some of these issues are not confined to those who are organised CSA victims, but have also been experienced by other parents whose children have been removed from their care. Whatever the reality of these individual cases, some practitioners believe that there are mothers who – having been failed by children's social care as children – are now being revictimised by the same services in relation to their own children. These may be isolated cases, but this issue may warrant further investigation, which is not possible within the confines of this book. As well as the consequences for the victims and their children, there are also concerns that this is impacting on others coming forward to disclose past abuse. They are unlikely to do so if they are concerned – rightly or wrongly – their children will be removed as a result.

Where there are any concerns about a mother or father's ability to protect their child where they have a history of CSA, the individuals should be subject to the same assessment process as any other parent. The fact that they were previously abused does not automatically mean they are unable to safeguard their own child. While such information may be disclosed during their child's assessment, it is how they have coped with the trauma that they suffered and how that has impacted on their life and that of their child that is the key issue. Tanya is testament to the fact that not all such parents struggle to safeguard their children:

> social services…I ain't really had much to do with them, since back then… Well, I've moved on a lot. Cos I boxed it all up and shut it all out and then… I've done a lot of stuff. I've been fortunate enough to be able to…shut it to one side and just be myself, and make something for me and my kids. And that's most important thing. I don't let it beat me. Never. (University of Sheffield Symposium, 2016)

Summary

In this chapter we have considered how best practice ensures that practitioners recognise and respond effectively to risk, that they question and analyse a child's behaviour in relation to known indicators of CSE and organised CSA, and respond appropriately if a child fails to engage with them. We discussed thresholds, risk assessment tools – particularly in light of Brown *et al.*'s (2016) comments regarding a lack of evidence for these – and levels of risk. We favour using different terminology from low, medium and high risk in order to avoid practitioner presumptions of low risk meaning no risk, and to acknowledge that some medium- and high-risk indicators are not indicators of risk but are actually indicators of abuse. We illustrated this with an example of such from Rotherham LSCB's CSE toolkit.

We have considered some additional component parts of effective practice: knowledge and skills to recognise early indicators, preventative work, sharing information, creative engagement with the child and their family, being able to assess, understand and learn where they fail to engage. We have also discussed the value of therapeutic responses, although we recognise that this is not necessarily appropriate for all victims and survivors. We have recognised the value of early intervention and preventative work, and work which addresses the needs of the family and child in a holistic way, and increases protective factors by involving families in plans and actions regarding their children. We have looked at the parts that families and multi-agency partnerships play. Part of effective interventions has to include a robust, multi-agency planning and review process, which involves the child and their family or carer. We also discuss issues for practitioners working with adults who either disclose historic CSA or are being targeted as vulnerable adults – especially where they have learning or physical disabilities, but also in relation to women who have had children with their intimate terrorist 'boyfriends'. While Chapter 7 discusses strategic and senior manager responses in detail, we emphasise here the importance of effective partnerships and having strategic oversight on local CSE and organised CSA issues. A fundamental issue that underpins all such practitioner work is effective supervision and support. This is vital to ensure that staff remain focused, clear minded and resilient, a critical factor in achieving positive outcomes for the child and their family.

In the next chapter we will consider police responses to CSE and organised CSA and some of the innovative practice that is developing across the UK in response to identified challenges.

Chapter 5

Key Considerations for Criminal Investigations and Tackling Perpetrators

Introduction

There have been significant changes to police responses to organised child sexual abuse in the last two years. Following the publication of the Jay report (2014), most police forces – as well as Local Safeguarding Children Boards and their partners – have all carried out internal evaluations in order to reassure themselves they were not as vulnerable as South Yorkshire Police to accusations that they failed to protect children. The personnel and resources available to CSE policing teams have increased significantly in the face of overall decreasing budgets, and there have been several subsequent successful prosecutions against offenders. In addition, there have been changes to legislation which reflect the growing awareness of CSE, organised CSA and related offences. The Sexual Offences Act 2003 was amended by the Serious Crime Act (SCA) 2015 to make reference to child sexual exploitation instead of child prostitution. The SCA also introduced new offences in relation to controlling or coercive behaviour in intimate relationships and sexual communication with a child. Other legislation relating to people trafficking and modern slavery, for example, has increased the number of CSE-related offences, making investigations more possible and allowing the inclusion of different types of evidence.

While we acknowledge that tackling the perpetrators of organised sexual abuse of children is often difficult and beset with significant challenges, that does not inevitably mean it is impossible. Indeed, the successful outcome of Operation Clover trials in February 2016 and October 2016 at Sheffield Crown Court, as detailed below and in Chapter 6, demonstrates exactly what can be accomplished when senior officers commit the staff and resources required to launch operations to investigate and prosecute suspects, even when it is many years since some of the offences were committed. The first trial involved 15 witnesses who had been victims of the five men and women convicted, and these perpetrators received a total of 102 years' imprisonment. This is the reality of what can and should be achieved. But as this and the following chapter demonstrate, such operations require a combination of different professional backgrounds, approaches, skill sets and expertise in order to achieve the desired outcomes for victims and survivors.

This chapter outlines issues in relation to gathering and analysing information for intelligence purposes; working with victims; different approaches to conducting operations using examples from different forces and other available options when witnesses do not give statements. This chapter is pertinent to all professionals working with children who are at risk of or who are involved in organised CSA, or their families. All such practitioners have a role in sharing relevant information, and supporting them through any subsequent criminal justice process.

Sharing information with the police

Any CSE/CSA investigation is reliant on receiving information, but 'information' only becomes 'intelligence' once it has been systematically analysed by trained professionals, and currently that is usually only the police. 'Safeguarding children and protecting them from harm is everyone's responsibility' (HM Government, 2015, p.5). Any practitioner, therefore, who is concerned that a child is being sexually exploited or abused – that a crime has been committed or is likely to take place – has a duty to report that information to the police. For example, practitioners may have information about a perpetrator of CSE or organised sexual abuse, which they may have been given by a child or young person with whom they are working, by their parents, siblings, friends, neighbours or another member of the public. Such information could, for instance, relate to a perpetrator who carries a firearm, the supply of drugs, the registration number of a car that is used or addresses where victims are taken. Alternatively, the information could be as a result of events that practitioners witnessed themselves. Practitioners should always share information with the police; it is for the police to decide whether it can be developed or investigated further. Practitioners may assume that the police will have relevant information, when in reality it is often only when information is shared that the police can begin to identify possible crimes, perpetrators, victims and sources of evidence.

Analysing information for intelligence purposes

The police analyse the information they receive by grading it using National Intelligence Model (NIM) processes (Police ICT, undated). One of the NIM products used by the police and other law enforcement agencies is the National Intelligence Record (NIR). This is a process that enables analysis of information that is received. It is graded on a score of 1–5 in three areas (also known as the 5 x 5 x 5 system): i) provenance, ii) reliability and iii) dissemination. Yet good intelligence analysis is reliant on trained staff who understand the relevance of the information in the context in which they work. Forces are currently in the process of changing to a revised Intelligence Report (IR), which has essentially simplified the process so that some areas are grouped together.

Sometimes the difference between 'information' and 'intelligence' and agency responsibilities in relation to these matters get confused, as noted by Casey:

> Police failed to act on information given to them by victims and by Risky Business, by parents and by schools and even by their own police intelligence. Risky Business passed on all their information but were invariably told it was not good enough and that it was information and not intelligence. When police actually looked at the information that attitude changed, as evidenced by the successful police work that went on around Operation Central. '[Risky Business] produced good information. It wasn't [their] job to turn it into intelligence, that's the police's job... Out of the information, our analyst was able to create a huge chart about the perpetrators.'
> A police officer. (Casey, 2015, p.48)

Casey also cited a former senior police officer from Rotherham who said, 'intelligence and information is imperfect, and that police couldn't always look for clarity from people with complicated lives' (p.39). He said they had learned from Risky Business about the importance of soft intelligence and rumours; that they had to respond to receiving this type of information. This is a key point: having a system and culture that enables the police to be receptive and respond to such information can be key to successful prosecutions. In Bradford, information gathered and analysed by an intelligence team ultimately led to a number of convictions. In an interview with Adele, as part of the research for this book, a police intelligence analyst observed, 'The police tend to go after known offenders but it is intelligence that provides the police with the leads and lines of enquiry regarding the unknowns.'

In South Yorkshire Police there is a single point of entry (SPOE) for information. Once the information has been graded as intelligence it is disseminated to the appropriate policing district, and then to the relevant units. The district intelligence officer conducts assessments of suspects using a risk matrix. Similarly, West Yorkshire Police in Leeds use a risk matrix. In South Yorkshire, those who are high risk (who score over 40) are discussed at weekly meetings in relation to potential investigation and disruption tactics, and come under the remit of the Integrated Offender Management Team. Those who score between 20 and 40 are not considered high risk, so action may not be taken. But this may be due to gaps in intelligence; were they to be examined in more detail information about previously unknown offending behaviour may be uncovered and they would then come in the high-risk group.

Intelligence problems

LSCBs are responsible for agreeing joint information-sharing protocols, so all practitioners should know what information to share, when and with whom. It is essential that the processes for the sharing of such information are communicated to all staff, so everyone understands their responsibilities. This is discussed in more detail in Chapter 7. In Rotherham, sharing of information was particularly problematic. While Risky Business gave Rotherham police endless information, what happened to it when it arrived at the district police station was a source of concern, as it appeared it was often not inputted into the intelligence system. Over ten years later there were still problems with the intelligence process:

> Instead of the police being able to easily access social care files via the social workers they were supposedly working with in a joint CSE team, they had to obtain information through the Freedom of Information team in an entirely separate part of RMBC. Waiting for this to be processed caused significant and unacceptable delays. This is an unusual interpretation of Section 29 of the Data Protection Act (1998) and could be easily solved by the implementation of a protocol. This sums up the total ineffectiveness of local approaches to multi-agency working. (Casey, 2015, p.93)

While the situation in Rotherham was extreme, there will inevitably also be difficulties in sharing information with the police and partner agencies in other parts of the country. Practitioners in health, social care, education and the voluntary sector will have information that could be very useful to police investigations, but there are two main barriers to disclosing. First, they may not know how to physically get the information to the local police, because the processes involved are not publicised sufficiently or are not sufficiently robust to work effectively. Second, practitioners may not feel comfortable or confident about what will happen to information they share, and whether it will have repercussions for their client/patient or themselves, as a result.

Staff need to be able to trust the police when sharing sensitive information, to understand what will happen as a result and have faith in the outcome of sharing such material. While multi-agency working has progressed significantly in recent years and CSE co-located teams are more commonplace, there will be places where difficulties remain. Local police districts should work with all relevant partner organisations to raise awareness of the information/intelligence process, including what happens to the information once it has been received and what they can expect from the police in return. Where police CSE intelligence units are not co-located with partner agencies, this can lead to them working in isolation and important information from partners being missed. If partner agency staff were trained, in NIM for example, so that they could analyse their own information as part of the process of sharing it with the police, this could significantly aid investigations.

In the case of historical victims, they may not want to make a formal complaint to the police, but their abuser may still pose a threat to children. In these cases, information obtained needs to be analysed for intelligence purposes in order to allow initial investigations to begin. This avoids the need for an immediate police visit to the victim, as required by National Crime Recording Standards (Her Majesty's Inspectorate of Constabulary, undated), and instead allows time for a relationship to be built with them where they can make an informed decision about coming forwards as a complainant.

Regardless of how information is shared with the police though, there should not be an expectation that professionals from partner agencies actively seek information from young people. There is a difference between sharing information they have been told or made aware of, and actively questioning young people in an effort to find out more in order to pass it on to the police. The need for further information should not dominate or change a practitioner's relationship with a young person. It needs to be obtained naturally and carefully and at the young person's own pace, otherwise they may start to question the basis of the relationship with the worker and begin to disengage.

Whether the report is of a current or historical crime, one challenge is that – in order to receive relevant information – the police need to 'enable awareness' of what could be potentially significant CSE or organised CSA information. This requires large-scale campaigns with a wide range of professionals and the public. An additional barrier is sharing information between police forces. Information uploaded onto the Police National Database (PND) differs from region to region and information sharing between forces is still governed by the need for specific formal written requests. Furthermore, each force has different policies regarding the creation of nominal records for a possible person of interest, who may not have been charged with any offence or where information is only partially known. Until these inconsistencies and issues are resolved, opportunities for offenders to avoid detection when working across police boundaries remain.

Good practice in sharing information

Operation Retriever, run by Derbyshire Police, culminated in nine men being convicted of offences ranging from rape to intimidating witnesses in relation to 27 teenage girls (BBC Online News, November 2010). Staff involved cited it as an example of the successful use of information and knowledge shared by professionals and the public, which was not necessarily previously known to the police. Sharing such information subsequently allows the police to identify people and locations of interest and to map and profile emerging patterns and models of offending behaviour. It enables them to identify areas where specific responses are needed, for example by way of disruption (discussed later in this chapter), and identify young people who may be vulnerable or at risk and refer them to services provided by other practitioners. Police in Leeds have taken this one step further by examining local profiles and working within a multi-agency partnership to address issues of vulnerability which are influential in the involvement of young people in organised CSA. *The Brief*, issued by partners in Leeds (Leeds partner agencies, 2015), is an example of how they raise awareness of CSE – including social networking issues – with partner agencies who work with children and their families.

Police forces have adopted different ways of addressing some of the challenges related to intelligence. Some have developed proactive and innovative methods of seeking further information. This includes, for example, scrutinising reviews left on TripAdvisor in relation to a hotel which is believed to be used for organised sexual abuse to see if guests have mentioned noise nuisance or seeing young people with older adults in suspicious circumstances. Some have adopted close working relationships with specialist projects, schools and other organisations which have regular contact with young people. In some areas, community officers visit educational and residential premises and become familiar and trusted. Information is therefore shared more easily and with confidence that it will be dealt with appropriately. As part of initiating and maintaining motivation for practitioner involvement, in Bradford their information is directed to a specific police email account. This sends an automatic acknowledgement of receipt and reassures the sender that it will be actioned. West Yorkshire and Derbyshire forces have developed specific information-sharing guidance and protocols for practitioners, as well as guidance on what and how to share, ensuring consistency. As one officer put it, 'Explicit reporting results in specific recording'.

Some forces have considered how information received by call handlers, working in police control rooms, is understood and correctly recorded when someone first makes contact with the aim of sharing CSE-related information. In Derbyshire, information-sharing forms reference Operation Liberty (Derbyshire Safeguarding

Children Board, undated), which is the county-wide, long-term police CSE operation. Awareness of this is raised through professional training, policies and procedures, as well as posters and campaigns in the workforce and wider community. This encourages callers to highlight to call handlers that the information they are sharing relates to CSE. Professionals and members of the public will only share information with the police if they know that such information is being sought. The more direction they are given regarding how and what to share, the more likely it is that the information the police receive will be relevant. Additionally, in Derbyshire, trained call handlers work to the Thrive model: Threat, Harm, Risk, Investigate, Vulnerability and Engage. This enables them to recognise potential indicators of CSE and CSA and ask callers if they have any such concerns about the young person.

Another approach is to ensure that call handlers receive intelligence training and are NIM compliant and, therefore, can assess the information when it arrives with the force, reducing the need for it to be analysed by another team. This cuts down on the time it takes for information to be graded, enabling it to be inputted onto police systems and available for investigations or enquiries more quickly, as well as reducing the number of staff required to deal with each piece of information. Where call handlers have been trained to recognise information relating to CSE and organised CSA, people, cars and locations of interest are flagged on systems. This results in information being better linked and brought to the attention of the relevant team. However, officers raise two issues in relation to this approach. First, police systems require a regular review of individual flags and in the absence of any recent activity about the subject the flag may be removed. Second, the flow of information received by the police may become overwhelming, making it more difficult to identify relevant material.

Across the country, members of the public are also prompted to share their information anonymously with the UK charity Crimestoppers. This often results in information being shared that would not otherwise be known to the police. It can therefore be regarded as a more efficient way of obtaining information from the community at large. Information gleaned from a young person who has been missing or absent (as discussed in Chapter 4) following their return and completion of a safe and well interview conducted by a return home worker should always be submitted onto intelligence systems as per local protocols.

Responding to received intelligence

There are three types of intelligence arising from information sharing:

- Actionable: which contains lines of enquiry that can be followed up and acted on immediately.

- Developmental: information which requires further development. This may involve recording on police systems so it can later be linked to any additional information, or may involve the police actively seeking further information and making further enquiries.

- Historical: this relates to past events. This presents much more of a challenge in terms of investigation as there is unlikely to be corroborative evidence such as DNA and CCTV, and witnesses, offenders and locations may have changed or no longer exist.

In most cases, it is actionable intelligence that receives priority. It is important, however, not to ignore the other two categories. As noted earlier, a historical complaint may involve an offender who is still a risk to children. Information received may be the missing piece of a jigsaw, which then enables an investigation to begin. As demonstrated throughout this chapter, information and intelligence are crucial to police operations and investigations. There are occasions, however, where information can be progressed with few resources required. A case example from West Yorkshire Police shows how the development of information resulted in the protection of a vulnerable child and the identification of a crime.

A young person was reported as missing. Information shared by a third-sector worker was that a member of the public had mentioned how some young people visited a flat above a business premises when they went missing. The police visited the property and although the young person was not there, they obtained the names of the adults living at the premises. Information on the police system revealed that the current missing young person had previously visited the former home of one of these adult men and he had received a police warning. When the young person returned home, her underwear was taken and forensically tested. It provided DNA evidence of sexual activity with the male concerned. He was subsequently arrested. The premises and the other men living there were flagged as being of interest to the police. What started as a search for a missing young person resulted in the arrest of one man for sexual offences and the identification of others who could pose a risk to children in the area, who were subsequently monitored.

It should not be assumed that intelligence is always shared with appropriate police colleagues. Information sharing is also an issue within and between police forces and districts, as well as with partner agencies. If community officers are not in possession of relevant facts and do not know the local police priorities, including who are persons of interest, their response to situations is less likely to be able to reflect best practice. Forces should ensure that all relevant staff are briefed when high-risk young people are missing, including relevant information and risk assessments. There are also different responses when the young person is found (which may include asking a parent or carer to collect underwear for forensic testing). Where forces do not brief their staff on such cases, vital information can be missed, the response to the young person may be inadequate and their vulnerability will be increased.

At times, the amount of information shared with the police may be overwhelming, particularly in CSE and CSA cases. This is an important issue for all police forces to address, as it is often small pieces of information or seemingly irrelevant information that can be significant. Some forces have responded by creating teams to sift through that information; some task the dedicated CSE teams to analyse it, others have regular briefings with partner services working with vulnerable young people to try to manage and compartmentalise the information being shared. In Derbyshire a multi-agency Tasking and Coordination Group (TCG) reviews intelligence every three weeks and agrees a strategy. Additionally, intelligence officers review information submitted via Operation Liberty and other sources every 24 hours. Where appropriate, immediate action is taken regarding high-risk cases or situations, which is subsequently reviewed by the TCG.

Following up information can also impact on police workloads. A visit to a house may subsequently involve the arrest and interview of potential offenders; speaking to possible victims; forensic examination of the premises, including removal and analysis of bedding, furniture, carpets, wallpaper and clothing; property such as mobile phones and cars being seized and forensically examined; door-to-door enquiries being conducted and other people of interest being followed up, some of who may be in a different policing district or force. In Derbyshire, trained crime officers can assess and triage, or prioritise forensic submissions. If, for example, there are a number of electronic devices at a property, a decision to seize them may be based on whether the device belongs to, or is used by, the offender or an initial examination suggests it may be of interest. This facilitates a targeted forensic examination which is likely to be quicker and more cost efficient. Officers in the force are encouraged to engage in robust decision making rather than taking a risk-averse approach.

Dedicated teams and partnership panels

Investigations of organised CSA are complex, resource intensive and challenging. There may not be a willing complainant, forming professional relationships with potential witnesses takes time, sensitivity and persistence, and evidence may be hidden or difficult to find. Investigations are costly and can take years. From a senior management perspective, it may sometimes be difficult to identify positive outcomes for resourcing CSE teams and intelligence work, but across the UK police forces have developed innovative and intelligent ways to respond to CSE and organised CSA, and continue to do so. Most force areas now have dedicated CSE teams, often with multi-agency partners. Where these teams work best is where there is a dedicated social care presence, as opposed to a contribution by practitioners who carry a caseload. In Derbyshire, the CSE Hub and Spoke Project works with CSE issues across the county, although at the time of writing it is currently under review. Co-working on individual cases ensures that individual practitioners are not left handling emotionally charged and difficult cases alone, which assists with staff welfare and performance. Additionally, the multi-agency membership ensures that families' holistic needs are addressed. Open-plan offices and regular briefings facilitate discussions and identification of relevant information and patterns, as well as improved ownership of challenges, obstacles and potential solutions.

Chapter 4 described how some areas, such as Wakefield, have a multi-agency CSE panel which considers cases to map and profile CSE on a countywide scale. The Derbyshire Tasking and Coordination Group is also a multi-agency forum; membership includes independent case advisors, health, education, the CSE team, the Vulnerability Unit and Safe and Sound (CSE project). It meets every three weeks with a focus on locations, hotspots, offenders and possible victims, agrees responses including disruption, and reviews action taken. This 'check and balance' approach, combined with a daily review by intelligence officers and regular CSE team briefings, offers a structured and dynamic approach which addresses individual cases, local patterns, and identifies information to be followed up and further developed. Such examples mean that local policing and resources are led by an analytical process that identifies what criminal activity might be taking place and where. This is proactive, intelligent policing which makes the best use of resources and is more likely to produce effective responses in tackling CSE crimes.

Working with victims to prosecute offenders: a victim-focused approach

The Rotherham Post-Abuse CSE Steering Group, which consisted of CSE survivors, drafted guidance – based on their experiences – for police officers and other practitioners to consider when working with victims and survivors of organised CSA, especially in the period of initial contact and during investigations. We would like to thank them for giving us permission to share this guidance; the issues discussed in this chapter and Chapter 6 should be read with this in mind.

- Speak to other agencies including those in the voluntary sector and gather intelligence about victims before making contact. This will help determine where people are emotionally.

- Treat every individual as an individual. One shoe does not fit all.

- Build a relationship – the following will help:

  - be honest

  - be friendly

  - listen

  - find a victim's interests.

- Be open about your own life experiences. You don't have to share too much but make yourself human.

- Praise the victim. It takes strength and bravery to disclose.

- Ask questions but don't interrogate.

- Give victims as much time as they need to disclose. Some people have carried this for a lot of years. Your agenda may be to get people arrested; however, some people need time, confidence and trust.

- Have one allocated professional to a victim. Over-facing with lots of professionals can be too much and ultimately it could make people pull away from you.

- Don't *ever* blame a victim; a child cannot consent to their own abuse. It is also not up to them to remove themselves from it. Some victims could still be at a stage where they feel they have consented (remember grooming and brainwashing go hand in hand).

- Families suffer too. They are also sometimes the stronger witnesses to what happened to the victim.

- Don't approach a victim in uniform or marked cars as it could bring attention to them. Remember, some people live in areas where perpetrators still reside.

- Don't presume everyone wants female police officers. They want someone whom they feel safe with and who believes them.

- Choose appropriate venues that the victim prefers.

- Some victims are still involved with perpetrators and other criminals.

- Most still do not understand they were groomed; this needs to be worked on first and may take time.

- Reassure them that they are not on their own in this.

- Don't ever just ask questions if family members are around. They may never have told their partners, children and so on about this.

- Determine the line between survivor and offender. Part of grooming is to groom a victim to commit offences.

- Understand all forms of grooming and abuse. You can't challenge it if you don't understand it.

Key Considerations for Criminal Investigations and Tackling Perpetrators

- Ask individuals how they want to be addressed: victim or survivor. Some may take offence.

- Share information with the correct agencies. This can help stop the abuse and help with gathering intelligence.

- A CSE support worker will be needed when approaching victims to assist with any needs.

- Make the victim aware of all services providing support and arrange the support for them if it is needed.

- Not all victims understand the correct terms of CSE, so speak so that they can relate and understand.

- Prepare for all behaviours from a victim – it's extremely distressing to disclose.

- Ask what they want and need – this is about them not you.

- Don't make arresting people the main focus – it is not.

- If someone refuses to talk, don't knock on their door and ring every day hoping they change their mind. Put other support in first.

- Don't mention social services – sadly a lot of people feel if social services are aware of their past abuse their children will be taken away from them.

- Don't make your rank part of the introduction – who cares, really?

- Don't say things like 'we know what we are doing – we are the experts'.

- It's okay to look shocked when someone tells you what happened to them; it makes you human.

- Don't offer support and then threaten to take it away if someone won't come forward.

- Be patient. They have lived with this for years – a couple more months may be what they need to understand that they can come forward.

- Be honest about what needs to happen next.

- Don't go away and not get in touch for weeks or months.

- Don't visit someone without at least knowing something personal about them. Take time to do your research.

- Ask yourself, if this was my child what would I expect?
  (Rotherham Post-Abuse CSE Steering Group, 2015)

Much of what is detailed in this guidance may now be routine practice by police officers involved in such operations, but these considerations should always be at the forefront of practice by all practitioners working with children and adults who have been victims of organised CSA.

Historical complainants

As already discussed in this book, children involved in CSE and CSA often do not recognise themselves as victims. Some may be adults who were abused as children and who have tried to put the abuse behind them. Historical complaints of CSA can present some challenges to the police. As noted earlier, evidence which corroborates the abuse may no longer exist and key witnesses may have moved out of the area. In addition, victims may regard the police with hostility and suspicion, especially if they have had previous poor experiences, such as Tanya demonstrated in her Foreword. Often they do not want to provide a formal complaint or statement, as they may be afraid of the consequences. Forces have had to recognise that a different approach from that taken towards other victims of crime is needed; staff have required training to recognise the victim behind the challenging behaviour and lack of cooperation. One member of staff from West Yorkshire Police described a conversation with an officer regarding a missing young woman who was a victim of organised CSA. 'The officer said to me, "She's a nightmare." I said, "No. She's been through a nightmare."' This reflects a change in police culture.

Innovative approaches include working in partnership with other services to help build relationships with victims and gain their trust, as well as working with case advisors who review and advise on building rapport. It is important for the police to take the time to consult those professionals who know the person concerned and how best to approach them. Victims may not have told their parents, partner or their own children about the abuse. They are unlikely to want to introduce the trauma back into their lives. It has to be recognised that this stage of any investigation takes time, dedication and sensitivity. It could be argued this should only be undertaken once the police are confident that the investigation is likely to continue and may result in charges against offenders, if the victim and possibly other witnesses assist the police. When a victim does come forward with a complaint of a crime, this may be a difficult time. Trauma that they have worked hard to overcome may resurface, and existing coping strategies may break down. This is discussed further in Chapter 6. What is vital is that a police investigation is handled sensitively, is victim focused and addresses any risk from the perpetrator to them or any child with whom they have contact.

Building trust and relationships includes listening to victims about their concerns and what would make them feel safe, and regular contact on their terms to keep them updated and reassured. One approach, as will be discussed in more detail below, is for a multi-agency partnership to resolve issues of housing, finances and meeting their needs before obtaining a statement. In an interview with Adele as part of the research for this book, a police officer commented, 'How can you expect them to give a statement when they are worried about having a roof over their head tomorrow, losing their kids, putting food in their kids' stomachs or having their house burned down?' Another officer described how a victim was given a mobile phone so that she could contact the right person when she was ready to talk, and could come to the police when she was ready and on her terms. The same officer eloquently described his ethos on police trying to engage vulnerable witnesses: 'Disclosures are given, not gotten. Don't put the pressure of your investigation on the child.'

Some police forces spoke of moving away from traditional methods of investigation to those that have involved victimless prosecutions, or obtaining corroborating evidence to place less reliance on the evidence of the child or historical victim. This includes gathering information from as many sources as possible such as DNA, CCTV, professional witnesses, third parties (which may include practitioners working with the child, the family, carers), other victims and information from professional agencies. It also includes tasked witnesses, usually a family member or carer, who is assigned a specific undertaking by the police, such as giving them the child's underwear when they return home after being missing. Where there are concerns that a suspect is financially profiting from the abuse of children, and that money is being laundered through businesses, property or other possessions, information from the Department for Work and Pensions, Her Majesty's Revenue and Customs, the Land Registry Agency and the Driver and Vehicle Licensing Agency may be relevant. Where circumstances warrant, the police may consider placing a suspect under surveillance as per the Regulation of Investigatory Powers Act 2000. The use of third-party information is often a key line of enquiry in CSE and organised CSA cases and can enable investigating officers to see 'the bigger picture'.

A final challenge for many forces has been the number of suspects and potential victims identified. Some forces, more than others, conduct follow-up lines of enquiry, where there are ongoing investigations and attempts to obtain and develop intelligence regarding persons of interest. As one officer stated, 'Your enthusiasm and supervision limits how far you will go.'

Launching investigations
Case example: Operation Clover, South Yorkshire Police

The first trial for the Operation Clover team resulted in five people being convicted. Arshid Hussain was sentenced to 35 years and Basharat Hussain to 25 years for 38 offences, including rape, indecent assault, abduction, false imprisonment and making threats to kill. Bannaras Hussain pleaded guilty to offences of rape and indecent assault and was sentenced to 19 years. Qurban Ali was sentenced to 10 years for conspiracy to rape. Karen MacGregor received 13 years and Shelly Davies was given an 18-month suspended sentence having been found guilty of false imprisonment and conspiracy to procure a woman under 21 to become a 'common prostitute'. MacGregor was also convicted of conspiracy to rape (BBC Online News, 26 February 2016; BBC Online News, 24 February 2016). The second trial for Operation Clover resulted in eight men being convicted. Sageer Hussain, brother of Arshid, Basharat and Bannaras, was convicted of four rapes and one indecent assault; Basharat Hussain was again found guilty – this time in relation to one indecent assault; Mohammed Whied was convicted of one count of aiding and abetting rape. Ishtiaq Khaliq was convicted of one rape and three indecent assaults; Waleed Ali was found guilty of one rape and one indecent assault; Asif Ali was convicted of one rape; Masoued Malik was convicted of one rape, one count of conspiracy to commit indecent assault and one of false imprisonment; Naeem Rafiq was found guilty of one count of conspiracy to commit indecent assault and one of false imprisonment. The eight men were jailed for a total of 96 years.

The initial investigation into Arshid Hussain by South Yorkshire Police was launched as a serious crime enquiry, which identified the Hussains as significant targets. As a result, a major crime team was established with a senior investigating officer (SIO) appointed. The major crime team approach utilised a police database – Holmes – which had been designed for homicide cases. It is a very procedural system, reliant on staff not missing any line of enquiry. In such an investigation, gaps and undermining material need to be examined, as well as evidence already collated. The first 12 months of the Operation was the research phase. Victims were not visited during this time, as it was agreed that this would not occur until officers were properly equipped and ready. They analysed all available documentation during this period in relation to the victims and the Hussains, including files previously held by Risky Business and reports prepared by Adele, as part of her research on the Home Office funded pilot 2001–03, and Angie during her employment with SYP. As a result, 196 victims were identified, as well as the Hussains and another five key nominals. The overriding and recurring theme during this research phase was the Hussains, confirming to the team that they were the suspects on whom they should focus. At any time, however, a force may have to respond to presenting issues that may have to take priority. During the research phase there were two murders – one of which involved a manhunt – and these took up significant officer and police staff resources. Consequently, by the end of the first year the investigation had not achieved as much as had been expected.

Towards the end of 2014 there was a renewed impetus in relation to Operation Clover, possibly influenced by the publication of the Jay report in August of that year. New senior officers were brought in, and a different investigative approach was developed that combined major crime and public protection – two areas of policing with very different working practices. While Operation Clover had at first utilised a major crime approach as noted above, it was later acknowledged that this was inappropriate when working with victims of abuse. If major crime officers met with a victim, where they denied they had been abused or refused to talk to them, that was usually the end of the process. Officers may have tried to visit once more, but if they had the same response the victim's case was closed.

South Yorkshire Police took an innovative approach in merging public protection and major crime approaches in Operation Clover. Major crime officers and staff lacked safeguarding and multi-agency knowledge and skills honed by public protection teams; the public protection officers and staff did not have investigative skills or the experience or capability to run the Holmes system. Combining both approaches resulted in upskilling on both sides. A review of Operation Clover by the National Crime Agency in 2015 concluded it was working well. However, it was not always easy to find skilled officers interested in working CSE cases. The very negative publicity in relation to Rotherham and changed working conditions meant that the Criminal Investigation Department (CID) was no longer a popular career choice. Vacant detective posts and sickness levels meant that sometimes officers had to be co-opted into the team, rather than volunteer to join. While this ensured that experienced officers worked on the investigation, close supervision and oversight were necessary to ensure that officers were using a victim-focused approach.

The SIO for Operation Clover was very experienced in major crime investigations, and the detective sergeant was a veteran in public protection. An externally appointed former detective superintendent with CSE-related investigative skills was also employed in the role of 'critical friend' to both Rotherham Council and South Yorkshire Police in relation to their CSE response, with a particular focus on victim management and community engagement. What commenced as an investigation into the Hussain brothers subsequently became a much larger investigation with a further trial scheduled in early 2017, yet the maximum number of officers on the team only ever reached around 25. This was significantly different to Operation Stovewood, conducted by the National Crime Agency, which secured funding to increase officer numbers from 69 to 117 during 2016–17 (The Telegraph Online, June 2016). (Operation Stovewood is examining criminal allegations of non-familial CSE and abuse, conducted at the request of SYP following publication of the Jay report (National Crime Agency, 2015).)

Making initial contact

Once Operation Clover had identified the 196 victims, each person was risk assessed using a matrix. Children, young people and adults currently being abused or at risk were prioritised for contact by specialist officers. This exercise had to be conducted very sensitively. It takes skill and confidence to knock on someone's door and ask whether they have been sexually abused. The Clover team were careful not to 'badger' victims into giving evidence, nor to be seen to do so by victims or their families. As a consequence of using the safeguarding, victim-focused approach of the public protection officers, victims started to give Achieving Best Evidence (ABE) interviews and statements (Ministry of Justice, 2011). The team also analysed the intelligence information obtained from victims, which enabled them to decide from where else they could capture evidence.

Achieving Best Evidence interviews

Most people do not reveal their most intimate and traumatic events to people they hardly know. This applies equally to victims giving ABE interviews. They may also subsequently regret providing a statement at all. It must be appreciated by all involved – including legal defence teams and judges – that victims' accounts can change during the course of the investigation and that there are often good reasons why this may happen. Giving the first interview may prompt flashbacks or further memories to emerge, which may consequently change their account, sometimes providing more detail. This is useful information for prosecution barristers to impart to juries during opening statements in a trial, where the fact that the victim has 'changed' their evidence is otherwise likely to be used by the defence team. Instead it can be presented by the prosecution as evidence of trauma, and used to demonstrate the impact that abuse has on victims. This may involve calling an expert witness to give such evidence during the trial.

Victims have to decide what information they are willing to disclose at interview; that may be dependent on the relationship they are developing with the officers. Their impressions of the police and the dynamics between them will influence their disclosures. As referenced above, this is particularly relevant for victims who were ignored or simply not believed by officers when they previously tried to report sexual abuse crimes. Operation Clover officers accepted that some victims would never have trust in them because they had been previously let down by South Yorkshire Police and, therefore, would not ever be able to work with them. But others – such as Tanya – have been able to put their experiences behind them to an extent, in order to achieve the prosecution of their abusers.

ABE interviews can be very traumatic for a victim. They can trigger flashbacks and panic attacks, which in turn can affect their psychological health and manifest in volatile and erratic behaviour, increased drug or alcohol use, or self-harming, all which are usually viewed as being 'self-destructive'. At the very least, following interview they are likely to experience low mood, low self-confidence and anxiety, as well as being concerned about repercussions they may face from their abuser or their associates. This can be a crisis point for victims; their individual risk level after interview is likely to increase significantly. It is a point at which they may need a lot of additional support from other services such as health, mental health teams, independent sexual violence advisors (ISVAs) and the third sector. The use of special investigators in a CSE investigation team is important, but other members of the multi-agency team have a vital role to play in supporting the victim through such difficult times. While a successful prosecution is desirable, the wellbeing and safety of the victim is paramount. If the victim is not able to proceed with the trial process, for whatever reason, the team should encourage them to withdraw.

It is at this stage that the close working of the multi-agency team is so crucial for victims. As will be discussed in more detail in Chapter 6, they need to be safeguarded and protected in order to consider giving evidence. The Clover team used Maslow's Hierarchy of Needs (1943), developed to understand human motivation, as a model for assessing the needs of victims and what support they first require (also used in police hostage negotiations). These needs are (in order of priority):

1. biological and physiological: including food, drink, shelter, warmth, sleep

2. safety: including security, order, stability, freedom from fear

3. love and belongingness: including friendship, affection and love from family, friends and relationships

4. self-esteem: including achievement, independence, prestige, self-respect, respect from others

5. self-actualisation: including realising personal potential, self-fulfilment, seeking personal growth.

(adapted from McLeod, 2016)

Viewed from a victim's perspective it is clear how important it is to fulfil their biological, physiological and safety needs in particular, before they are able to participate in any investigation. The approach adopted by Operation Clover was to call to the victim's house and speak directly to them. Officers from Clover always visited in person to see the victim, a mix of male and female officers in plain clothes in attendance. Officers from the team did not call in a marked car or wearing uniform, although this did sometimes happen in situations outside their control. If a victim decided to make a disclosure at 2am and rang the police to report the crime, for example, it had to be an initial response by uniformed officers in order to be able to react swiftly.

All officers work to statutory guidance *The Code of Practice for Victims* (Ministry of Justice, 2015), which sets out all elements of support to which a victim may be entitled. Once a victim has given evidence and has agreed to testify at court, they are also known as a 'witness'. It is essential that they have a designated point of contact throughout the investigation and trial, that they know how to contact them and what to do if they have any fears or concerns. Within Operation Clover, the Victim Engagement Team (VET) was separate from the main team. Standing members of the VET included the police victim contact officer; a children's social care social worker; an adult social care social worker; Victim Support; court services; Young Women's Christian Association (YWCA); Grow (a voluntary sector women's support organisation); police witness liaison and the mental health crisis team. Housing services and Department for Work and Pensions were also involved as required. The role of each agency was agreed in relation to the plan drawn up with each victim, so they knew the purpose of each practitioner's involvement.

One issue that concerned Jay (2014) was that South Yorkshire Police staff were only interested in victims if they were prepared to give evidence, otherwise they did not want any involvement. This approach has now been reversed. Victims are now not under any pressure to give evidence and can join and leave the process at any time. There was understandably some initial scepticism from victims regarding this significant change, but generally the police believe this is now accepted. A model was developed that had three access points for victims: pre-trial, during the trial and post-trial/ post-abuse support. This is considered in more detail in Chapter 6, as is the victim contact plan.

Disruption techniques

While in many cases there are indicators of CSE and CSA, the police may not be able to make arrests due to a lack of evidence. There are, however, a number of other steps they can take which can disrupt the relationship between the offender and victim, and deter future criminal activity.

Increased visible police presence near CSE hotspots (locations associated with CSE), and public areas such as parks and shopping centres, means that criminal activity may be deterred and intelligence collected. This may include the identification of young people potentially at risk as well as possible suspects. As will be discussed in Chapter 7, some police forces and their partners are using crime reduction interventions and making changes in specific locations. In some areas, people such as park wardens and security officers have been trained to recognise the signs of offending behaviour and pass this information on to the police. Further intelligence can be sought on specific individuals, locations, vehicles and businesses. As discussed earlier, flags can be placed on police systems against such targets which alert staff, prompt them to gather information and also make CSE officers aware when relevant information is available. A number of forces have systematically reviewed what intelligence is known and what is required. They subsequently approach services such as licensing, safer neighbourhood teams, the fire service, and environmental health, looking at who is best placed to visit persons or locations of interest, observe and gather further intelligence. Derbyshire County Council's Community Cohesion Team, for example, was successfully able to assist the force in such a way.

Where a relationship between an individual adult and child or children is identified as being of concern, the adult can be served with a Harbourer's Warning, also known as an Abduction Warning Notice. This provision was made in the Child Abduction Act 1984 for children under 16 years of age, and extended to those under 18 where the child is in the care of the local authority. This notice should only be served when a formal statement has been obtained from the child's parents, or the local authority where the child is in their care. Child Abduction Warning Notices are issued to a specific person in relation to a specific child. That person is made aware that the child is in their company, care or house against the wishes of their parent or carer. The notice informs them of the age of the child, and of action that is prohibited following the serving of the notice (for example, allowing the child into the property again, or having further contact with them). Breach of a Child Abduction Warning Notice is not an offence in itself, although it may support a prosecution in the future by demonstrating that the perpetrator knew the age of the child and had previously been warned. If the person continues the relationship and/or allows the child to stay at their property, however, they may be prosecuted under the Children Act 1989 and/or the Child Abduction Act 1984. Alternatively, an injunction may be sought, which if breached can lead to imprisonment.

A Harbourer's Warning may deter some abusers, but it will not deter all. What it does do, however, is enable the police to flag on their system that the Warning has been served and that there is concern that the person may be involved in CSE or CSA offences. This may prove to be significant if information is later shared in relation to them, or information is sought by another police force. Where someone has been identified as a possible perpetrator this should make them a priority for police attention. Also, if evidence of a sexual relationship can be proven, there is an additional offence, as the following case example from Adele's private practice shows:

> Abi was in the care of the local authority, but living with her grandparents. A 37-year-old man was served with a Harbourer's Warning in relation to contact with her. Her grandparents were asked to gather evidence when she went missing, including giving her underwear to the police. Subsequently, after she had been missing one night, the adult male's DNA was found in Abi's underwear. He was charged with sexual activity with a child, as well as offences under the Children Act 1989 and Child Abduction Act 1984, to which he pleaded guilty. He received a custodial sentence.

Legislation such as anti-social behaviour provision and civil orders (such as Sexual Harm Prevention Orders and Sexual Risk Orders under the Anti-Social Behaviour, Crime and Policing Act 2014) can also be useful in deterring abusive behaviour. Additionally, potential offenders can be subjected to scrutiny on a number of different levels. If, for example, they own business premises and there is reason to believe the premises are being used to commit offences against children, licensing, health and safety and environmental legislation can all be used as a reason to visit and enter the property and gather information. If the property is owned by the local authority or a private landlord, steps can be taken to remove the adult or another tenant. Business locations identified through intelligence analysis as potentially being of concern can be visited and staff spoken to by officers. Where businesses do not cooperate with local campaigns, such as *Say Something If You See Something* (Derby Safeguarding

Children Board, undated), which encourage businesses to contact the police if they have any concerns about activity with children or young people in or around their premises, further enquiries can be made to see if there is any cause for concern. If the offender owns a car and the police believe it is being used in the commission of offences, they can be made the subject of a stop and search procedure. The more ways information can be sought, the better subsequent intelligence about that person and their activities will be. This, in turn, will inform actions taken against them.

Another form of disruption activity can focus on the child. Good multi-agency assessments should explore why they are involved in a relationship with a perpetrator or placing themselves at risk, and what interventions can be done to address this. Offering alternative activities that meet the child's needs, for example having a mentor they can talk to, or making home, care or school more attractive to them, can all be effective disruption methods. This should involve participation with the child's family or carers. Jay revealed examples of the worst possible past practice by the police who twice arrested fathers who were trying to rescue their daughters from their abusers (Jay, 2014, p.36). But good practice finds that relationships with parents and carers can be invaluable, and they can provide much information, as discussed in Chapter 4. In Leeds, the police and a local project visit the family home and consider with parents and carers how they can assist the investigation. This might involve borrowing the young person's phone while at the police station so that the contents can be downloaded and later examined; giving parents advice and prompts to take specific action; the recovery of clothing when the young person is away from the home; and obtaining itemised mobile phone bills for police examination for numbers and any call patterns relating to missing episodes, for example.

When the police share with and receive information from partner agencies about suspects and children who may be at risk, it is more likely to lead to multi-agency interventions that protect children and prevent abuse. Where information suggests a young person is in the early stages of being grooming or recruited, regardless of whether a criminal act has yet been committed, information should be shared with safeguarding services and partners, such as education, so that early interventions can take place. It is often considered that disruption can only be employed once the abuse has started, but it is most effective as a prevention technique.

Disruption techniques, therefore, can prevent, obstruct or end abusive relationships. They can help the police identify nominals for further scrutiny, identify other young people at risk, who were previously unknown to services and also result in intelligence which can identify associates, locations and vehicles not previously known to the police. They can ultimately lead to investigations and charges against perpetrators being brought. In cases where intelligence cannot be developed, and seemingly a dead end has been reached, recording of such information is vital. In one force, an officer created a record, indicating that a person was suspected of being involved in CSE. Some 18 months later, that person was reported by a member of the public as being involved in the physical assault of a young person. Enquiries by another police force led to evidence being identified that the male was involved in a relationship with another under-age female. The subsequent investigation resulted in his successful prosecution.

Cases where there are no complainants

One of the features particular to these cases is that there may be a lack of complainants. The previous chapters discussed why a victim may not want to speak to the police about their abuse. There are, however, a number of approaches the police may consider. These include:

- focusing on developing the intelligence they have and following up relevant leads

- developing relationships with local practitioners and businesses to encourage information sharing

- appointing a liaison worker who becomes known to young people, some of whom may be thought to be involved in CSE or CSA, via a local service or school

- approaching parents and carers of children who are thought to be involved, to see if they can provide information and potential evidence

- liaising with other professionals to develop lines of enquiry, which may assist potential future investigations

- looking at any other possible sources of evidence.

CSE and organised CSA are not standard crime types and therefore often require a creative approach. There have been cases where so-called 'victimless' prosecutions have been successful – cases where abusers have been convicted without a child having to give evidence. Not all of these are current examples – in 1999 Nottinghamshire Police ran a successful police operation that utilised evidence from toilet attendants, park wardens and local surveillance, as well as information passed on from local children's residential homes. These cases show that with the right resourcing and determination, evidence can be found to support prosecutions. Good police work, in conjunction with the force's multi-agency partners, continues throughout the lead up to the trial, and throughout the trial process. This is discussed in Chapter 6.

A final point is that of training. A well-informed and trained police force should have officers and staff who are alert to indicators of CSE and CSA. Those staff will also have a clear understanding of their responsibilities in identifying, recording and passing on relevant information. In future years, the knowledge gap between dedicated teams and other police force members needs to close in order for the police forces across the UK to have a consistently effective response to CSE.

Summary

This chapter has discussed some of the key issues that exist for police and partner agencies in tackling the perpetrators of CSE and organised CSA, and launching investigations against such suspects. It raises a number of fundamental points that need to be considered to improve the likelihood of investigations being successful.

The process of obtaining and analysing information from multi-agency practitioners and the public is an area that still poses some considerable challenge for forces, especially in relation to receiving focused information which is analysed by trained police staff. Yet progress has been made and operational gains as a consequence are apparent. Joint police and partner agency good practice models are now evident in many areas of the country. These include dedicated CSE police officers, often co-located with multi-agency practitioners from children's social care and specialist third-sector organisations. Police operations which target such nominals now also work very closely with partner agencies, whereas they would previously have been solely the domain of CID who usually only liaise with a few other law enforcement agencies.

We believe that the increase in both the number of joint teams and the quality of the work they undertake is a testament to how much progress has been made in this area. Previously, we felt that the 'commitment' to multi-agency working could be shallow and piecemeal, and that there was not a genuine appreciation of what each partner could bring to the table and how this could benefit all involved – particularly victims and their families. While the learning from Rotherham has at times been hard to digest, we believe that the wider understanding of the multi-agency arena – in particular third-sector agencies – has been one area where there has been considerable achievement. Significant improvements are also evident in the area of witness care and the approach of multi-agency teams building relationships with victims and focusing on addressing their priority needs, before contemplating any possibility of police interviews and statements. The needs of victims are now coming first, as opposed to previously when they were last or indeed not considered at all.

With the use of a number of different disruption techniques in relation to both individuals and businesses involved in the sexual exploitation and abuse of children, such offences may be prevented and individual children better protected. This approach is more likely to work with lower level offenders, however. Those embroiled in other serious and organised crimes, such as the supply of drugs, may be less likely to be deterred from sexually abusing children unless they think such activity is resulting in unwanted police attention. Operation Clover has been used as a case example in this chapter (and also features in Chapter 6), providing a unique insight into how SYP completely changed its approach in order to deliver a successful prosecution against the main perpetrators of organised CSA in Rotherham. Arshid and Basharat Hussain received some of the longest sentences for sexual offences the police force has ever seen. It was a defining investigation and trial, both for South Yorkshire Police and some of the Rotherham victims.

Chapter 6 now examines how the police and partner agencies support witnesses once charges have been brought against their 'intimate terrorists' (Johnson and Leone, 2005) and other abusers of organised CSA.

Chapter 6

Child Sexual Exploitation, Organised Child Sexual Abuse and the Criminal Justice Process

Introduction

As Chapter 5 provided some insight into police operations and multi-agency teams working together with victims to tackle the perpetrators of organised child sexual abuse, this chapter discusses victims' experiences of the criminal justice process. Some of the accounts given in this chapter show how the current criminal justice system can cause further distress to traumatised victims, which is also often witnessed by their families in court. While we recognise the importance of giving defendants a fair trial, this should not be at the expense of witnesses. They also deserve justice.

This chapter provides an outline of the criminal justice system in England and Wales. It discusses the rights of witnesses and the support for victims, including pre-trial therapy, court preparation plans, special measures, support following giving evidence and post-trial, and a victim exit plan. It examines issues of safety and risk, particularly in relation to witness intimidation. Finally, it discusses current and forthcoming pilots in relation to improving the experiences of child victims, both in court and during the whole of the criminal justice process.

The criminal justice system in England and Wales

The criminal justice system in England and Wales is described in *Working Together to Cut Crime and Deliver Justice*, the criminal justice strategic plan published in 2007, as follows: 'The central purpose of the Criminal Justice System is to deliver an efficient, effective, accountable and fair justice process for the public' (HM Government, 2007, p.13).

All cases within the criminal justice system start with a complaint that a crime has been committed, followed by a police investigation (although this may be very brief). The Crown Prosecution Service (CPS) advises the police on cases for possible prosecution, and reviews cases submitted to them by the police. Their decision to prosecute is based on two tests: whether there is enough evidence to prove the case, and whether it is in the public interest to bring the case to court. The threshold for the first test is not always an easy one to reach (particularly with cases of historical abuse). This explains why investigations can take months, and why some cases do not go forward to court. When cases do go to court, the prosecution must prove with the available evidence that the defendant is guilty 'beyond reasonable doubt', which is the standard of proof in the criminal courts. The defendant does not carry the burden of proof but instead has a presumption of innocence; 'innocent until proven guilty' (European Convention on Human Rights, 1953; United Nations Universal Declaration of Human Rights, 1948).

The UK has an adversarial system of criminal justice. This is where two opposing parties (the prosecution and the defence) seek to persuade the judge or jury that the evidence supports their case, i.e. in the prosecution case that the defendant is guilty of the charges, and in the defence case that the defendant is innocent. This is quite different to the inquisitorial system adopted in some countries such as France, where a judge or group of representatives investigates a case and reaches a decision. The relevance of this will be discussed later in this chapter. A defendant has the right to give evidence to support their case but if they do so, they will be open to cross-examination. This is the process by which the legal representation of the opposing party can ask questions. A defendant also has the right to remain silent and not give evidence. A judge must allow a fair and transparent process where certain evidence may not be allowed as it may be regarded as being prejudicial to the defendant, or an abuse of their human rights. Article 6 of the Human Rights Act 1998 gives defendants the right to a fair trial. For example, any evidence which may be regarded as irrelevant to the charges before the court or which may give the jury a prejudicial view of the defendant will be excluded.

Article 6 also states that a defendant has the right 'to examine or have examined witnesses against him and to obtain the attendance and examination of witnesses on his behalf under the same conditions as witnesses against him'. This explains a key issue with the UK's current legal system that many practitioners and members of the public may not be aware of. In criminal proceedings:

- the complainant is the CPS, who effectively represents the Monarch (currently HM Queen)

- the defendant is the person charged with specific offences

- the victim is a witness in the case against their abusers.

The witness has rights, but they are neither the same nor equal to those of the defendant (their abuser). As such, witnesses can be compelled by an order of the court to attend trial, where they will be required to give evidence in support of the case against their abuser. In the process of ensuring a fair trial, their evidence will be tested. In other words, they will be cross-examined.

Victims' experiences of giving evidence at court

'What happened, what they did to me at court was worse than the abuse.' Lilly is a young woman still profoundly traumatised by her abuse and the eventual court case. Instead of feeling that her abuse was recognised, that she was protected and her abuser punished, she regrets ever coming forward and telling anyone what happened to her. After giving an interview at the police station, Lilly (who was then just 16) was allocated to an out-of-area placement, allegedly for her own safety. In reality, this placement was a hostel without 24-hour staffing, located in a red-light area of an unfamiliar town where she was constantly approached by adult men for sex. Lilly was told that she had to pay for her accommodation and was left with hardly any money for food. She had no sources of support in the town. Two weeks after she arrived, she came face to face with her abuser who had tracked her down via social media. As a result, she was placed in a series of hostels until finally being placed with foster carers. In the months leading up to the trial, Lilly was constantly contacted by her abusers. They repeatedly threatened to kill her.

Lilly agreed to work with the police and be a witness in court. Giving evidence by video link, she was determined to show her abusers that she was not frightened of them any more. When she came out of the witness box she collapsed. The worker from the specialist project that was supporting her told us what happened:

> I remember when we went to court, as an adult and as a professional I was actually quite intimidated, but she was petrified… I remember one of the things that she said to me were 'When I go in and when I give my evidence I am going to show them that I am not scared of them any more. I'm going to be really brave and I'm not going to cry and they are not going to make me feel like I need to hide any longer.' We sat in that room, we maybe waited for an hour… We came out of that room, it were a very tight-fitting corridor and there was another door that was the door that Lilly had to go in and give evidence. She was terrified, especially at having to give evidence

alone. It seemed to go on forever…when she came out I stood up and I remember looking at her and she said to me, 'I've showed them that I'm not scared' and then she was sick, burst into tears and collapsed. And I remembered thinking that all that the judge had seen, that the judge and the jury and everyone else who were in the room, is this hard-faced young woman sat there petrified inside but adamant to just prove that she's not scared. And she sobbed and one of the things that this young woman used to do, regular, every night when she went to bed, is check under her bed to make sure that they had not broken in; she had nightmares that they were climbing through her window. She'd had messages that if they drove past where she lived and saw her, they would shoot her. They'd found her on [social media]. And for years she had suffered this, day in, day out. And I remember the day that she came out of that witness room that she was probably more terrorised than she had ever been, through the fear of what she had been through. But nobody but me saw that side of her vulnerability. If they had turned that camera around at that moment, we would have gotten a conviction.

The jury found Lilly's abuser not guilty. What they thought they saw on the video link screen was an apparently adult female who was aggressive, defensive and defiant. Lilly's abuse had been prolific, sadistic and extensive. As a result she is unlikely to be able to have children. She has difficulty leaving her home. She is one of a number of victims of organised CSA across the country who has been left wondering why she put herself through the ordeal of giving evidence at court.

Andrew Norfolk reported in *The Times* newspaper throughout 2013 what he witnessed in a number of different courts across the country as cases came to trial:

girls who suffered years of sexual abuse from a street grooming gang were reduced to anguished sobbing during aggressive cross-examination by defence lawyers.

One victim, who was 'passed around and used as meat' from the age of 13, was cross-examined for 12 days in what became 'an almost forensic examination' of her past... A senior judge later denounced the trial as 'an unmitigated disaster'. Another judge said: 'We should all be very ashamed that our criminal justice system allowed it.'

One victim in the case wept when she was forced by a defence barrister to read aloud graphic details of a childhood sex attack by her stepfather that was totally unconnected to the case.

One victim in the Stafford trial, aged 18, was apparently so traumatised by her time in the witness box that she was said to be suffering flashbacks and panic attacks. She was sent for a four-hour psychological assessment to determine whether she was fit to continue.

A second girl, trafficked and sold for sex to restaurant workers, was also reduced to tears after she was labelled 'very wicked', 'very cruel' and 'a compulsive liar' by...a defence barrister. (*The Times*, May 2013)

Norfolk also reported how victims of abuse were cross-examined in court:

At one stage of his cross-examination, [a defence barrister] told her to 'stop fiddling...and try to concentrate'.

Another defence barrister went so far as to ask whether she repented her sins. She did not understand the question.

On the final day of her cross-examination, pushed beyond endurance, she broke down. (*The Times*, May 2013)

As young people are already traumatised by their abuse, experiences such as these in giving evidence will inevitably cause them further trauma. We discussed issues of trauma and behaviour in Chapter 3. One common feature is how young people feel that they are to blame for their abuse, that they are somehow responsible and that people will judge them. This is also drilled into them by their abusers. The criminal justice system, in allowing cross-examinations of young people and vulnerable victims to be conducted in this way, reinforces those beliefs, causing them further trauma and impacting on their mental health. It is not just young people for who such experiences can have tragic consequences. Frances Andrade, a 48-year-old violin teacher, committed suicide in January 2013 following her cross-examination in a trial at Manchester Crown Court. Her husband recalled that she felt judged and was accused of lying. Frances had not chosen to go to the police herself, but was identified during investigations relating to a complaint by another woman and hence felt compelled to attend court to give evidence. Her abuser was subsequently found guilty of five charges of indecently assaulting her as a teenager; other charges were dropped earlier during the case. This appeared to have also been a trigger for her suicide, as she thought he would be acquitted of all offences (The Guardian Online, February 2013).

Cross-examination

Cross-examination is the process by which evidence presented to the court is interrogated by the legal representatives – who in crown court trials are usually barristers – of the opposing party. They seek to expose inconsistencies, errors and other issues to use to their advantage in persuading the court of the defendant's innocence, or guilt. In essence, the legal team seeks to undermine the witness's evidence and destroy their credibility in the eyes of the jury and court. It can often be a lengthy, hostile experience in which witnesses feel manipulated and criticised.

These are some of the examples of questions, observed from Adele's private practice, put to child witnesses during cross-examination over the last ten years:

Were you a virgin when you first had sex with my client?

How many men have you had sex with since your relationship with my client ended?

You have been described as a 'Walter Mitty' character and a 'drama queen'. Isn't it the case that this whole trial is about you lying and getting attention as a result?

Isn't it the case that you know my client is a wealthy man and this is all just some scheme that you and your friends have made up in order to get some money?

Other cross-examination approaches consist of focusing at length on incidents that happened months or years ago, of which the witness is unlikely to have a clear recollection. As discussed in Chapter 5, assertions may be made from the fact that victims of abuse often recall trauma piecemeal – through flashbacks, nightmares and in fragments. Often they later recall abuse that they did not mention in the initial police station interview. This is frequently used by defence barristers to claim that the witness is lying and that they have embellished their original account. Much is often made of the witness's credibility, their behaviour and conduct. The consequences for the judge and jury making a wrong assessment of the evidence is that a potentially innocent defendant may spend time in prison, deprived of their liberty and human rights. It is little wonder, therefore, that witnesses often feel as if they have been involved in a battle.

A mother of a 14-year-old child, who had been groomed online and abused by a large number of individual perpetrators, wrote an account for Adele for use during professional training. In this appalling case, she felt that she and her husband had been involved in a constant battle starting with getting the police to treat what had happened to their son as a crime. There were a number of perpetrators who abused her son, and as they were acting as individuals rather than as an organised group, there were several trials. Their son was required to give evidence at each. A number of perpetrators pleaded guilty on the day he was due to give evidence. Although he was spared the ordeal of giving evidence in those cases, in a number of trials he was not. Below is her account of what she witnessed in supporting her son through several trials stretching over a number of years:

In our experience, the character of a child victim is too easily attacked by skilled defence counsel using convoluted questioning techniques, innuendo, harassment, verbal intimidation and bullying... As parents we listened to the perpetrators make up lies and complete fabrications that we could totally have proved to be untrue, but as we were not called as witnesses we could say nothing...We felt we had not protected or kept our son safe from these vile and callous paedophiles, but then felt we had let him down once more by allowing him to be abused again in court. Remember he is the victim, but he was treated like a perpetrator. It is heartbreaking to sit there and listen to a defence barrister tear your child to pieces and there is nothing you can do about it. They called him a liar and a fantasist, but remember they had the details of the men who had already pleaded guilty and had been sentenced. The summing up by the defence barrister is truly horrific, and to my shame having listened at a previous trial, I could not bear to listen at a subsequent trial and left the courtroom. I was told later by the chair of a charity which was supporting us in court, that she was relieved neither my husband nor I had heard what this barrister had said, and that she will never share it with us.

Witness rights

Witnesses do have rights, but as noted above, arguably not as many rights as the defendant. They cannot refuse to attend court to give evidence if they have been served with a witness summons. If they try to, a warrant can be issued enabling the police to arrest them and bring them to court, detaining them until it is time to give evidence. In reality, few police officers would wish to do this and this should have been covered in the trial management plan. But ultimately the police may have no other option if the witness refuses to attend court. In comparison with the defendant, the witness has no legal representative. While the CPS is there to present a case based on their complaint and their evidence, the witness is not actually party to the proceedings. This can often result in witnesses feeling disadvantaged from the start of the trial, especially if they are not properly prepared and supported.

Witnesses are, however, entitled to different types of support, including the right to special measures if they are a child or vulnerable adult witness. Introduced by the Youth Justice and Criminal Evidence Act 1999, these include:

- provision of therapy prior to trial
- assistance if the witness is frightened or distressed about attending court
- assistance of an intermediary appointed by the court to help them give best evidence at court
- examination in chief (their evidence) given via a pre-recorded interview (usually a police station interview)
- provision of live link or screens (if this is how the witness prefers to give evidence)
- no cross-examination by the defendant in person
- restricted questioning (for example, no questions about the witness's sexual history allowed without permission from the court)
- removal of the public gallery (this does not always include the press)
- removal of wearing of wigs and gowns by judge and barristers
- reporting restrictions, including not publicising the witness's identity.

Additionally, the CPS has a number of different policies regarding witness care, including care and treatment, code of practice, provision of therapy and safeguarding children. As illustrated by Operation Clover and Operation Retriever in Chapter 5, all witnesses should receive a care package that addresses their assessed needs before, during and after trial. This may include access to a sexual assault referral centre (SARC) where they can access a range of support services, including counselling. They may also be allocated an ISVA (independent sexual violence advisor or advocate) or CHISVA (a children's ISVA). Their role is to support the victim throughout the process, accompanying them to appointments and court if required. The Advocate's Gateway provides guidance on best practice when dealing with vulnerable victims. Additionally, the national charity Victim Support often has a key role to play. As the trial draws closer, the witness will also have access to Witness Support, whose role is to support them when they go to court to give evidence.

These measures go some way to make attending court a less traumatic experience for the victim. It has to be acknowledged, however, that the support witnesses receive in one area may not be available in another, resulting in a 'postcode lottery'. Many professionals, victims and family members argue that the special measures also do not go far enough and that witnesses can experience 'secondary abuse' as a result of their court experience. Current proposals and pilot schemes in the UK are examining different ways of addressing these issues. This is discussed in more detail later in this chapter.

Effective support for victims and families during the criminal justice process

Even the most resilient victims can find the experience immensely difficult. Tanya described her experience of working with practitioners and the criminal justice process as more stressful than the abuse she suffered at the age of 11 and 12:

> I just want it to be over with. I just want all the stress to go. I just feel like my stress levels have gone so high since, like, I've started being in contact with everybody. I just feel like my stress levels are the highest ever. Even compared to back then. I think my stress levels are the highest at the moment. I just want the stress to go and I just wanna be what I were, what I were aiming to... I were on the ladder, to becoming good, the best, so I just wanna be back to that. (University of Sheffield Symposium, 2016)

The support needs of witnesses should be identified through assessment and a subsequent trial management plan, following the first police interview. This plan should be regularly reviewed during the investigation and the trial process, as the needs of the victim and their family will change during this time.

Before trial

The starting point to effective support before trial is having a victim-centred approach as discussed in the previous chapter. In an interview with South Yorkshire Police, officers from Operation Clover described the importance of building a relationship of trust with a witness and to recognise that they were at their most vulnerable once they had spoken to the police. This is because they often have to re-live experiences during interview that they have tried hard to suppress. They may also have started to consider the consequences of giving a statement to the police, for example having to give evidence against their abusers. The needs of the victim and their family must be considered and addressed from this point, not just when the trial is imminent. Any plan and associated interventions need to address issues of concern for the victim. This can include a range of needs from access to therapy and support, to rehousing them and their family. It can also include ensuring that they feel as safe as possible, which we consider in more detail later in this chapter.

Chapter 5 referenced Operation Retriever, a Derby Police operation launched in 2008. Retriever had an exemplary victim-centred approach, which in part was as a result of the involvement of Safe and Sound, a specialist CSE charity in the city. Once victims had been identified and perpetrator arrests made, the police investigation operated in conjunction with a multi-agency team; young people and their welfare were its central focus. The young women who were the victims in Operation Retriever received support from Safe and Sound and also had access to therapeutic interventions. Their overall needs were identified through assessment, and addressed through planned interventions. They established and maintained relationships with the police. Issues of witness intimidation were responded to promptly. In this case, the young women were supported and made to feel safe.

Those who gave evidence at Crown Court and consequently saw their abusers convicted and imprisoned did so with the support and active involvement of a number of professionals. The fact that a large number of young women were able to give evidence against their abusers is testament to the success of the multi-agency interventions. Some years later, follow-up data showed that a significant proportion of those young women were in education or employment. Without the support of the multi-agency practitioners, these young women may not have been able to lead 'normal' lives. The key principles from Operation Retriever can be seen in the trial management plans of operations today. As the officers from Clover observed, if victims are taken care of and their needs addressed, they are more likely to be able to give best evidence at trial.

Recognising the victim's perspective

It is important to recognise that the witness may still have conflicted feelings about their abuser. As has been discussed, many CSE victims believe they are in love with the abuser and are in a relationship with them. They may be infatuated by them and would do anything for them, even ultimately at the expense of their own safety, wellbeing and family. They are deceived by their abuser into thinking that the love they feel is mutual, that they will get married or live together openly, as other couples do. Peer-on-peer abuse can normalise the grooming and abuse. Victims who have been abused online can often believe that they were in some way responsible for what happened to them.

If a victim considers talking to someone when they first have doubts about the relationship or friendship group, it might lead to a police station interview. As a result, the police may hope for:

- a formal complaint

- other witnesses to come forward, including an expectation that the victim provides names of others

- an investigation which leads to the arrest, prosecution and conviction of the abuser/s.

Practitioners should, however, also consider the enormity of the potential consequences on a victim already struggling with the psychological impact of the trauma of their abuse, and perhaps living in an area where their abuser and associates may still be very active. While they may feel relieved to be safe and free from the abusive relationship, they may also feel a range of emotions as more information is revealed to them, usually by the police, about their abusers. This includes fear, guilt, shame, doubt, confusion, loss, anger, humiliation, self-disgust, self-blame, flashbacks and the recall of traumatic memories. It is, therefore, essential to ensure that victims are supported to have a realistic assessment of their needs, along with early access to therapeutic intervention and practical support, including someone to whom they can talk openly about their feelings. Any plan should include the goals of both the witness and professionals such as the police and social care, and be reviewed regularly and adapted accordingly, particularly as the trial date approaches. The plan should also include how to keep victims and their families informed of any progress or any substantive changes to the case. There are times when to a professional there is seemingly nothing to report to a victim, especially if there are delays or periods of inactivity, but it may be just those times when it is important to keep in contact, so they know they have not been forgotten and that such periods are normal during lengthy criminal justice processes.

Victim contact

Operation Clover, discussed in Chapter 5, established a Victim Engagement Team (VET), which focused on witnesses and their needs. Witnesses had a chosen designated point of contact from the multi-agency VET throughout the investigation and trial. The victim contact sheet and plan were developed in consultation with the victim, stating how and when the witness would like updates or contacts from the police. This resulted in an individual plan, specific to the victim's needs and wishes. As one officer remarked:

> It's got to be an evolving policy to meet the victim's needs. Credibility is vital. Victims will test officers to see if they are telling the truth and to see if they will actually be there for them. We hope that we are winning the trust of victims through reliability. No victim, no case, so it is of mutual benefit.

Some victims wanted daily contact, others wanted very little at all. Some people preferred a phone call or a home visit; others wanted to receive contact via text message. It is essential that the right level of support is achieved for each individual witness – not too much that they feel overwhelmed, but not too little that they feel unsupported and abandoned. It is also likely that the contact plan evolves during the pre-trial period. If there is a long time between giving evidence and the trial start date, the victim may possibly want less contact mid-way, for example, but require a considerable increase prior to the trial commencing. Each victim's needs are different and the plan should be based on what they want. As one officer stated, 'No one victim is the same. It is about finding what is right for each child.'

Some victims choose third-sector or other agency professionals as their designated contact person, rather than a police officer. This may be because they already know the worker, have developed a rapport and feel supported by them or because of their previous experiences of the police. This may, however, lead to an erroneous assumption that there is no ongoing contact from the police in the lead up to the trial. A lack of direct police contact can sometimes be misinterpreted as no ongoing police involvement.

Pre-trial therapy

As discussed earlier, the CPS has published guidance (Crown Prosecution Service, undated) regarding the provision of therapy before and after trial for children and vulnerable adult witnesses. As the guidance, which is compatible with Articles 3 and 12 of the United Nations Convention of the Rights of the Child 1999, acknowledges, 'Witnesses are fundamental to the success of the criminal justice system'. There is a common interest in facilitating access to therapy which enables a victim to:

- explore what has happened to them in a safe and supportive environment

- address some of the beliefs that they might have (such as it was their fault)

- start to develop coping strategies and access support that helps restore and protect their emotional wellbeing

- learn how to start moving on.

If victims have been supported in these areas, they are far more likely to engage with the criminal justice process and be able to give their best evidence.

The CPS guidance concerns what therapy and support are permissible without concerns being raised that the witness's evidence has been assisted or contaminated. One challenge for therapists, however, is that their records are subject to the rule of disclosure. Essentially this means that their otherwise confidential therapy records may be requested by and disclosed to the defence team as part of evidence in the proceedings. This is permissible if anything in those records may impact on the decision to prosecute, and includes anything that may prove or disprove the issues disputed by the prosecution and defence. Although the guidance is clear on what records may be regarded as being relevant and that they cannot be produced without a court order, from the therapist's position 'confidentiality cannot therefore be guaranteed in advance' to their client (Crown Prosecution Service, undated, 3.15). Therapists should ensure from the outset that witnesses are aware that their therapy records could be subpoenaed. The benefit of providing therapy, even in these difficult circumstances was summed up succinctly by a South Yorkshire Police officer: 'Providing therapy to victims before trial is essential, otherwise it's a bit like having a broken leg and being told you can't have a cast.'

Needs of the family

As discussed in Chapter 1, being a victim of abuse impacts on the whole family. Having to be a witness at court can also have a similar effect on family members, who often accompany the witness and see and hear parts of the trial that the witness does not. However much they support their child in giving evidence, the experience will leave a lasting emotional impact on them all.

In the long months leading up to a trial, parents and siblings in particular may have a sense of feeling stuck and being unable to move forwards with their lives. There is likely to be additional stress as the family tries to manage their child's and their own anxiety about giving evidence, and the trial as a whole. The needs of the family, as well as the strengths and support that they can bring, must be considered when assessing support and developing a plan with the young person before, during and after the trial. Practitioners should not forget the needs of immediate family and, while they may not be directly responsible for their care, providing relevant information and advice about services they may benefit from can be immensely helpful. This may benefit the victim too, as family members accessing their own support and therapy may be better able to support their child or sibling. Parents and siblings may need to talk in confidence about conflicting feelings or issues they do not want to discuss in front of their child. Parents in particular are likely to repeatedly revisit the abuse in their mind, including their perceived failure to protect their child or recognise what was going on. They may also have intense feelings of anger towards the perpetrators and others. To ignore the needs of the family in any planning process means that potentially positive and protective factors may be weakened. As one parent told a group of professionals in London: 'Remember to listen to the parents; they are there to pick up the pieces when everyone else has walked away' (PACE, 2016, p.3).

Addressing issues of safety and risk

In recent years, holding offenders in custody on remand has become increasingly more difficult. This results in suspects being on bail, sometimes for many months. It is therefore essential in any court case that witnesses feel safe and that any intimidation or threats by their abuser, or more likely their associates, are dealt with swiftly. This is an essential part of witness support, as is providing investigation and trial updates and access to therapy. Effectively addressing threats involves pre-emptive listening to witnesses about what they think are risks for them. Having often been involved with their abusers for years and subjected to previous intimidation and violence, victims are best placed to help the police assess their risks, predict triggers and consider effective interventions. Involving witnesses in this way is likely to increase their sense of safety, as it can make them feel consulted, listened to and in control, while also being looked after. It empowers the victim and makes them feel part of the plan to protect them.

Another requirement is to clearly communicate to the abuser their obligations while on bail, clearly explaining what behaviours are prohibited (for example, sending a victim a message via social media or phone), and the consequences of failing to adhere to these prerequisites. This can be communicated to them in a number of ways, including court bail if charges have been brought, and police bail during investigations. Sexual Harm Prevention Orders and Sexual Risk Orders may offer an alternative way to protect witnesses, as a breach of the order can result in a custodial sentence and it may be easier to obtain a civil order than obtain restrictive bail conditions.

There also need to be practical measures in place to protect the victim. While bail conditions and civil orders may act as effective deterrents, where a defendant is likely to try to intimidate the victim, they are only as good as the practical measures taken to protect them. This may include staff visiting the victim's home and improving security by fitting better locks or installing an alarm system. Some police forces flag a victim's address on their system, so any officer responding to a call out of hours will see the significance of the flag and respond promptly and appropriately.

Victims and their families should be briefed on what action they can take if they feel threatened or in danger, and who they can call overnight or at weekends. Some prosecutions can take a long time before the trial is actually able to start. For example, a media article dated February 2016 reported a trial that was not due to commence until January 2017 (The Star Online, February 2016). Trying to keep a witness safe for such a long time if suspects decide to try to intimidate a witness can present challenges to the multi-agency team, particularly the police. Keeping the witness motivated to give evidence in court may also be difficult at times, especially if their mental health is suffering as a result of the forthcoming trial.

In some cases it may be necessary to move the young person and their family out of the area, in order to better protect them. This is something that should be considered carefully, as the implications can be extensive. Despite the threats that exist, support for them from family and friends in the area in which they currently live may be more beneficial and outweigh the risks. Moving a family away from familiarity can also cause a witness to feel unsafe. It can also cause them additional stress and guilt, as they may feel responsible for the family having to move, including parents losing jobs and siblings having to leave friends and schools behind. Services where resources are stretched may find it difficult to fund staff to travel to see the witness and their family, which may limit the effectiveness of their interventions. In other words, moving a family out of an area may make them more vulnerable. If the risk to a family is so great that this is being considered, an alternative approach is to consider why an offender is at liberty or what else can be done to protect the victim, their family and the general public from them.

Another key issue is to identify and risk assess the known associates of the victim's abuser. In most organised CSA cases, there are a number of friends and associates involved. Taking action against the abuser but not considering the risk posed by the associates is unlikely to be effective. When a perpetrator is out on bail, they are unlikely to make threats against the victim themselves; their associates are more likely to do it on their behalf. Many young people involved will reveal the involvement of associates in their abuse, albeit perhaps on a peripheral level, but still associates in abuse and sexual violence nevertheless. This needs to be taken into account when considering any bail conditions or terms of a civil order.

Victims must have confidence that the police and criminal justice system will protect them, and offenders must know that threatening and intimidating behaviour will not be tolerated. In Operation Retriever, the police arrested and charged any person who they suspected of intimidating witnesses. Operation Clover in Rotherham noted that a review was held of responses to victim reports of intimidation following an incident when a response by uniformed officers did not recognise the significance of an apparently minor incident on a witness. Victim care plans subsequently became very prescriptive about what action officers should take in certain circumstances, for example if the alarms are triggered at a victim's property. It is also worth noting that after an incident involving social media during Operation Clover, an associate was arrested, charged and convicted of offences relating to witness intimidation. This sent out a clear message to associates that such illegal behaviour would be responded to robustly and also reassured witnesses that they would be kept safe and that Clover staff took their concerns seriously.

A final point is to acknowledge that victims may have conflicting feelings about their abusers. As one survivor said, 'After everything he put me through, if I had seen him at court and he said sorry, I would have forgiven him.' Anticipating young people's reactions and behaviours is therefore a key element to any plan. Some young people may not feel able to talk about this openly. However we feel about their abusers as practitioners, the victims need unconditional support in working through their conflicting emotions. As the trial approaches, so does the chance of them expressing their feelings through unpredictable behaviour. They will be under growing pressure, so the agreed support and reassurance need to be stepped up and there must be good contingency planning in anticipation of any such challenges that occur. Victims of abuse should not be expected to be solely responsible for their own safety.

Preparing the witness for court

An essential element of support is how police or multi-agency teams inform and develop a witness's understanding of what is required of them and exactly what that will involve. This includes making them aware of how long the investigation may take before the CPS decides about whether to charge their abusers; that the trial date may be a long time ahead; that their confidential records may be examined as part of the investigation; but most importantly what happens when they go to court.

Any plan needs to have the best possible preparation for the witness's experience of going to court, including conveying an understanding to them of what will happen on the day – how they will get there, who they can take with them for support, what childcare issues will be put in place, where they will wait, how long they might have to wait and why. It should also include what steps will be taken to prevent them coming face to face with their abusers, their families or their associates. In developing the plan, staff should work with the witness to decide what special measures they want to employ in order to lessen the stress of giving evidence in court. Staff should also ensure that the witness knows who will be in the courtroom when they give their evidence, where they will be sat and whether or not the victim can see them and they can see the victim. Where the witness is in agreement, they should also be taken to court beforehand. This helps to familiarise them with the environment in which they will give evidence, which is particularly important if they will be speaking in the court itself (rather than on video link). Witnesses can then become familiar with the route from their home to the court, how long it will take, who will take them and through which doors they will arrive in the court. These may be minor considerations for professionals involved in the trial, but this will not be the case for the victim.

In Operation Clover, pre-trial court runs were used to identify things that needed further thought or planning. As detailed in the previous chapter, this included trialling an after-school club for one witness, as her children had never attended childcare provision before. Trialling this before her case came to court enabled her to then focus on giving her evidence in court, rather than worrying about her children in what would have otherwise been an unfamiliar childcare setting. This type of planning removes areas of uncertainty. It prevents the witness from worrying unnecessarily and makes them feel valued and nurtured. Most importantly, it allows them to start mentally preparing for the task ahead.

Witnesses need to be prepared about what questions they may be asked by the defence team. A designated person needs to prepare them for cross-examination and help them to understand that while it is a challenging process, it is not a personal attack. It is helpful for witnesses to understand why solicitors and barristers act as they do in court and why they might ask certain questions. This is in order to test the evidence that the witness provides, in order to represent their client to the best of their ability; the cross-examination should be conducted without personal judgement or prejudice. It may be useful, without coaching, to help the young person reflect on what aspects of their behaviour might be questioned, giving them time to think about how they might respond.

In terms of pre-court planning, it is important to give the child advice on appearance, including hair, make-up and clothing. Defendants will be given such information by their defence team and often attend court well dressed. They appear to be the physical manifestation of what their legal representative tells the court they are (for example, an otherwise respectable adult who was misled by a young person online, or who made a genuine mistake). In Lilly's case, as discussed earlier, she was not given advice on appearance and turned up at court wearing a smart but low-cut top and heavy make-up. While this was part of her defence mechanism – her armour – to a less-informed member of the jury she looked anything but the vulnerable child victim she actually was. Witnesses should not be put at such a disadvantage, particularly when such issues are usually easily remedied. Appearance is often neglected as part of pre-trial preparation, as practitioners seem to expect young people and vulnerable witnesses to instinctively know how to dress. Nothing in their lives up to now has prepared them for this experience, so it is unlikely that they will understand the importance. Practitioners who spend time supporting a young person to choose appropriate clothing and decide how they are going to do their hair and make-up (a different suit of armour) will simultaneously help build their confidence.

One Operation Clover officer described how the trial management plan included such issues as knowing that one witness would not be able to eat before giving evidence. The team brought energy bars and drinks to court to give her some nutrition before giving evidence. In his words: 'You cannot plan enough.'

Special measures

Advising and involving witnesses in decisions about the use of special measures, for example screens or video links, is another element of supporting victims to give best evidence. Although using a video link is the preferred option of many victims, because it does not involve being in court with the defendants, the witness needs to be aware that it can have less impact for the jury. In video links, jury members cannot see the witness, and therefore cannot see the impact that being cross-examined is having on them. In one court case, a vulnerable witness began intensely scratching her arms in distress during cross-examination and the trial had to be halted to enable her to receive first aid. The defence barrister could not see the impact the questions were having on the witness, but the jury could. Although distressing for the witness, her behaviour illustrated in very real terms for the jury the trauma that her abuse had caused, and how difficult it was for her to come to court and give her evidence.

Each witness is an individual with their own feelings and requirements about coming to court. Although they may get intense support from experienced professionals, ultimately it is only they who can assess and decide on what is right for them. Some victims may be so fearful of being in the same room as their abuser, that giving evidence is not a realistic prospect. For others, being in the courtroom may represent a significant step in their journey of recovery. Only by practitioners informing them and involving them in an ongoing assessment about their requirements at court can they give their best evidence. As an officer from Operation Clover commented: 'Everyone reacts differently. One victim came out bouncing around in frustration as she had wanted to be in the box for longer. Some take pride in doing it. Others struggle significantly.'

One young woman, who self-harmed in the witness box, afterwards expressed to the officers that she felt stronger and empowered by the experience of giving evidence. For her, the process, although very traumatic, was also extremely important. Good victim care and support enabled her transition from giving difficult evidence to feeling proud of what she had achieved.

Support for witnesses after giving evidence

Protecting the wellbeing of the witness after they have given evidence is crucial. Where there is a successful conviction, there may be fear of reprisals from the abuser's associates or family. Things may have been disclosed in evidence that the witness or their family did not know. At the very least, the witness has had to re-live the trauma, and has gone through the difficult experience of being cross-examined. For some, such as Lilly, their ordeal does not end with a prosecution. After the end of the trial, when they often feel exhausted, witnesses can become extremely vulnerable. The trial management plan needs to consider their wellbeing after giving evidence. Are they safe to go home? Is there a chance that they might self-harm? What interventions might need to be put in place before the victim goes home? Who is taking them home and who is supporting them once there? These are not questions ordinarily contemplated as part of a criminal trial, but when dealing with vulnerable witnesses this part of the process is essential. Justice is not justice if the witness comes to further harm as a result of giving evidence at court.

Post-trial support

As seen throughout this chapter, giving evidence is only one part of the trial process. Support is essential throughout the duration of the trial, including helping witnesses and families understand delays, judicial or legal decisions and decisions about evidence, and managing the impact of what is being reported in the media, including social media.

The support plan should also plan for the impact on the victim of the verdict. As many journalists now tweet live from court, consideration needs to be given to how to manage information provided to the victim when they are not in court, especially when often there is no indication of when a jury may return a verdict. In one court case, a family was forewarned that a verdict was likely that day and asked to refrain from looking at social media or news channels. It was agreed that a named person would keep them informed, who would visit the family that day if any emerging issues needed explaining. In Operation Clover, victims who wanted to attend court for the verdict were supported in doing so. A separate waiting room was provided for them, and police and witness support agencies assisted with transport to and from court, as well as giving practical support such as using another exit from the court to avoid the media.

Communicating the outcome of the trial is an important part in helping witnesses to move forward. Part of this is helping victims and their families or carers understand the outcome and the reason why a verdict has been reached. It is essential that someone qualified to deliver this information properly is identified, especially for those witnesses who do not want to attend court for the verdict. For witnesses whose prosecutions are unsuccessful, they need particular support from the multi-agency team. This eventuality should have been built into the plan, and the agreed interventions put into place as necessary. Such victims may be particularly vulnerable, and they may suffer intense feelings of distress and self-doubt. If there are concerns about their safety and wellbeing they may need an urgent referral to mental health services, if these are not already involved with the victim.

Victim exit plan

A final point to consider is the exit plan. Practitioners may become so focused on the outcome of the trial, they lose sight of the witness. Attending court is highly likely to have been a traumatic experience for the victim. Even when abusers are convicted, as discussed earlier, this is not without witnesses having suffered greatly through cross-examination. In some cases, the conviction itself is a traumatic experience for the victim; someone they loved has been convicted and sentenced to a (often) long term of imprisonment as a result of their evidence. However relieved they may seem outwardly, they may still feel internally conflicted.

In the lead up to and during the court case, for better or worse, a witness is very focused on the trial and its outcome. When it is over, they can feel disorientated and uncertain about the future, especially as the often intense support provided as part of the trial plan can start to dissipate. In order to adequately support the witness, the exit part of the plan needs to be considered just as carefully as any other aspect. The police, especially the liaison officers, along with the ISVA, are likely to have built a close relationship with the victim, but it is not viable or appropriate for them to continue this long term. As part of the trial plan, consideration should have already been given as to what the witness and their family need once the trial has concluded and in the future, and who is best placed to provide that service, although it must be acknowledged that this may change. If this is done, victims are not left feeling abandoned or merely used to get a conviction, and practitioners are not left feeling that they have deserted victims. A carefully prepared and delivered plan should help witnesses regard the trial and outcome as a positive point in their lives. At the conclusion of the trial, some witnesses feel their lives can now really start.

In the case example of Operation Clover, officers acknowledged there were some difficult discussions regarding the support to victims after trials had concluded. Some senior officers wanted to withdraw immediately and did not see it as their responsibility post-trial.

An exit strategy was devised for the victims in the Clover trial. This resulted in:

- one witness who did not want support

- one who was retained by the mental health crisis team

- five who were supported by adult social care

- others being supported by voluntary and community organisations.

One Operation Clover officer described his definition for a successful outcome at court: 'What matters most is not success at court – it is how the victim feels afterwards.'

Proposed changes to the criminal justice processes

This chapter has considered the considerable challenges involved once charges are brought against an offender and a trial date is set. It has described some of the comprehensive and innovative planning and measures taken by police forces and multi-agency teams to enable witnesses to attend court and give best evidence. Those measures cannot, however, compensate for the fact that going to court is a difficult experience for child victims of sexual abuse, some of whom have become vulnerable adults.

In 2013, the Government announced new measures to make it easier for victims of sexual abuse to attend court (Ministry of Justice, June 2013). These included:

- specialist training for lawyers

- new measures for victims, including the right to make a personal statement and have it read out in court; automatic referral to support organisations; information about their case at each and every stage; and an assessment of their needs at the earliest opportunity

- a new Victims' Information Service, including a helpline and website where witnesses can access support and information

- separate waiting area from the abusers' waiting area

- opportunities to give evidence away from court buildings

- pre-trial recorded cross-examination for child witnesses (Section 28 pilots) launched in December 2013 and running in Leeds, Liverpool and Kingston-upon-Thames.

Section 28 pilots

Section 28 (s28) of the Youth Justice and Criminal Evidence Act 1999 introduced the concept of a more child-orientated process, focused on improving the experiences of child witnesses before, during and after trial. It provides for the early assessment and provision of support for witnesses. In the s28 pilots, child witnesses give evidence and are cross-examined in front of a judge, with a recording made to show to the jury at the trial. This can take place at court or the police station and occurs as early as possible in the proceedings. The questions to put to the child in cross-examination are agreed in advance with the legal representatives and judge. Each barrister may have a set time in which to ask the approved questions. Questions cannot be repeated by different barristers, unless there is a compelling reason to do so. This is very different to the current experience that child witnesses have at court, and as described above. The s28 pilot approach prevents the child witness having to wait months before giving evidence. It does not preclude a witness being recalled at trial, but only if points emerge that were not evident at the time of the recording, and this is the exception rather than the norm. It could also represent an end to trials where children are subjected to hostile and traumatic questioning, which sometimes extends for days.

There has been no formal evaluation of the pilots at the time of writing this book, although one is imminent. Two police forces involved in the pilots were positive about the outcomes for witnesses when speaking to Adele. Whether the pilot will be implemented as practice across the UK remains to be seen.

The Barnahus model

For Anne Longfield, the Children's Commissioner for England, the s28 pilots and current special measures do not go far enough in addressing the challenges children and vulnerable witnesses face in the current criminal justice system:

> When it is suspected that a child has been sexually abused, they currently often have to be interviewed many times by the police, social workers, and medical professionals in an attempt to gather evidence so that a case can go to court. It is a complex, gruelling process which often breaks down and which can take many months. This can be incredibly traumatising to the child and may delay their access to therapeutic support. (Children's Commissioner, 2016)

She has proposed a separate model for children who have been sexually abused, based on the Icelandic Barnahus model (Children's Commissioner, 2016). This model is markedly different from the UK's current system. When a child makes a disclosure or exhibits indicators of sexual abuse, arrangements are made for them to attend the Barnahus (which essentially means 'children's house'). Once the child is there, one interview is conducted by a forensic interviewer, who is a qualified child psychotherapist. Where a child has made a disclosure, an investigative interview is conducted which is observed by video link by a range of professionals, including the police, prosecutor, defence solicitor, judge, and a legal representative for the child appointed by the state. The interview is controlled and supervised by a judge, and recorded. Practitioners observing the process put questions to the judge, who makes a decision regarding their validity. If approved, the judge passes the question to the forensic interviewer, who asks the child the question. In this way the evidence is explored and tested in a safe environment, which does not cause trauma.

This unique process also results in all assessments being conducted in one place, without the child repeatedly having to discuss their abuse with a number of unknown professionals. The needs of the child and family are considered at the earliest possible opportunity, and interventions offered without delay. If a forensic examination is required, it can take place on the same day without the child needing to leave the building. Evidence is captured and tested without either the rights of the child or the potential offender being compromised. The model was explained by Bragi Guðbrandsson, General Director of Icelandic Government Agency for Child Protection (2013). It has revolutionised responses to sexual offences committed against children across Europe and has now been implemented in Norway, Greenland, Finland, Denmark, Lithuania, Croatia, Turkey, the Netherlands, Portugal and parts of the USA.

In Iceland, the model was implemented 15 years ago. The number of complaints investigated by the CPS has doubled, as has the number of convictions. There have also been significantly better outcomes for victims and their families. The Barnahus model is being piloted in several different areas of the UK in 2017, including in the original pilot areas of Durham and London. The Children's Commissioner is urging all police and crimes commissioners to consider running the pilot in their area. If fully implemented, it could result in an overhaul to the current English criminal justice system in relation to sexual offences against children, including the way the police, judges and defence lawyers currently work. There are challenges that need to be addressed by the pilot, including how the model will sit within our adversarial justice system. Having considered the experiences of those children who have given evidence in adult courts over the years, however, we find it difficult to argue that a review of our criminal justice system in this area is not long overdue.

Summary

This chapter has discussed in some detail, with supporting examples from victims and professionals, some of the issues that currently exist for witnesses who give evidence against their abusers in Crown Court trials. It examines the practical advice, information and assistance that witnesses and their families need in relation to their forthcoming trials, so that they are as well prepared and supported as possible. In addition, it demonstrates the importance of listening to the witness, to ensure that their individual preferences and needs are part of the ongoing assessment. Witnesses and their families need to be prepared for difficult questions from the defence team; cross-examination is never a pleasant experience. In the past, practitioners have shied away from this for fear of unsettling the child or their family, and making them reluctant to attend court. In reality it is the unknown that is the more terrifying; the more preparation and information they have, the more familiar and less intimidating it should be. Failure to advise and plan with the witness is likely to result in traumatic experiences that can scar children and families for life.

We have provided above some traumatic but truthful accounts of what happened to victims when they gave evidence in court about their abuse. It lays bare some of the ugly truths about our current justice system. While there is impetus for change in some professional quarters, it cannot come fast enough in order to spare future witnesses such ordeals. This chapter has dealt with what we hope is the end of the abusive experience for victims and ends at a point where their recovery should now gather pace. The final chapter explores strategic responses of agencies and senior managers that should facilitate prevention and early intervention in relation to victims and perpetrators of child sexual exploitation and organised child sexual abuse and preclude victims from having to endure such traumas in the future.

Chapter 7

Strategic and Senior Management Responses to Child Sexual Exploitation and Organised Child Sexual Abuse

Introduction

We have addressed the practice of multi-agency practitioners throughout this book. Ultimately, however, what happens on the frontline is the responsibility of senior strategic leaders in individual agencies, overseen by Local Safeguarding Children Boards and Safeguarding Adults Boards. This final chapter discusses the role of the LSCBs and SABs and their constituent partner agencies and senior managers in safeguarding children and adults from organised sexual abuse. It outlines their responsibilities as defined by *Working Together to Safeguard Children* (HM Government, 2015) and the *Care and Support Statutory Guidance* (Department of Health, 2016), including the provision of policies, procedures and training. In particular, issues of accountability, challenge and organisational and professional cultures are discussed, as well as cross-border working.

The role of the LSCB in monitoring peripheral services such as taxis, licensing and the leisure and hotel industry is also discussed.

Roles and responsibilities: the legal and policy framework

The first act of Parliament enabling state intervention for the prevention of cruelty to children was passed in 1889 and legislation has been building on this ever since. The protection of children, organised within the processes in which we currently work, was implemented under the Children Act 1989, which gave every child the right to protection from abuse and exploitation and imposed a duty on local authorities to make enquiries to safeguard their welfare. The bodies which were then monitoring work at a local level were the area child protection committees (ACPCs). These were not set up under legislation, however, so did not have any statutory teeth. This was remedied under the Children Act 2004, which established LSCBs.

Working Together to Safeguard Children (HM Government, 2015) is the statutory guidance for all agencies working with children and young people. It is regularly revised, the most recent edition being published in 2015. It states:

> Local authorities have overarching responsibility for safeguarding and promoting the welfare of all children and young people in their area. They have a number of statutory functions under the 1989 and 2004 Children Acts... This includes specific duties in relation to children in need and children suffering, or likely to suffer, significant harm, regardless of where they are found, under sections 17 and 47 of the Children Act 1989... Whilst local authorities play a lead role, safeguarding children and protecting them from harm is everyone's responsibility. Everyone who comes into contact with children and families has a role to play. (HM Government, 2015, p.5)

It defines safeguarding and promoting the welfare of children as:

- protecting children from maltreatment

- preventing impairment of children's health or development

- ensuring that children grow up in circumstances consistent with the provision of safe and effective care

- taking action to enable all children to have the best outcomes.

Local agencies, including the police and health services, also have a duty under section 11 of the Children Act 2004 to ensure that they consider the need to safeguard and promote the welfare of children when carrying out their functions. (HM Government, 2015, p.5)

Under Section 10 of the Act, partner agencies have a duty to cooperate with local authorities in the duty to promote children's welfare, from strategic responses through to operational delivery of safeguarding interventions. Professionals are responsible for fulfilling their roles and responsibilities consistent with the statutory duties of their employer. Local agencies have a clear duty to take action where their staff have concerns.

Working Together to Safeguard Children (2015) is underpinned by two clear principles. First is that safeguarding is everybody's responsibility: 'everyone who comes into contact with children and young people has a role to play in identifying concerns, sharing information and taking prompt action' (p.9). Second is taking a child-centred approach. All too often where there have been safeguarding failings, it is the result of professionals not keeping the child as the focus of their assessments and interventions, not hearing what children are trying to communicate to them or not understanding how the abuse is impacting on them. In *Working Together to Safeguard Children*, children said that they need the following:

- Vigilance: to have adults notice when things are troubling them.

- Understanding and action: to understand what is happening; to be heard and understood; and to have that understanding acted upon.

- Stability: to be able to develop an on-going stable relationship of trust with those helping them.

- Respect: to be treated with the expectation that they are competent rather than not.

- Information and engagement: to be informed about and involved in procedures, decisions, concerns and plans.

- Explanation: to be informed of the outcome of assessments and decisions and reasons when their views have not met with a positive response.

- Support: to be provided with support in their own right as well as a member of their family.

- Advocacy: to be provided with advocacy to assist them in putting forward their views.

(HM Government, 2015, p.11)

These views of children should underpin safeguarding practice by all multi-agency practitioners.

The role and functions of the Local Safeguarding Children Board

The LSCB has a range of roles and statutory functions in relation to safeguarding and promoting the welfare of children in its area. These include coordinating what is carried out by a person or organisation on behalf of the LSCB and ensuring the effectiveness of such action. The Local Safeguarding Children Boards Regulations 2006 set out the functions of the LSCB. In summary, these are:

(a) developing policies and procedures, including in relation to:

    (i) action to be taken where there are concerns about a child, including thresholds for intervention;

    (ii) training;

    (iii) recruitment and supervision;

(iv) investigation of allegations against people who work with children;

(v) the safety and welfare of children who are privately fostered;

(vi) cooperation with neighbouring children's services authorities and LSCB partners;

(b) communicating to local people and organisations about safeguarding and promoting the welfare of children, raising awareness of how to do this and encouraging them to do so;

(c) monitoring and evaluating the effectiveness of what is done by the authority and their Board partners individually and collectively and advising them on ways to improve;

(d) participating in the planning of services; and

(e) undertaking reviews of serious cases and advising the authority and their Board partners on lessons to be learned.

(HM Government, 2015, p.66)

Issues affecting LSCB effectiveness in responding to CSE and organised CSA

While all LSCBs have the same statutory responsibilities, in reality they may differ considerably from one local authority area to another due to each board's financial and staffing resources, the way in which the LSCB is constituted locally, the local area's population and demographics and commissioning and service delivery arrangements. Sometimes it is possible for an LSCB to work in partnership with other LSCBs in order to reduce costs and share good practice, particularly as smaller LSCBs may be under-resourced in comparison to those in larger local authority areas. LSCB staffing also varies, but usually consists at least of a board manager, an administrator and another 'development' officer tasked with a variety of roles so as to ensure that the LSCB is able to deliver on its statutory responsibilities, as outlined above. In some areas, LSCBs have now combined with Safeguarding Adults Boards in order to share staff and resources. While this is an understandable and cost-effective measure in an age of austerity, it tasks those officers with being very familiar with two different safeguarding agendas, which, although there are some overlaps, are also quite distinct.

LSCB configurations may also vary between areas. Some have the board serviced by a number of sub-groups dedicated to delivering specific statutory obligations, for example serious case reviews, or the development of policies and procedures. In addition to the board, others may have an additional structural layer in the form of an operational executive or similar, where operational managers and board officers meet. Although such meetings and sub-groups report to the LSCB itself, which should consist of the most senior officers from partner organisations, this may lead to a disconnect between the work of each separate group, with a consequent lack of understanding of the issues each faces. There may also sometimes be an unwillingness or disincentive for operational managers to be completely transparent or honest about any problems they are uncovering or experiencing.

The Wood Report: Review of the Role and Functions of Local Safeguarding Children Boards (Wood, 2016) was commissioned by the government in 2016. It summarises common themes for LSCBs, including differences between those assessed by Ofsted as good and those assessed as underperforming. The review found that there was varied performance among boards in terms of data collection and scrutiny, and the ability to challenge and evaluate performance input from children and young people appeared to need to improve. While training was provided it was not sufficiently evaluated, there were concerns about the resources required to conduct serious case reviews, and a lack of clarity around early help responsibilities and referral thresholds was identified as an issue. All of the above can impact on how LSCBs respond to issues of organised child sexual abuse specific to their local area.

In response to the Wood report, the government has said it will implement a number of measures. These include:

- introducing a more robust but flexible statutory framework which will support local partners to work together more effectively to protect and safeguard children and young people

- introducing a new requirement on the three key organisations – local authorities, police and the health service – in relation to local arrangements for working together

- an expectation on schools and other relevant agencies to cooperate with the new multi-agency arrangements (see Department for Education, 2016)

- removing the requirement for LSCBs to have set membership, and introducing the ability to develop local arrangements (HM Government, 2016).

These new arrangements will be underpinned by new legislation and statutory guidance, and revised inspection regimes. At the time of writing, details about the forthcoming legislation are yet to be made public. Whether these changes will be sufficient to better safeguard and promote the welfare of children and young people who are subject to grooming and organised child sexual abuse will be assessed over time.

Organisational and professional cultures

At the time of writing, official investigations into the conduct of a number of staff (including senior managers) from South Yorkshire Police and Rotherham Council in relation to CSE and organised CSA in the town are ongoing. Whatever the outcome of those investigations and whether any clarification is ever received as to why action was not taken when repeated concerns were raised and information shared, one of the significant factors was the attitudes of some staff towards children and young people who had become involved with men who were abusing them. This has been a recurring issue across the country in CSE cases; it is not unique to Rotherham (see Griffiths, 2013 regarding Rochdale; Coventry Safeguarding

Children Board, 2016: Bedford, 2015 regarding Oxford). In relation to Rotherham, Jay noted:

> The Leader of the Council [Rotherham], from 2000 to 2003, agreed that the culture overall was 'macho' and 'sexist'... He also referred to the 'bullying behaviour of some members'...'which had a very traditional culture, which was slow to change'... 'One of the current Cabinet members...also agreed with the description of bullying and strong male dominance'... Of the group of people interviewed, many confirmed this perception. (Jay, 2014, p.114)

Likewise, Casey reported: 'The Council's culture is unhealthy: bullying, sexism, suppression and misplaced "political correctness" have cemented its failures' (2015, p.9).

The Drew Review (2016) into SYP made no mention of sexist or machismo cultures, but in a police force that only appointed its first female officer to the Senior Command Team (rank of Assistant Chief Constable and above) in 2013, it was – as Angie can testify – a very male-dominated and sexist environment. Women senior managers in the Force did not always show a better understanding of child victims of organised sexual abuse. Some women officers held similar views to their male counterparts, and were equally dismissive of the suffering of the children they were tasked to protect. The sexist and macho cultures culminated in practitioners being unwilling to look beyond the problematic, presenting behaviour of the young person and failing – or indeed choosing – not to see the abuse they were experiencing. In turn, this led to young people being categorised as undeserving of the very interventions that would have helped protect them.

As already stated, Rotherham will not be exclusive in some staff in statutory agencies holding sexist views and having macho cultures. One of the positives to come out of the Rotherham-related publicity has been the shift in attitudes towards CSE on a national level. Organisations need to ensure, however, that a change in perception by staff is genuine, and not just a tick-box exercise at surface level. Changing entrenched organisational cultures is an exceptionally difficult objective to achieve and will take a long time, but it is vital that the process of change is implemented sooner rather than later. It may require the assistance of independent, specialist consultants to undertake research with staff and make necessary recommendations to instigate the required change. In essence, there are three stages:

1. Views and opinions of all staff should be sought in order to understand current prevailing attitudes and beliefs. This should include a number of different data collection methods, such as observation of staff and the different environments in which they work, surveys, interviews and group discussions. Some of the findings may be positive; some may be less palatable. But change cannot be achieved without first achieving this necessary step.

2. Once stage 1 has been completed and the current organisational culture is more comprehensively understood, senior managers must define the strategic direction, and decide what they want the organisation's culture and vision to be. The use of external consultants should help to ensure that managers who may hold the types of views the organisation wants to change do not negatively impact on the outcome of the exercise. The development of the new strategic vision should also include the process for achieving such culture change and clearly defined timescales.

3. In order to achieve genuine change in staff attitudes and behaviour, the process must include work-based discussions and training, including team meetings and supervision. This is the hardest step in culture change. The processes involved in stage 1 will need to be repeated to ascertain progress and identify obstacles which need to be addressed.

Challenge and accountability

As noted above, as part of its role and function the LSCB has a duty to monitor and evaluate the effectiveness of the local authority and partner agencies in safeguarding and promoting the welfare of children in its area and, where necessary, to advise them on ways to improve. It has a statutory duty to 'monitor and challenge the effectiveness of local arrangements' (HM Government, 2015, p.8). The whole premise of the LSCB is that it is independent, as is the chair, in order to be able to challenge ineffectual or poor practice and hold agencies to account (HM Government, 2015, p.70). While there needs to be close working between the LSCB and the local authority's children's services department, at times the closeness of this relationship may jeopardise the required independence and weaken the scrutiny and challenge required. This was recognised in *Working Together to Safeguard Children* (HM Government 2013) when the hiring and firing of the independent LSCB chair, which had previously been the responsibility of the director of the local authority's children's services, was given over to the chief executive of the council. In daily practice, however, the line management of the LSCB business or board manager is often allocated to a service manager in children's social care services. Where concerns about children's social care practice are brought to the attention of the board manager, it must surely make robust challenge more difficult if it relates to an area of responsibility for their manager, however independent the chair and the board business unit are from the children's services directorate.

The way in which individual LSCB chairs operate may vary, with some having an open and inclusive approach to meetings which encourages debate and discussion, and others focusing on fulfilling the business as set out in the agenda. While the latter is important, it is the former approach that enables considerations of practice or service funding concerns, for example, and is key to enabling challenge to take place in a supportive atmosphere. In a comment that does not solely apply to Rotherham, Jay noted:

> As meetings become larger the more difficult it is for the Chair to give due weight to the varying interests represented, to encourage full and open debate and reach definitive conclusions which attract the agreement of all present. In addition, the Chair has the

responsibility to ensure that decisions are acted upon, timeously and to a high standard. Not only does this make the task difficult for a part-time Chair, but it also raises questions about the concept of accountability as applied to such a large, disparate group of people. (Jay, 2014, p.61)

Likewise Casey (2015) reflected that while the LSCB in Rotherham met its statutory requirements, the issue of challenge was significantly lacking at that time.

Historically, the Board has failed to identify shortcomings within Children's Services and ensure action to improve. It carries out the required audits of casework, and makes effective judgements, but these audits are not used to drive improvements in practice, and the Board does not follow up or challenge this effectively enough. The Chair recognises RLSCB has not functioned effectively. In his oral report to Cabinet in December 2014 he acknowledged the failings of the Board and included an honest reflection of what he, as Chair, could have done differently. (Casey, 2015, p.119)

This is likely to also be an issue for LSCBs elsewhere in the country.

With increasing numbers of children's services departments across England coming under scrutiny for their service delivery and their ability to safeguard children and promote their wellbeing, this can – conversely – often make challenge more difficult and unwelcome in an environment where being seen to improve is essential. LSCB officers are unable to act in relation to concerns, however, unless they are made aware of them in the first place. Communication between frontline practitioners and line managers about any concerns may not always be filtered up to senior managers who are in a position to constructively challenge partner agencies. One LSCB conducted an audit of strategy discussion practice, which revealed an authoritarian approach by social work managers in relation to decision making at such meetings. They told us that while there had been dissatisfaction from health, police and other practitioners at ground level to this approach, this had not been conveyed to their senior managers for action. Frontline practitioners have a duty to report any concerns of poor practice, whatever their nature, if it has the potential to impact on outcomes for children. Suppressive management styles are unlikely to facilitate this, leading to poor practice and harm to children, as well as negative inspection evaluations of local service delivery.

While the Wood report was not specifically commissioned as a result of serious case reviews or learning lessons from cases of CSE or organised CSA, the overall findings resonate considerably with us; indeed, some issues have already been discussed in earlier chapters. In particular, Alan Wood's findings in relation to the ability of LSCBs to challenge partner agencies to evaluate their own performance, secure input from children and young people (that is, listen to their views and experiences), as well as their operational practice in relation to early help responsibilities and referral thresholds are very pertinent to CSE and CSA multi-agency practice. We hope that the forthcoming changes in legislation and statutory guidance will positively impact on the commissioning and delivery of such services, as well as other areas of safeguarding and child protection.

Understanding issues locally

The Association of Independent LSCB Chairs (2013) produced guidance for all LSCBs, with practice examples, posing a number of questions that each LSCB should consider in relation to CSE:

1. Understanding the level of CSE risk in the area: how does the LSCB know what the level of risk of CSE is in its area?

2. Local strategy: does the LSCB area have a comprehensive local strategy for CSE with clear links to missing children and trafficking strategies; has it considered a combined strategy with neighbouring areas; does the strategy include detail of how it will be evaluated?

3. Local awareness: how does the LSCB raise awareness with young people and how does it know that this increases their safety; how does the LSCB raise awareness of parents and

carers; how does it raise awareness in the local community including local business and especially hotels?

4. Assessing and addressing risks for individual young people: how does the LSCB ensure the vulnerability of individual young people is being assessed; how does it know that local services are effective in reducing individual risk?

5. Disruptions and prevention: does the area collate information to gain a picture of potential abuse and potential perpetrator; does it have evidence that action is being taken to disrupt exploitation or potential exploitation?

6. Supporting victims: how does the LSCB know that victims receive appropriate support once abuse is identified; is there a coordinated approach to supporting victims through and beyond any court processes?

7. Auditing and monitoring the effectiveness of the local response: how does the LSCB receive updates on the effectiveness of local action in relation to CSE?

In an open letter to LSCB managers, chairs, and local authority directors in the *Municipal Journal* (Gladman, 2016), Adele added to the above guidance by inviting them to consider the following questions in order to assess the effectiveness of their own local authority area responses to CSE:

1. Have you independently audited practice responses to CSE? Do you have a clear understanding of the challenges and how you are addressing them? Do you have clear objectives in specified timescales for review? Are you collecting and analysing relevant data that will enable a review of whether interventions and strategies are working?

2. Is quality multi-agency training being delivered that facilitates the development of professional development beyond what e-learning or Level 1 courses can offer? What about training for less obvious employees such as park wardens and leisure staff?

3. Have you developed public awareness campaigns, including awareness raising for parents and carers; and preventative work for children and young people in education?

4. Have you clear information-sharing protocols so that professionals and public alike know how and where to share information? Is anyone assessing whether information is being shared and if not, why not? Is that information being used effectively to map and profile patterns in your area, and inform future work including disruption interventions and police investigations?

5. Are your key practitioners equipped to deal with the challenges that CSE presents, including young people who continually place themselves at risk or fail to engage? Is contingency planning a regular feature of their work? And is your authority properly supporting them?

6. Is practice in your area good enough? Does it address trauma and future vulnerability? Does it support families and children in moving forwards?

7. Is there an effective criminal justice response to abusers? Are they actively challenged, deterred, investigated and prosecuted? If cases are going to court, are children and families adequately prepared and supported?

Understanding local issues must also include the sexual exploitation and abuse of boys and young men in the LSCB area. Where such services do not exist, it should not be assumed that means that there is no abuse taking place. It is far more likely that it is hidden and that victims feel unable to make such disclosures, particularly if there are no specialist projects. It may also be that no comprehensive research has been undertaken to understand the abuse of young males locally. LSCBs should consider seeking the expertise of organisations such as BLAST. Of particular interest is their experience of running Excellence for Boys (E4B), funded by the Department for Education. During this two-year funded project, BLAST worked with 20 existing

CSE services to ensure that they were inclusive of and accessible to boys and young men. E4B also aimed to raise awareness on a national level as well as to increase the numbers of boys and young men reporting CSE and being referred to CSE services (BLAST, 2015).

In order to assist senior managers to proactively address issues of CSE in their area, the Office of the Children's Commissioner published the *See Me Hear Me Framework* (Berelowitz et al., 2013), which puts the child at the forefront of any work undertaken by all agencies in relation to their abuse and their abusers. The framework was developed in order to assist agencies to comprehensively protect children subject to organised child sexual abuse. It incorporates a number of different factors in relation to strategic planning and operational interventions, offering both proactive and reactive initiatives.

The framework focuses on ensuring that the child who is at risk of, or is a victim of CSE is 'seen, heard, attended to and understood' (Berelowitz et al., 2013, p.11). It is about ensuring that their needs and experiences are central and at the heart of all decisions made and actions taken. It is about ensuring that the victim is visible to all professionals and that they clearly understand what is happening to them and the level of risk involved. It outlines seven essential principles that must underpin all strategic and operational work in order for it to be effective, all of which we have discussed throughout this book. They are:

1. The child's best interests must be the top priority;

2. Participation of children and young people is key;

3. Enduring relationships and support;

4. Comprehensive problem-profiling;

5. Effective information-sharing within and between agencies;

6. Supervision, support and training for staff;

7. Evaluation and review.

(Berelowitz et al., 2013, pp.12–13)

The framework proposes three main areas to consider:

- the voice of the child
- the voice of the professional
- protection of the child.

At the time of writing, the framework is currently under review.

Policies, procedures, training and supervision
Policies and procedures

As noted above, LSCBs have a statutory duty to develop policies and procedures in relation to safeguarding children and promoting their welfare. A policy is a statement that sets out how a body or organisation intends to conduct itself in relation to a particular issue, for example in relation to safeguarding children and young people at risk of CSE. The policy should provide guiding principles to help with decision making, so that all staff know the approach or ethos of the body or organisation to the issue in question. Procedures describe how the policy should be put into action, and should include who will do what, what steps they should take and which forms or documents to use.

Policy and procedure can also be supplemented by practice guidance, which gives additional information for frontline staff and managers in which to consider their working practices. In relation to CSE and organised CSA, effective guidance includes a definition, explanation of terminology, indicators of risk and what action to take. It may also signpost to other documents such as a risk assessment tool or information-sharing protocol. It is sensible to combine policy, procedure and practice guidance related to a particular subject into one document, to aid understanding of the issues and make finding information easier. It should not be unnecessarily long or complicated, but it has to include all the information that is needed for staff to understand what is required of them in any given situation.

Policies and procedures are vital to the effective running of any organisation. This is because they provide the framework for organisational practice and the minimum standards by which staff should be operating. If staff do not have written policies and procedures to read and understand as part of their induction or to consult during their employment, they may do things differently from other staff and the service young people receive may vary. This is particularly important when managers or more experienced workers are not on hand to consult. It is also important to be able to facilitate challenge among services where practices are believed to be deviating from what is defined within policies and procedures. This is vital for safe practice in any organisation, but particularly where children are vulnerable and have complex needs. It is essential that children all receive the same level of service from staff, however long they have worked for the organisation and however much experience they have.

LSCB multi-agency policies and procedures are not replacements for organisations having their own internal processes, nor should they be considered unnecessary as partner agencies have their own. All organisations should have internal policies and procedures in relation to safeguarding children and adults, for example how to make referrals, supervision, training, whistleblowing and allegations against colleagues, as well as those that relate specifically to their particular specialist areas of practice. LSCB policies and procedures are necessary because they provide consistency and standards across all agencies. They should be considered the benchmark for local practice and be consulted when individual organisations are drawing up their own procedures, to make sure they are compliant with those the LSCB has signed off via the LSCB policies and procedures sub-group or its equivalent. They should be written in a manner that is appropriate and understandable for staff and volunteers from all agencies who work with children and young people, or come into contact with them in the delivery of their services, for example when working with adults. This will range from small voluntary sector organisations to large public sector bodies such as hospitals and police forces.

LSCBs can develop the best possible policies and procedures, but if they are not used by staff, or if practitioners are not aware of how to access them or of why they are important and relevant to them, they simply become a tick-box exercise, devoid of any meaningful purpose apart from during inspections. Herein lies the inherent problem across the country with policies and procedures – they are not routinely used by staff and are not embedded into daily practice. This is not just the case with LSCB procedures, but can also apply with internal procedures for individual organisations too. In the case of LSCB policies and procedures, it is the responsibility of each partner agency to ensure that the multi-agency procedures are read, understood and consulted when required by their staff, in addition to their own internal procedures. This was exemplified by Jay:

> The Rotherham Safeguarding Children Board and its predecessor oversaw the development of good inter-agency policies and procedures applicable to CSE. The weakness in their approach was that members of the Safeguarding Board rarely checked whether these were being implemented or whether they were working. (Jay, 2014, p.2)

LSCBs, overseen by the chair and attended by senior officers from partner agencies, need to ensure that they have a systematic approach to policies and procedures. This needs to include multi-agency development, sign off, dissemination, informing all staff of changes, monitoring understanding and compliance. This must involve frontline managers, who play a significant role in informing their staff of procedural changes, checking that they have read and understood them, and monitoring this against their work-based performance through supervision and annual appraisal. It is vital that managers at all levels throughout the organisation understand the purpose of policies and procedures and do not just give lip service to their importance.

Poor quality practice or staff not being familiar with procedures can lead to:

- children and young people being put at risk

- complaints from children, young people and/or their families

- complaints from other professionals/agencies

- disciplinary proceedings being taken against a member of staff (which would not be valid if there was no effective procedure)

- grievance proceedings being instigated by affected staff

- legal action being taken by children or their families

- organisations being criticised and poor ratings resulting from statutory inspections, such as Ofsted.

As the Communities and Local Government Committee noted:

> Rotherham's structure of policies and plans were divorced from reality. As Professor Jay told us, Rotherham 'had no shortage of policies, procedures or plans. There were mountains of them, but the weakness was that nobody checked whether they were being implemented, or indeed whether they were any good'. (Commons Select Committee, 10 September 2014)

Embedding policy and procedures into daily operational practice is a key component in improving CSE- and CSA-related practice in all partner agencies. Training is one method of accomplishing this, along with effective induction processes, supervision, case audits and robust team discussions.

Training

In any local authority area, most of the safeguarding children training accessed by the children's workforce is organised, provided or commissioned by the LSCB. The training programme should be based on a needs analysis audit conducted annually by the LSCB training manager, and meet the needs of the services and organisations working with children and their families in the locality. Delivering high quality training in times of austerity and reducing budgets has become increasingly challenging for LSCBs. There are, however, key principles to be observed, particularly in relation to CSE and CSA training:

- Different levels of training should be available. While e-learning may have a place in raising initial awareness of a subject, it is highly unlikely to address all of the learning needs for practitioners working on a daily basis with vulnerable children. Additionally, the needs of a lunchtime supervisor will be very different from those of a designated lead, community family worker or police officer.

- Attitudes and beliefs should be explored and discussed so that any questions, reservations or myths are debated in a safe learning environment.

- Practitioners should be equipped to be able to recognise and feel confident in challenging poor practice.

- Sharing information and confidentiality issues should be explored.

- Training should inform participants when and how to act.

- Training should enable participants to understand different service roles, as well as what is expected of them as individuals and of their organisation.

- Training should help participants understand the behaviour and lack of engagement of young people.

- Participants should understand at the conclusion how they can seek advice, be able to recognise the relevance and importance of policy and procedures, and know how to access them.

- Training should challenge participants' thinking about how they and their organisation can raise awareness of CSE with young people, families and communities, and feed into local strategic responses to CSE and CSA.

- For key professionals working with children and their families, training should facilitate their thinking in relation to what robust practice looks like and measuring the effectiveness of their responses to CSE and CSA.

In local authorities where case audits, reviews or independent inspections have been undertaken, training also plays a crucial part in delivering key learning from such reviews. In individual organisations, training can be further developed in team discussions, case discussions and targeted learning events which address the specific developmental needs of practitioners in the team. The quality of training should be assured by securing the best possible person to facilitate it. The LSCB manager should ensure that the training materials reflect local priorities, as well as the policy, procedural and practice guidance expectations. Evaluations of the training should be scrutinised, in conjunction with the training being observed by an LSCB representative. It may be useful to conduct a follow-up evaluation with a sample group of attendees in the months following their attendance, to see what impact the training has had on their practice.

Staff support and supervision

Issues of staff supervision were considered in Chapter 4, in relation to practice. Here we discuss management responsibilities in relation to supporting and supervising staff.

Anyone who has seen media coverage, read press articles or books in relation to CSE and CSA cannot fail to be moved by the horrific experiences described by victims and survivors. The effect on staff involved in working with children and young people who have been sexually exploited and abused can be profound. The emotional stress of listening to young people recount intimate details of vaginal rape, anal rape, oral rape, gang rape, torture, physical assault, blackmail, trafficking, humiliation and threats should not be overlooked.

The same applies to staff who do not directly work with children and young people but who are still exposed to the information they share, such as intelligence analysts, business administrators and line managers.

As previously mentioned, supervision can take a number of different forms, including individual sessions with a line manager, individual sessions with an external supervisor, clinical supervision, group supervision and peer supervision. While staff may participate in one or more such types of supervision, these should be in addition to supervision with a line manager rather than in place of it. This is essential to ensure management oversight of staff working in challenging circumstances. Regular supervision in conjunction with frequent contact with line managers as part of daily practice should ensure that managers become aware of staff burnout, stress and possible mental ill health sooner rather than later and can constructively intervene to support a practitioner who is struggling.

As well as ensuring that regular individual supervision takes place, managers have other responsibilities in relation to staff support. These include ensuring that holiday leave is taken regularly; that time owing does not build up and is taken promptly; that flexible working patterns are available so they can spend quality time with their family and friends; that staff do not work additional hours without overtime payments or taking time back; that caseloads are manageable; that adequate time is given for case recording and that time is built in for training for personal development as well as for completing mandatory courses. Management styles should be supportive and protective of staff, and avoid being negatively critical and disseminating pressure which they may receive from their managers. Being able to work effectively and empathically with children and young people who have been or are being so badly abused and traumatised is essential. If victims cannot develop good, supportive relationships with practitioners who they can trust, the abuse they receive from their intimate terrorists and other abusers can be compounded and may continue for longer where they feel they have no one independent of family and friends to whom they can turn for help.

Quality assurance

Effective strategic responses to CSE and organised CSA inform good working practices, particularly when they come from information gathered and analysed relating to local profiles and models of offending. Developing multi-agency, rather than single-agency, strategic action plans is the only effective response due to the complexity of the issues and the number of services likely to be involved; several LSCBs have such action plans. Strategic responses should include quality assurance to assess the effectiveness of the local response. This should include consideration of factors such as those outlined below.

- Are the action plan, policy, procedures and practice guidance being implemented and are they resulting in good quality work where children are protected and their abusers investigated?

- What areas are identified as requiring improvement and how will they need to be addressed?

- What services or interventions have been identified as necessary, but currently are not available in the locality, or are under-resourced or have long waiting lists?

- Is there proactive as well as reactive practice being undertaken? This includes preventative work such as raising awareness among families and local communities and asking local businesses to take action to prevent, identify and report CSE and organised CSA.

- Are local priorities and responses informed by information gathered from services and is this regularly reviewed to identify changes in patterns and models?

- Is there regular and effective information sharing between services?

These questions can only be answered by undertaking audits and case reviews, as well as local assessments or profiles of what information is known about CSE and CSA and what challenges have been identified as a consequence. For example, Adele has undertaken case reviews and county-wide audits, and interviewed staff and children and young people using services in order to identify good practice and areas for improvement and make appropriate recommendations. The LSCB is the main forum where such scrutiny and strategic review should take place, and where good quality policies, procedures and local training are not having an impact on local practice, this needs to be addressed without delay.

Raising awareness and working with different communities

In Rotherham, the vast majority of the perpetrators of organised child sexual abuse were men of Pakistani origin. This matter has been widely reported (including Jay, 2014; Casey, 2015) and has been the focus of much media reporting and public discussion. While this is an important issue that should not be ignored, there is a wider debate that must take place. Paedophiles and sexual abusers come from all racial and ethnic backgrounds. While it is acknowledged that there are a significant number of Asian men coming before the courts to be tried for child sexual offences in other areas of the country too, if UK society solely focuses on one group of perpetrators this is more likely to enable abusers who do not fit that profile to carry on harming children with impunity. For example, nine men were convicted of offences against one teenage boy in May 2016 (Birmingham Mail Online, May 2016). He was repeatedly raped and sold for sex over the course of a year. Apart from one man, all those convicted were white British. The outcome of the trial hardly touched the national press; the ethnicity of the accused was not discussed. Likewise, the presence of two white women convicted alongside the Hussains hardly drew public comment. It appears that the only time ethnic origin is worthy of public debate is when the offenders are of BME origin; when they are white it is apparently not an issue.

LSCBs and their statutory partners must not shy away from difficult discussions with particular communities where it has been identified that there is an issue of abuse. To do so enables the perpetrators to continue to abuse their victims without consequence, and therefore does a disservice to that community within which there may be other victims of their sexual abuse. Where the police and local authorities are seen as failing to act against black or minority ethnic offenders it can have serious repercussions for other members of those communities and the wider town or city in which they live, as discussed in Chapter 1. Yet where debate does take place it has to do so in an environment of great sensitivity and tact, conducted by people experienced in working with different communities. CSE and organised CSA are not about race; they are about the sexual abuse, power and control meted out by – predominately – adult men against children. Sometimes there are racial elements to the abuse, and where there are organised criminal networks of perpetrators from one particular ethnic group acting together to abuse children, this must be addressed.

Many LSCBs have considered how to raise awareness among the public, including among new and emerging communities, which can be a particular challenge. In Derbyshire, a decision has been made not to brand approaches as 'CSE' as it can result in communities not recognising the relevance for them, or becoming defensive. Instead, natural opportunities are identified to raise awareness of CSE. These can be:

- through the work of the local authority community cohesion team, with new and emerging communities incorporating CSE into programmes around staying safe, technology and e-safety, the law, acceptable behaviour and customs, for example

- awareness can be raised through safer neighbourhood teams and the contact that they have with people on a day-to-day basis

- making use of large diverse employers such as the local authority, the police force, health and education by adopting a public health approach which raises awareness among its employees and consequently their families and communities.

Additionally, education has a significant role to play. In Derbyshire, the U Create initiative was used with school children to raise awareness about the risks involved with sexting. Campaigns were created by the children, which were uploaded onto YouTube and voted for by the public. The winning campaign won a spot on local radio stations, which again engaged the media and wider communities in the Derbyshire area, and this was therefore an approach that was not targeted at specific communities.

Other LSCBs have a more direct approach. For example, where a problem of CSE-related activity is identified through research and intelligence, one LSCB told us it responds with an operation that has four elements, as outlined below. It uses local community groups working with statutory services.

1. Prepare: aims for a sustainable solution. Local groups work with women, girls and family groups raising awareness, for example through using creative media such as dance.

2. Prevent: a mix of approaches including environmental responses to reduce physical areas of risk, such as derelict garages, alleyways, parks and shrubbery, licensing of food outlets, taxis, hotels – mandatory training for staff, CCTV installations. Those who refuse to participate are watched closely by the authorities.

3. Protect (children's social care led): includes the multi-agency co-located team, which consists of police, children's social care and specialist CSE staff.

4. Pursue: the traditional police investigative approach.

Whether an LSCB and its partners take a direct or indirect approach to working with particular communities will be a local decision, based on an evaluation of the situation. But such work also needs to ensure that it reaches as many people from all communities in the area, including locally born white populations. LSCB's preventative messages and raising-awareness agenda need to be received and acted on by all, not just a targeted few.

Working with peripheral services: taxis, food outlets, hotels and retail centres

Much CSE-related activity involves peripheral services. These can include:

- taxis to transport or traffic children to the venue in which they are to be abused

- food outlets such as takeaways where young people have been drawn to for many years but where they can become the target of exploitation

- hotels where children can be abused by one or more men in rooms

- retail centres such as shopping centres, where young people are allowed to go on their own to meet friends, and where again they can be targeted for the purposes of exploitation.

Often such services operate as part of the night-time economy, as well as being open for business during the day. Children are vulnerable to abuse during both the day and the night, especially those who have gone missing from home or care.

LSCBs and partner agencies should work with these sectors in order to raise awareness of how their services may be manipulated by CSE perpetrators, who either work in the service and meet children during their working hours or use the service for the purpose of meeting children with the aim of sexually abusing them. There are a number of good practice examples in this area from South Yorkshire,

Derbyshire, Greater Manchester and London. In Rotherham, the LSCB is working in partnership with the local authority to address concerns regarding some taxi drivers. This has included working with one of the independent commissioners (appointed by the government after the Casey review) to review individual drivers, following which approximately 40 had their licences revoked as a result of concerns about their suitability. All drivers now have to undergo safeguarding training and have CCTV in their vehicles. There is also a regular partnership licensing meeting, which shares information in relation to any concerns about individual drivers or companies. This, in turn, feeds into the LSCB's CSE sub-group and the CSE Multi-Agency Risk Panel. Concerns still remain in relation to a few drivers, however. The Communities and Local Government Select Committee heard evidence from South Yorkshire MPs, who believe a legal loophole allows taxi drivers to work in the town, even once they have been rejected by Rotherham Council for not meeting the required standards. They can receive their licences from other authorities which do not have the same conditions, and this allows them still to operate in Rotherham (BBC Online News, August 2016).

Rotherham LSCB, together with South Yorkshire Police, also trains hotel staff, including night managers, room service and cleaning staff. Due to an initial lack of response, they first resorted to cold-calling hotels in person and offering to attend their team meetings on site in order to provide training rather than staff have to attend sessions in other venues. The following case example shows how this has yielded results.

> An older male had taken a young woman to a hotel. Reception staff who had attended the awareness training sessions were suspicious and shared their concerns with the hotel manager. The older male ordered room service. The manager took food to the room and insisted on taking it into the room rather than just to the door. He saw the girl and asked if she was OK, to which she said she was. He remained concerned and reported the incident to the police, including the man's car registration details. The man was identified as being linked to the exploitation of another child, and as a result

of this information, he became a person of interest to the police and local authority.

Sheffield SCB has a dedicated licensing project, which works with all types of premises or events that require a license, such as body piercing businesses, public events, gambling premises and the licensed trade, including off-licences and businesses which employ children (for example, as performers). The project is involved in providing information leaflets; raising awareness and providing training sessions; attending licensing meetings and court regarding possible revocation of licences, disseminating best practice guidance; consultation, including advisory visits to business premises; and advocating safeguarding children leads in businesses. These case examples illustrate ways in which strategic partners can work together to increase public awareness of CSE and CSA, protect vulnerable young people, increase the flow of information to the police, identify those who may be a risk to children and where they are operating, and reduce opportunities for young people to be abused.

Cross-border working

While LSCBs and SABs are clearly defined by their local authority boundaries, perpetrators are obviously not confined to such perimeters. In fact they often travel regularly and widely for the purposes of CSE and CSA, including trafficking children and young people. Abusers quickly learn that there can be communication difficulties for agencies working across local authority borders and so exploit any loopholes for their own gain. The main issue that arises in relation to cross-border working is when children are found in an area in which they do not live and agencies have to communicate and share information with the home authority. This applies to children's social care, police and other agencies that have information about the child which needs to be shared with their counterparts in the home authority area. It is at this crucial time, when a child has been trafficked and is likely to have been abused and traumatised, that home agencies need to know what has happened to them and who was responsible. The home agencies need to receive this information to continue to build a picture about the scale of the abuse the young person is involved in, so that they can be offered the appropriate support and add to the intelligence picture in relation to the perpetrators. It may also be the first time that a child who has become involved in CSE or organised CSA has come to the attention of the authorities, and so sharing information with the home authorities is key to protecting that child.

When a child is found, the first priority is removing them to a place of safety. This will usually be the responsibility of the police, who are likely to have been called to the situation. Once the child has been made safe the police should follow their internal procedures for responding to such circumstances. Where it is suspected that a crime has been committed, they may wish to interview the child and take forensic samples for DNA analysis. This has to be approached with the child with great sensitivity. To be abused at home is awful enough, but to be away from familiar surroundings and not have anyone they know to be with them during their ordeal will be very traumatic. Where geographically possible, a parent, carer or the child's key worker should travel immediately to be with them during this time. Discussion should take place with the local children's social care, the home children's social care and the home police public protection unit as to the best way to proceed in the child's best interests.

The main issues are to return the child to where they are living safely and as quickly as possible, gather as much evidence as is appropriate and possible before the child is returned home, and share all the information about the child and the circumstances in which they were found with the authorities in the home area. Children's social care will also have their own internal procedures for responding to a child who is found in their local area, and these should be followed accordingly. The practicalities of travelling arrangements and who is responsible for paying for the child to get home should be dealt with sensitively and practically. It is to be hoped that this situation would not occur now, but ten years or so ago two young people were trafficked from Rotherham to the south of England, but managed to escape their perpetrators. The main concern for the two police forces at that time was not about the abuse the young people may have suffered or about finding out information about the men who perpetrated such crimes, but who was going to pay for their rail fares home (*Panorama*, 2015).

Although we are increasingly moving to systems that better enable information sharing across boundaries and services, we are far from having a national system within either social care or the police. This enables perpetrators to domestically, or internally, traffic young people and take advantage of arguments about remits, responsibilities and budgets. This is an area that needs addressing as a matter of priority.

Adult services

Chapter 4 discussed some of the practice issues for multi-agency staff who work with adults who have been a child victim of perpetrators or with young adults who are currently either at risk of or experiencing abuse due to their involvement in organised sexual abuse. The case below, provided by a third-sector organisation, is an example of the type of organised sexual abuse that some adults can suffer too.

> Cheryl, who had grown up in care, was living in a small town in the Midlands. When she was 18, she met an older man who promised her love, stability and an exciting new life in another area of the country. Cheryl agreed and he 'drove' her to a city, about an hour and a half away. Within minutes of their arrival he disappeared, leaving her on the street; she never saw him again. Instantly a woman appeared and started talking to her. Cheryl explained what had happened and the woman then offered her a room in her flat. Later the woman explained that Cheryl would need money to pay for rent, food and so on, and the only way she could do that was to go to other houses to have sex with the men there. The woman advised Cheryl to use drugs so she would know less of what was happening to her, but Cheryl refused, although sometimes she did drink alcohol in order to cope. She was regularly trafficked throughout the city; a driver

would pick her up, deliver her to houses where she had no choice but to have sex with the men there, and then return her to the flat where she was living. She finally managed to escape when – having been raped by four men – they literally threw her out onto the street, saying she was useless.

In order to avoid some of the failings that have been evidenced throughout this book, it is vital that adult services and SABs learn from the errors of the past in relation to how some of their counterparts in children's services responded to CSE and organised CSA. Casey expressed disquiet about the transition of victims from children's to adult services:

> We have serious concerns about the group of young people during their transition to adulthood: that is, over 18. It was unclear to Inspectors what happens to victims of CSE at this point. RMBC do not view these young people as victims with ongoing support needs, and instead see their role in terms of a statutory Children's Social Care responsibility which ends when the children turn 18. Some interviewees suggested that services were just turned off. Adult services did not have an effective system in place to ensure a smooth and effective transition for this vulnerable group. Indeed, the criteria for receiving adult services mean that the victims may not meet the need for continued support even though they remain vulnerable, and in some cases continue to be sexually exploited... 'They've got a poster with my birthday on it when I turn 18 and then they don't need to bother with me.' A victim of CSE. (Casey, 2015, pp.93–94)

Senior managers need to ensure that sufficient resources, both from a staffing and financial perspective are committed to this area. We spoke to one woman who had had four allocated social workers in a nine-month period prior to the court date for the trial of her abusers at which she was required to give evidence. Three of them, she said, had been agency workers who were only required to give one week's notice. She said they each started working with her saying, 'We'll be here for you...we're not going anywhere', but within months they were gone. As the police described this woman as someone who did not present them with many challenges, it is not suspected that the issue lay with their working relationships with her; it was more likely to be an issue of management support and organisational issues. Ultimately, however, it was the woman herself and her family who were most affected by such practice issues.

While it is hoped that the circumstances that occurred in Rotherham will not be found to the same extent elsewhere, it is worth considering the recommendations from research and inquiries and applying them to adult services. The sector has an opportunity to be more proactive, and it is strongly recommended that this chance is taken. The impact of abuse and trauma does not dissipate at 18; proactive interventions may support child victims in becoming survivors rather than vulnerable adults. The more entrenched their issues and maladaptive behaviours become, the more difficult and costly the response. There is a clear logic, therefore, to early intervention in adult services.

Jay's recommendations for children's services can be applied to adult services, and should be considered by them and SABs.

- Senior managers should ensure risk assessments on those who have been the subject of organised abuse should be current, high quality and clearly recorded on file. The assessment should also include professional judgement, as numeric tools are not able to adequately summarise the situation.

- The risks to those in residential care need to be minimised, especially if they become exposed to sexual exploitation. Managers should take a strategic approach to supporting residents, and also to children who are transitioning from children's to adult services.

- The local authority should make every effort to reach victims not yet in touch with services.

- The remit and responsibilities of multi-agency teams should be agreed and communicated to all staff, and regularly reviewed to ensure they are consistent with the need and demand for services. There should be one overall manager for the service.

- Services should recognise that survivors are likely to require support and therapeutic intervention for an extended period of time and should work with local partners to secure the delivery of post-abuse support services.

- All agencies should resource and support quality assurance work in relation to sexual exploitation and abuse under the auspices of the safeguarding board.

- Local authorities and safeguarding boards should work with communities and individuals from minority ethnic communities on the issue of sexual exploitation and other forms of abuse.

- Issues of race should be tackled as a priority if it is found to be a significant factor in the local criminal activity of organised sexual abuse.

(adapted from Jay, 2014, pp.117–118)

As discussed in Chapter 3, the Office of the Children's Commissioner reports (Beckett *et al.*, 2013; Berelowitz *et al.*, 2013) identified a number of common failings in the response to tackle and address sexual exploitation. These are also relevant for adult services to take on board, and therefore have been adapted to read for practitioners and managers in adult services.

- Forgetting the victim: those at high risk, or who are already victims, are often ignored or discounted. They are often seen as 'putting themselves at risk', rather than the perpetrators being a risk to them.

- Failure to engage: professionals and agencies lack awareness and understanding in how to engage and work with those who are the victims of organised sexual abuse, particularly in relation to their specific needs. The individual's views of their own needs should be discussed with them; this would also aid professional understanding.

- Lack of leadership: a lack of leadership among senior local decision makers, who fail to understand the gravity of sexual exploitation and organised abuse, can result in insufficient resources being committed and a lack of a coordinated multi-agency response.

- Limited or no strategic planning: an absence of strategic planning and an action plan can result in differing approaches and an uncoordinated response across agencies. While strategic planning was found to have improved a year later, progress at a strategic level had not filtered down to frontline practice (Berelowitz *et al.*, 2015).

- In denial: there is a tendency for denial about the realities of sexual exploitation and organised abuse; professionals therefore do not believe what victims tell them.

- Failing to recognise victims: victim and perpetrator stereotypes still exist, which results in other patterns of abuse being ignored and victims left 'unseen' and unprotected, for example in relation to gangs.

- Agencies working in isolation: some agencies hold information not shared with the police, social care services and others, or sharing information is not as effective as it could be.

- Delayed response: a delayed strategic response at senior level hampers frontline practice and the provision of services to victims.

- Results not monitored: agencies do not review actions; there is no common agreement on goals and desired outcomes.

Finally, from a strategic perspective, the following information should be shared between local children's and adult services, in order to ascertain whether there is/are:

- a profile of children and young adults currently found to be most likely to be at risk in the local area

- particular residential homes (children's and adults) which have been/are targeted by perpetrators

- a profile of offenders (if single perpetrator or organised groups, for example)

- specific hotspots and locations (such as takeaway shops, hostels, party houses or transport hubs)

- local structures for response (for example, voluntary and statutory sector service providers, referral pathways, multi-agency working arrangements).

Often one of the challenges for adult services is to effectively address issues for victims and survivors resulting from their historic trauma and coping mechanisms, which have often become habitual and dysfunctional. Established partnership working between children's and adult services should assist in addressing such issues. Adult services should be aware of past abuse, and interventions, and be able to identify best ways forward. A balance needs to be achieved between meeting the adult's needs, including giving them time and support to come to terms with the trauma, and addressing potentially ongoing safeguarding issues (for example, if a crime has been disclosed).

Summary

This final chapter has discussed strategic and senior management responses to organised sexual abuse in relation to children's, and also adult services. The legal and policy framework in relation to children's services has been considered, in conjunction with the role and functions of the LSCBs. The response of adult services under the auspices of the Care Act 2014 and the accompanying statutory guidance has also been discussed. Some of the issues impacting on the effectiveness of these statutory bodies have been summarised, and pending proposals for change outlined. Adult services have a unique opportunity to learn from some of the errors of their counterparts in children's services; this chance should not be overlooked.

Reduced budgets have undoubtedly impacted on service funding and the delivery of interventions for children and adults who have been involved in organised sexual abuse, and on tackling and investigating perpetrators. It is the responsibility of senior and strategic managers to provide their practitioners with the best possible working environments their budgets can buy. But while adequate funding is – of course – key, it is not just financial support that makes a difference. Where poor practice prevails and practitioners have no practice guidance, procedural clarity or management support in relation to what they are supposed to be doing, increased budgets will not result in improved service delivery. There is far more to good practice than just money; it is what is done with those funds that is so vital. Money needs to be spent wisely, particularly in these austere times, and on interventions that work. Much can be done to ensure that staff are delivering best practice to the children and families with whom they work.

As discussed earlier in this chapter, this involves senior managers robustly changing negative and inappropriate organisational and professional cultures, particularly in relation to racist and sexist opinions and disparaging attitudes towards children and young people involved in child sexual exploitation. It also comprises managers listening to their staff and taking action in relation to what they say is and is not working and what resources are required. As is also noted previously, one of the benefits to emerge out of the Rotherham scandal has been improved practitioner and public understanding of the reality for children who become involved in organised child sexual abuse. Many people now understand it is not of the child's making, not of their choice and not within their control. While there has been a wholesale shift in attitudes towards those young people, we cannot be complacent that there are not still pockets of out-dated, ill-informed and unpalatable thinking (Lloyd, 2016). The issues of challenge and accountability are not solely for those at a strategic, senior management level. They also apply to all practitioners whose own colleagues or partnership peers express negative opinions about children or their families, or indeed stereotypical views about perpetrators of child sexual abuse. This is not about political correctness, but about seeing the bigger picture and having our eyes open to the realities of such abuse. Who are *all* the victims and survivors; who are *all* the abusers; what is the impact on the children, their families and wider society; what can we do better this time to prevent child sexual exploitation and how can we intervene with both victims and perpetrators early in order to prevent further harm?

While policies, procedures, training, supervision and quality assurance may not necessarily be the most riveting of subjects, they are essential to improving, supporting and maintaining good practice. They ensure the practice standards that children and their families should receive. But while practitioners should do their utmost to deliver best practice, ultimately it is the responsibility of senior managers to ensure that the services and interventions available for child and adult victims of organised sexual abuse are more than just fit for purpose. Senior managers are accountable for providing quality services, which work with some of the most traumatised and vulnerable young people in the country. Victims and their families have suffered enough; it is up to us all to ensure that their experiences are not further compounded by poor quality care and support. Significant improvements have already been made across the country; we need to ensure that such progress is embedded in daily practice by all, for all.

Conclusion

This book is dedicated to learning from the experiences of victims and survivors of child sexual exploitation in Rotherham. Accounts from victims, survivors and families have been woven throughout to aid our understanding, not only of the levels of trauma and abuse meted out by perpetrators, but also the compounding impact of poor practice by the professionals who wholly failed in their statutory duty to protect them (Jay, 2014; Casey, 2015). While much of what we have written may have been difficult at times to read and process, we owe it to the victims and survivors to listen to their stories and take action to ensure that events such as these never happen again. Reflecting on poor practice, as well as identifying positive professional responses, helps us see what changes need to be made in the present and in the future, as well as what challenges lie ahead.

We hope that, through this book, we have given students and practitioners more than a basic understanding of the main issues related to child sexual exploitation and organised child sexual abuse. We hope it has given practitioners food for thought when undertaking practice assessments, planning and decision making, and generally working with children, young people, and young adults who are at risk of, or who are experiencing, significant harm by sexual predators.

At the very least we hope that it has given readers more knowledge and therefore confidence in responding to and communicating with children, and that children will be better understood and protected as a result.

Before we make some final comments and a number of proposals, we would like to take this opportunity to summarise some of the main discussions in each of the preceding chapters, to remind ourselves of the salient points covered in this book. Clearly the main emphasis of this book is about understanding and responding to the experiences of children who are groomed, sexually abused, traumatised and terrorised, in Rotherham and beyond. Yet as demonstrated by Chapter 1, The Consequences of Statutory Agency Failure in Rotherham, there have been huge consequences for other groups of people as a result of the failures of senior managers in the town. We discussed the consequences for family members, but particularly parents, who had to endure not only seeing their child change dramatically before their eyes while simultaneously being unable to protect them, but also had to suffer the uncaring, unprofessional and sometimes very critical 'practice' of some of those tasked with the responsibility of keeping them safe. Rotherham businesses have suffered as a result of the tarnished reputation of the town and the repeated marches of right wing agitators, demonstrating against the involvement of men from the Pakistani heritage community. That community in turn has been vilified, stigmatised, criticised and targeted – fatally in the case of Mushin Ahmed – yet the majority are law-abiding people who will have been equally horrified at the actions of the abusers. While, yes, the community leaders should have done more to tackle the perpetrators and those at risk of following in their abusive footsteps, they were also let down by Rotherham Council and South Yorkshire Police, who failed to address these issues proactively. Politicians and local councillors, senior managers in the police and children's social care are all responsible for failing to tackle child sexual exploitation and abuse, and the devastating consequences for the town.

Chapter 2, Defining and Identifying Child Sexual Exploitation and Organised Child Sexual Abuse, outlined the key issues of which practitioners must be aware in order to be able to identify CSE and take appropriate action when they have any concerns that a child is being groomed by perpetrators for the purposes of sexual exploitation and abuse. While the majority of organised sexual abuse cases being prosecuted before the courts have involved offences committed against girls and young women, the chapter discussed how boys and young men are very much a target group for some perpetrators. Yet as there is less recognition of boys' involvement in CSE and the general perception is that it is older, male abusers who usually target girls, boys may feel less able to disclose sexual abuse in case they are not believed. Apart from specific case examples, the language used throughout this book is deliberately gender neutral in order to help practitioners to think outside the usual narrow focus. The issue of age was also examined, emphasising that a child's vulnerability does not end at their 16th birthday when they reach the age of lawful consent to sex. It is power imbalances within friendships or relationships that can be a key indicator of potential abuse. Different models of grooming and exploitation were considered – the 'boyfriend', 'party house', peer-on-peer, gangs and online paradigms – to help practitioners recognise such scenarios, which they can then apply to any such relevant information a child, or another person, shares with them. Physical, emotional, environmental and other indicators of abuse were discussed, to further aid practitioners to be able to identify a child at risk of significant harm. As has been repeated elsewhere in this book, it is essential that all practitioners working with children and their families understand CSE and sexual abuse, as ultimately if they do not take appropriate action it can result in a child experiencing ongoing abuse and harm.

Chapter 3, Understanding the Impact of Grooming and Organised Child Sexual Abuse, outlined the complex nature of this type of abuse, and how cruel, violent, controlling and sadistic the acts can become. Practitioners should not dismiss a child's account of abuse on the grounds that they think it is too outlandish to have taken place.

Unfortunately, this is the *modus operandi* of many perpetrators. The chapter discusses how abused children are, unsurprisingly, only likely to disclose their abuse to someone they can trust, and that relationships are far more likely to be established with staff who are knowledgeable and confident in the issues covered throughout this book. The chapter also considered the different reasons why some children may be vulnerable, but stressed that ultimately all children may be susceptible if they should become a target of skilled and manipulative abusers. The psychological trauma as a consequence of their abuse is likely to be considerable, and if left unrecognised and untreated can lead to the child experiencing significant and complex problems well into adulthood, some of which never recede. Good practice and prompt responses from practitioners working with children and families can significantly reduce a child's level of risk, and can hinder abusers' attempts to exploit them. Poor practitioner practice, however, including the use of inappropriate language and sceptical attitudes, can prevent a child from being able to establish a good working relationship, which in turn is likely to inhibit disclosure. When practitioner emphasis is on what they believe to be the child's lifestyle 'choices', in reality it can result in increasing the child's risk by erroneously normalising and validating abusive relationships. When the child's behaviour is the focus and the crimes of their intimate terrorist or other abusers are ignored, the child is put at additional risk by those who are tasked to protect them.

In Chapter 4, Taking Effective Action within a Safeguarding Framework, we examined in detail what best practice should look like, and considered some of its component parts. Key issues included recognising warning signs of being groomed or abused, without making immediate assumptions that a child is either being or not being exploited or harmed. Using professional judgement in combination with the child, the family and colleagues from partner agencies is vital. Where a child is already involved, early interventions from knowledgeable practitioners are crucial for better outcomes for them. As in Chapter 3, we emphasised that the response they get from staff is an essential element of that protection process.

We discussed thresholds, indicators and toolkits, and the current practice and research debates regarding evidence. We noted the importance of including the family where they are a protective factor in the child's life – holistic interventions – and how their involvement can be therapeutic for them as well as their child. We outlined some issues for practitioners in adult services, particularly those who work with adults who are vulnerable but also those whose children have been fathered by their abusers. A most crucial issue that underpins all practitioner work with children and adults involved in CSE or organised sexual abuse, however, is effective managerial and organisational support and supervision. Without such processes and systems in place, staff will suffer as a result of having to respond to often relentless trauma and abuse. This impacts on the staff, sickness records, work performance and organisational reputation. But ultimately it is the child, and their family, who will suffer the most.

Chapter 5, Key Considerations for Criminal Investigations and Tackling Perpetrators, discussed key issues for police and partner agencies in tackling the perpetrators and conducting investigations. The process of receiving and analysing information from multi-agency practitioners and the public was examined in some detail, including some of the challenges that exist for police forces. Joint working partnership models are operating in many areas of the country; these include dedicated CSE police officers who should preferably be co-located with practitioners from children's social care, and specialist third-sector organisations. The chapter discussed different disruption techniques that can be useful in relation to individual offenders and businesses. Disruption, however, is far less likely to be an effective, preventative tool for serial offenders embroiled in sexual abuse and other serious and organised crimes, such as the supply of drugs. This is particularly so for the intimate terrorist, who can manipulate and control their victim over time, sometimes – as has been seen – with impunity. The only time CSE and abuse disruption techniques may be useful with such perpetrators is if they become concerned that unwanted police attention may impact on their more profitable criminal enterprises. South Yorkshire Police's Operation Clover was used as a case example in this chapter, providing a unique insight into police investigations in relation to historic crimes committed by the main perpetrators of organised child sexual abuse in Rotherham.

Chapter 6, Child Sexual Exploitation, Organised Child Sexual Abuse and the Criminal Justice Process, examined some of the issues for witnesses who give evidence against perpetrators in Crown Court trials. It discussed the advice, information and intensive support that witnesses require in order to best prepare them for the court experience and eventual outcome. Individual care plans are essential to ensure that the needs of each witness are considered in detail and implemented as planned. Failure to address such issues may result in them not being able to give evidence or the experience having such a negative impact that they subsequently suffer significant mental health issues. The chapter also highlighted examples of the appalling treatment that some victims have received from defence barristers, while giving evidence in court. It is acknowledged that some changes have been made to reduce the potential negative impact of testifying during trials, and the chapter discussed some of these special measures. It is also recognised that, under the rule of law, defendants are innocent until proven guilty. It is vital, however, that all who participate in the court process ensure that the victim's appearance does not compound their already abusive experience at the hands of the perpetrators, for both them and their family.

Finally, Chapter 7, Strategic and Senior Management Responses to Child Sexual Exploitation and Organised Sexual Abuse, discussed issues for strategic and senior managers in children's services. It outlined the legislative and policy frameworks for the sector, and the responsibilities and challenges for Local Safeguarding Children Boards. It also considered the responsibilities for adult services and the Safeguarding Adults Boards, in light of their statutory duties under the Care Act 2014. Adult services and SABs must learn lessons from their counterparts in children's services and LSCBs, to ensure that the same errors are not repeated in relation to adults requiring care and support either as a result of the abuse they suffered as children, or that which they suffer as young adults. Tools which aid staff and give practice direction were discussed in some detail, including policies, procedures, supervision, training and quality assurance processes. These are vital apparatuses required to support staff, monitor practice and manage their practice performance. They should not be scrimped on in times of financial austerity, otherwise it is the service received by children and young adults which will suffer, with the possibility that they are left exposed to continued sexual abuse and trauma. This also applies to organisational cultures, where entrenched poor attitudes and beliefs need to be challenged, particularly when based on erroneous and dangerous stereotypes of children and young people involved in CSE.

The chapter also discussed the strategic response to working proactively with communities, with the aim of preventing young people becoming perpetrators and raising awareness of grooming and online dangers to reduce the likelihood of victimisation. It must be stressed that this is not just a police or local authority responsibility; all partner agencies have a role to play, overseen by LSCBs and SABs. This also applies to other types of proactive crime reduction interventions, such as with local businesses, hotels, shopping centres and leisure areas. It is a multi-agency response that is required, including members of the public, in order to reduce the risk of harm to children, young people, young adults and their families.

As authors of this book, we still feel angry and very passionate about what happened to many children and young people in Rotherham, both at the hands of the perpetrators who subjected them to such depraved sexual acts and psychological terror, and the subsequent lack of compassion and competent practice from the statutory agencies who left them unprotected and endangered to ongoing abuse. We were unable to influence the outcomes for children and young people at that time, despite our best efforts. It is to be hoped that through this book we will have more success. Having summarised the main points from each chapter, we now make our concluding comments on issues of particular concern to us.

We expect our young people to understand the premise of a healthy relationship. But why? How often do we as parents, carers or professionals specifically talk to our children and young people about what healthy relationships look and feel like? Undoubtedly, not often enough. Maybe to avoid embarrassment and discomfort we often avoid discussing such issues, but this in turn can enable inappropriate and abusive relationships to flourish. Perhaps though, it is also because a 'healthy relationship' is difficult for us to define ourselves. Relationships are rarely perfect, but as adults – unless there is coercion and control – we are able to decide for ourselves what are important characteristics in a person with whom we are involved. Likewise we can make decisions in relation to a person's traits we consider to be flaws, and whether we are willing to ignore them, and which may ultimately cause a relationship to break down. Children and young people, however, do not usually have the emotional maturity and life experience to be able to make those judgement calls. They have not yet learned to be sceptical of what seems too good to be true. Often young people believe that something is good for them because it feels good to them. So while they might initially question why this older, good-looking person, with money, is showing an interest in them, they take the situation at face value and are not able to assess the situation further in order to give themselves a true answer. Children frequently believe that someone is a nice person because they look nice.

Children who have previously been abused, who may be far less trusting of adults, are also still vulnerable to being targeted by sexual predators. Their previous experiences can make them vulnerable in other ways, for example their need to be in what they think is a healthy relationship. We must not forget that relationships, especially those which have an illicit or forbidden element to them, are also very appealing to young people. Excitement is a considerable motivator for them and we often overlook this, despite being able to remember similar feelings when we were their age if we think hard. What we as professionals and parents consider dangerous or risky, young people often regard as exciting and appealing. To an extent that is normal teenage behaviour; being targeted by sexual predators is not.

The initial stages of CSE and organised sexual abuse involve grooming and gaining control over the victim. Where professional assessments and decisions place the responsibility for their own safety and abuse on the shoulders of those victimised, this also reinforces the power of the abuser. This not only increases the risk to the abused young person but also to other vulnerable young people who may be currently targeted by the perpetrator, as well as to future victims. It must also be considered that if a vulnerable child does not have the ability to recognise and avoid the risk in the first place, is it realistic to assume that they have any power to extricate themselves from a sadistic relationship once they have been abused and traumatised? Adult victims of domestic violence and abuse find it difficult enough to exit such relationships; those difficulties will be compounded for a child who wants to get away from their intimate terrorist, but who does not have the life experiences and knowledge to help them to leave.

We propose that there is a commitment by the Department for Education and its partners, to encourage and support parents, carers, education services and other practitioners alike to have open and honest discussions with all children and young people about relationships. This should include the attributes of a healthy relationship, as well as discussing different types of abusive relationships and the warning signs to which children should be alert. While we acknowledge that good work in relation to this is being done in some places, there clearly needs to be a more comprehensive and robust approach taken, with additional support available, as children are continuing to be abused in such ways.

For young women in particular, their preparation for adolescent relationships comes from the idealised world of Disney or Hollywood. For young men and women questioning their sexuality, however, there is a double jeopardy. As noted above, as a society we are still not comfortable talking to children about sex and relationships, and this is exacerbated when discussing same-sex issues. How many films or books, for example, for teenager and young adult readers have characters in same-sex relationships? LSCBs must ensure that they address the needs of boys, young men and lesbian, gay, bisexual and transgendered (LBGT) young people in their local area as well as girls and young women. As referenced in Chapter 7, this is not an option; this is the law. We propose that LSCBs and SABs review the services they offer to LBGT groups to ensure that they are not inadvertently discriminating against such children and young adults, which unintentionally culminates in excluding them from mainstream CSE services and, again, leaves them unprotected and vulnerable to continuing abuse by perpetrators as a result of senior officer oversight.

As we discussed in Chapter 3, intimate terrorists and other abusers are very skilled at grooming and abusing children. They share information with others, including how to target children for their own abusive ends and how to reduce their risk of being surveilled, investigated and arrested. They adapt their *modus operandi* accordingly, in order to reduce their level of risk and capture. It is vital that all relevant agencies share information and work together using good practice approaches to keep up with such paedophiles. We as practitioners – together with the public – must all be vigilant and proactive when we have any suspicions or concerns about a child, because the reality is that some adults will continue to be sexually interested in children, and want to exploit their vulnerability in order to commit abusive and traumatic acts. Key to the arrest and conviction of perpetrators is practitioners and the public sharing information with the police. As considered in Chapter 5, there are some significant problems with police forces receiving, analysing and acting on information. While we discussed a number of issues in relation to intelligence, here we propose one fundamental change: that multi-agency practitioners and all police staff are trained to become National Intelligence Model compliant, in order that they can analyse information they receive or witness before submitting it to the police. Undergoing such training is not lengthy or complicated, but the advantages it could bring investigations into perpetrators of organised child sexual abuse would be significant, with the added benefit of substantial cost and staff time savings.

Of the eight convicted in the second Operation Clover trial, removing Basharat Hussain from the equation who was 40 years old, the men were aged between 30 and 34. As they were convicted of offences committed 13 years previously, they were then aged between 17 and 21 years old. Following conviction, the Crown Prosecution Service spokesman noted the prominent role that Sageer Hussain in particular took in befriending the victims, and in relation to one particular young woman, passing her on to his friends and other associates (BBC Online News, October 2016). He was aged just 17; he was still legally a child himself. This demonstrates the need to better understand, through research, the attraction of organised CSA to young men, particularly in the context of their attitudes to girls and women – and possibly other members of society too – that they simply exist as victims for their own gratification. Without understanding the underlying problems, we will not be able to effectively tackle the root causes. We would welcome comprehensive research studies conducted into the offenders of CSE and organised CSA, to aid our comprehension of these appalling crimes. This would provide an evidence base for work to divert young people away from such perpetrator lifestyles, as well as interventions aimed at those convicted of crimes related to organised CSA.

We discussed terminology in the Introduction, particularly in relation to the term 'child sexual exploitation'. We have used this phrase throughout the book in relation to the true meaning of 'exploitation', which is at the grooming and initial stages of a child becoming involved. When we have discussed the types of sexual offences that are commonly committed by perpetrators, such as vaginal, anal and oral rape, sometimes by multiple abusers, we have used the term child sexual abuse, and sometimes in the context of organised crime: organised child sexual abuse. When we have been discussing the needs of adult victims and survivors, we have referred to sexual abuse or organised sexual abuse. We need to ensure that we use language appropriate for the individual and reflect their actual experiences. By talking about 'child sexual exploitation', or any other term that does not wholly and adequately explain the abuse, do we detach ourselves from the horror and reality of what is happening to the child? Sanitised phraseology that does not make clear the type and severity of the abuse may simply protect our sensitivities and make such incidents less offensive, while leaving the child exposed to continuing abuse, with practitioners failing to comprehend the types of offending and resulting trauma that the child is experiencing. We recommend that practitioners think carefully about the language and terms that they use in relation to the exploitation and sexual abuse of children, to ensure that they are reflecting the reality of the child's situation.

While the National Crime Agency (NCA) includes child sexual exploitation as one of the threats it is tackling, and police operations such as Operation Clover investigate using the same procedures as employed to tackle other types of organised crime, there may be less of a practitioner and public perception that child sexual abuse comes within the definition of organised crime.

> Organised crime can be defined as serious crime planned, coordinated and conducted by people working together on a continuing basis. Their motivation is often, but not always, financial gain. Organised criminals working together for a particular criminal activity or activities are called an organised crime group. (National Crime Agency, undated)

While the NCA does not specify the number of perpetrators that constitute an organised crime group, the United Nations Office on Drugs and Crime (undated) notes it is 'a group of three or more persons that was not randomly formed'. While this is in relation to transnational crime, there is no reason why it should not apply on a national basis too. It is evidence of how few perpetrators are required to operate on an organised basis, and be considered a significant threat. We also propose, therefore, that child sexual exploitation and organised child sexual abuse are more widely considered by multi-agency practitioners, the media and the public as crime types that constitute the definition of organised crime.

We would like to conclude with two final comments. First is to reiterate a very important quote from Chapter 1:

> I strongly believe that in future those who occupy senior positions in the public sector must be responsible to account for any failure to protect vulnerable children from deliberate harm or exploitation. (Laming, 2003: 1.27, cited in Heal, 2003, p.54)

The responsibility of ensuring that we implement the right response in relation to children who are being sexually exploited and abused, their families and the perpetrators lies with all of us, but no one more so than the senior strategic leads in children's social care and the police. It is their statutory duty, their moral obligation. Creating cultures where staff are able to positively challenge colleagues is down to all practitioners, but ultimately it is the responsibility of the head of each organisation. To use a policing term, it is the 'direction and control' that is key to how an organisation responds to either emerging or entrenched issues, whether they are related to child sexual exploitation, organised sexual abuse or other significant concerns. It concerns how a constabulary or other organisation is run, as opposed to the day-to-day practice decisions or actions of its staff. Direction and control is the responsibility of chief constables and chief executives; it is they who are ultimately accountable for their organisation's responses. They are often quick to acknowledge successes; they need to be equally open about their organisation's failings and where their own responsibilities lie in such matters. That is the level of responsibility that, when they take up office, is bestowed on them – the status and power with which to act, and for which they get very well remunerated. We both continue to work with a number of different organisations and individuals in an attempt to comprehend what happened to the common sense and compassion of senior managers during those years covered by the Jay report. As Professor Alexis Jay, now chair of the national Child Sexual Abuse Inquiry, firmly said:

> 'I treat with some scepticism calls for us to forget the past,' she said. 'Only by understanding the lessons we can learn from that and the

possible failings and cover-ups that might have taken place in certain institutions will we go forward with confidence.' (BBC Online News, October 2016)

We wholeheartedly agree.

Our second concluding point is to end by reciting some of Tanya's Foreword; it is too important and powerful only to be used once. While some of what she says is Rotherham specific, it applies far beyond this specific town. Please remember her words when you are considering what action to take; when you meet a child who you think is being sexually exploited and abused.

I believe that if social workers would have listened to my mum the first time she told them what was happening to me, then my life could have been so much different – I would have put trust in and listened to professional advice. I believe workers then knew what needed to be done and had the knowledge, but was too scared to stand up and admit this was a problem and it needed addressing in fear of losing their jobs and being victimised by senior members of staff. One thing I have learnt from this whole thing is being silent is what made this town become such a mess.

Speak out and don't be scared to challenge and stand up for what is the right thing to do. I am so happy to be able to use this very bad and unfortunate part of my life to talk out and try and change the way things went wrong. My personal opinion is that the only way to move forward is for workers to be prepared to challenge every little thing they come across. Yes, it's a lot of work, but in the long run it will come naturally and society will change the way they think about the failures that once was, and look forward to putting trust in South Yorkshire Police and Rotherham children's services again.

References

Alter Ego Theatre Company (undated). Available at www.alteregocreativesolutions. co.uk/chelseas-choice, accessed on 10 May 2016.

Anonymous (Girl A) (2013) *Girl A: My Story.* London: Ebury Press.

Anti-Social Behaviour, Crime and Policing Act 2014. Available at www.legislation.gov. uk/ukpga/2014/12/contents/enacted, accessed on 30 September 2016.

Association of Independent LSCB Chairs (2013) *Guidance for Local Safeguarding Children Boards on Child Sexual Exploitation.* Available at www.lscbchairs.org.uk, accessed 13 June 2016.

BBC Online News (24 November 2010) *Derby rape gang 'targeted children'.* Available at www.bbc.co.uk/news/uk-11819732, accessed on 7 December 2016.

BBC Online News (9 May 2012) *Rochdale grooming trial: Nine men jailed.* Available at www.bbc.co.uk/news/uk-england-17993003, accessed on 3 October 2016.

BBC Online News (12 January 2015) *Breck Bednar murder: Lewis Daynes sentenced to life in prison.* Available at www.bbc.co.uk/news/uk-england-30786021, accessed on 18 August 2016.

BBC Online News (24 February 2016) *Rotherham abuse: Hussain brothers 'were infamous'.* Available at www.bbc.co.uk/news/uk-england-35595008, accessed on 7 December 2016.

BBC Online News (26 February 2016) *Hussain brothers jailed in Rotherham abuse case.* Available at www.bbc.co.uk/news/uk-england-35670538, accessed on 7 December 2016.

BBC Online News (29 February 2016) *Mushin Ahmed death: Two men jailed over racist Rotherham killing.* Available at www.bbc.co.uk/news/uk-england-south-yorkshire-35688543, accessed on 4 July 2016.

BBC Online News (19 August 2016) *Taxi loophole 'puts Rotherham children at risk', say MPs.* Available at www.bbc.co.uk/news/uk-england-south-yorkshire-37124926, accessed on 7 December 2016.

References

BBC Online News (17 October 2016) *Child sex abuse inquiry: No reduction in scope, says Alexis Jay.* Available at www.bbc.co.uk/news/uk-37680906 accessed, on 20 October 2016.

Beckett, H. with Brodie, I., Factor, F., Melrose, M. *et al.* (2013) *'It's wrong...but you get used to it': A qualitative study of gang-associated sexual violence towards, and exploitation of, young people in England.* Children's Commissioner, London. Available at www.childrenscommissioner.gov.uk/sites/default/files/publications/Its_wrong_but_you_get_get_used_to_it.pdf, accessed on 7 October 2016.

Bedford, A. (2015) *Serious Case Review into Child Sexual Exploitation in Oxfordshire: From the Experiences of Children A, B, C, D, E, and F.* Oxford Safeguarding Children Board. Available at www.oscb.org.uk/wp-content/uploads/SCR-into-CSE-in-Oxfordshire-FINAL-FOR-WEBSITE.pdf, accessed on 16 October 2016.

Berelowitz, S., Firmin, C., Edwards, G. and Gulyurtlu, S. (2012) *'I thought I was the only one. The only one in the world': The Office of the Children's Commissioner's Inquiry into Child Sexual Exploitation in Gangs and Group Interim Report.* Office of the Children's Commissioner.

Berelowitz, S., Clifton, J., Firimin, C., Gulyurtlu, S. and Edwards, G. (2013) *'If only someone had listened': Inquiry into Child Sexual Exploitation in Gangs and Groups Final Report.* Office of the Children's Commissioner.

Berelowitz, S., Ritchie, G., Edwards, G., Cabrita Gulyurtlu, S. and Clifton, J. (2015) *'If it's not better, it's not the end': Inquiry into Child Sexual Exploitation in Gangs and Groups: One Year On.* Office of the Children's Commissioner. Available at www.childrenscommissioner.gov.uk/sites/default/files/publications/If%20its%20not%20better%20its%20not%20the%20end_web%20copy.pdf, accessed on 17 August 2016.

BLAST. Available at www.mesmac.co.uk/projects/blast, accessed on 10 October 2016.

BLAST (2015) *Excellence for Boys Project: Summary of Initial Findings.* Available at http://assets.mesmac.co.uk/images/efb-summary-findings.pdf?mtime=20151109125549, accessed on 1 October 2016.

Birmingham City Council v Sarfraz Riaz and Others (2014) EWHC 4247 (Fam). Available at www.familylawweek.co.uk/site.aspx?i=ed138138, accessed on 1 September 2016.

Birmingham Mail Online (20 May 2016) *Teenage boy was 'sold' in Birmingham by abuse gang.* Available at www.birminghammail.co.uk/news/midlands-news/teenage-boy-sold-birmingham-abuse-11363801, accessed on 10 October 2016.

Brown, S., Brady, G., Franklin, A., Bradley, L., Kerrigan, N. and Sealey, C. (2016) *Child Sexual Abuse and Exploitation: Understanding Risk and Vulnerability.* Coventry University. Available at www.eif.org.uk/publication/csa-risk-and-vulnerability, accessed on 16 September 2016.

Canadian Broadcasting Company: *The National* (18 March 2015) *Hundreds of Girls Sexually Exploited in Rotherham, England.* Available at www.cbc.ca/player/play/2659333584, accessed on 6 November 2015.

Care Act 2014. Available at www.legislation.gov.uk/ukpga/2014/23/contents/enacted, accessed on 12 September 2016.

Casey, L. (2015) *Report of Inspection of Rotherham Metropolitan Borough Council.* Available at www.gov.uk/government/uploads/system/uploads/attachment_data/file/401125/46966_Report_of_Inspection_of_Rotherham_WEB.pdf, accessed on 9 October 2016.

Channel 4 (December 2015) *Hunting the Paedophiles – Inside the National Crime Agency*. Available at www.channel4.com/programmes/inside-the-national-crime-agency, accessed on 22 October 2016.

Children Act 1989. Available at www.legislation.gov.uk/ukpga/1989/41/contents, accessed on 1 June 2016.

Children Act 2004. Available at www.legislation.gov.uk/ukpga/2004/31/contents, accessed on 1 June 2016.

Child Exploitation Online Protection (CEOP) (2013) *Threat Assessment of Child Sexual Exploitation and Abuse*. Available at https://ceop.police.uk/Documents/ceopdocs/CEOP_TACSEA2013_240613%20FINAL.pdf, accessed on 9 October 2016.

Children and Young People Now (9 September 2014) *Rotherham DCS told to quit by parliamentary committee*. Available at www.cypnow.co.uk/cyp/news/1146486/rotherham-dcs-told-quit-parliamentary-committee, accessed on 24 October 2015.

Children's Commissioner (2016) *Children's Commissioner for England says Icelandic 'Barnahus' approach could double convictions of child sexual abuse in West Yorkshire*. Available at www.childrenscommissioner.gov.uk/news/children%E2%80%99s-commissioner-england-says-icelandic-%E2%80%98barnahus%E2%80%99-approach-could-double-convictions, accessed on 19 October 2016.

Clutton, S. and Coles, J. (2007) *Sexual Exploitation Risk Assessment Framework: A Pilot Study*. Barnardo's.

Coming Out of the Darkness conference, 11 March 2016. Available at www.comingoutofthedarkness.co.uk, accessed on 28 January 2017.

Commons Select Committee (9 September 2014) *Rotherham child sexual exploitation and Home Office Reviews explored further*. Available at www.parliament.uk/business/committees/committees-a-z/commons-select/home-affairs-committee/news/140904-rotherham-ev, accessed on 6 November 2015.

Commons Select Committee (10 September 2014) *Independent inquiry into child sexual exploitation in Rotherham*. Available at www.parliament.uk/business/committees/committees-a-z/commons-select/communities-and-local-government-committee/news/rotheram-ev, accessed on 6 November 2014.

Community Care (15 September, 2016) *Social workers 'not equipped' to identify risks of social media, reviews say*. Available at www.communitycare.co.uk/2016/09/15/social-workers-equipped-identify-risks-social-media-reviews-say, accessed on 6 October 2016.

Cooper, F. (2012) *Professional Boundaries in Social Work and Social Care: A Practical Guide to Understanding, Maintaining and Managing your Professional Boundaries*. London: Jessica Kingsley Publishers. Available at http://jpkc.fudan.edu.cn/picture/article/320/00/da/391bb47a43659403fac63ac3d1d7/749193e0-c1d5-4ced-a500-bfbde5f538b7.pdf, accessed on 16 January 2016.

Coventry Safeguarding Children Board (2016) *Serious Case Review Child G, Child H, Child I, Child J, Child K*. Available at www.coventry.gov.uk/downloads/file/21223/cse_-_serious_case_review_overview_report, accessed on 1 August 2016.

Crimestoppers. Available at https://crimestoppers-uk.org, accessed on 10 October 2016.

Crown Prosecution Service (2013) *Operation Bullfinch men sentenced – Oxford*. Available at www.cps.gov.uk/thames_chiltern/cps_thames_and_chiltern_news/operation_bullfinch_men_sentenced___oxford, accessed on 8 October 2016.

Crown Prosecution Service (undated) *Provision of therapy for vulnerable or intimidated adult witnesses prior to a criminal trial – Practice guidance*. Available at www.cps.gov.uk/publications/prosecution/pretrialadult.html, accessed on 20 April 2016.

Daily Mail Online (3 October 2014) *Police struggling to cope with soaring number of child abuse images circulating online warns NSPCC*. Available at www.dailymail.co.uk/news/article-2779459/Police-struggling-soaring-number-child-abuse-images-online-warns-NSPCC.html, accessed on 20 August 2016.

Daily Post Online (11 September 2014) *North Wales couple who sexually abused and gave boy drugs to face jail*. www.dailypost.co.uk/news/north-wales-news/north-wales-couple-who-sexually-7757366, accessed on 6 October 2016.

Derbyshire Safeguarding Children Board (undated) *Child Sexual Exploitation: Operation Liberty*. Available at www.derbyshirescb.org.uk/professionals-and-volunteers/child-sexual-exploitation/default.asp, accessed on 16 October 2016.

Department for Education (2009) *Safeguarding Children and Young People from Sexual Exploitation: Supplementary Guidance*. Available at www.gov.uk/government/uploads/system/uploads/attachment_data/file/278849/Safeguarding_Children_and_Young_People_from_Sexual_Exploitation.pdf, accessed on 30 September 2016.

Department for Education (2011) *Tackling Child Sexual Exploitation Action Plan*. Available at www.gov.uk/government/uploads/system/uploads/attachment_data/file/180867/DFE-00246-2011.pdf, accessed on 30 September 2016.

Department for Education (2012) *What to Do if You Suspect a Child Is Being Sexually Exploited*. Available at www.gov.uk/government/publications/what-to-do-if-you-suspect-a-child-is-being-sexually-exploited, accessed on 4 May 2016.

Department for Education (2014) *Statutory Guidance on Children Who Run Away or Go Missing from Home or Care*. Available at www.gov.uk/government/uploads/system/uploads/attachment_data/file/307867/Statutory_Guidance_-_Missing_from_care__3_.pdf, accessed on 22 October 2016.

Department for Education (2016) *Keeping Children Safe in Education: Statutory Guidance for Schools and Colleges*. Available at www.gov.uk/government/uploads/system/uploads/attachment_data/file/550511/Keeping_children_safe_in_education.pdf, accessed on 22 October 2016.

Department of Health (2016) *Care and Support Statutory Guidance*. Available at www.gov.uk/government/publications/care-act-statutory-guidance/care-and-support-statutory-guidance, accessed on 19 October 2016.

Department of Health, Home Office and Department for Education and Employment (1999) *Working Together to Safeguard Children*. London Stationery Office. Available at http://webarchive.nationalarchives.gov.uk/20130107105354/http://www.dh.gov.uk/prod_consum_dh/groups/dh_digitalassets/@dh/@en/documents/digitalasset/dh_4075824.pdf, accessed on 3 January 2016.

Derby Safeguarding Children Board (undated) *Say Something if you See Something*. Available at www.derbyscb.org.uk/media/derby-scb/content-assets/documents/procedures/say-something-campaign/Say-something-if-you-see-something-presentation.pdf, accessed on 19 October 2016.

Drew, J. (2016) *Drew Review: An independent review of South Yorkshire Police's handling of child sexual exploitation 1997–2016*. Available at www.drewreview.uk/wp-content/uploads/2016/03/SYP030-Final-report.pdf, accessed on 6 August 2016.

Eaton, J. and Dalby, N. (2016) *We need to talk about CSE Toolkits*. Available at http://safeandsoundgroup.org.uk/blog/we-need-to-talk-about-cse-toolkits, accessed on 16 October 2016.

Equality Act 2010. Available at www.legislation.gov.uk/ukpga/2010/15/contents, accessed on 4 July 2016.

European Convention on Human Rights (1953). Available at www.echr.coe.int/Documents/Convention_ENG.pdf, accessed on 18 July 2016.

Firmin, C. (2016) Contextual, integrated and holistic practice: next steps in responding to child sexual exploitation. University of Sheffield Symposium (8 July 2016) *Child Sexual Exploitation: Learning from Rotherham and Beyond*. Available at www.sheffield.ac.uk/law/research/clusters/ccr/learning, accessed on 22 October 2016.

Franklin, A., Raws, P. and Smeaton, E. (2015) *Unprotected, Overprotected: Meeting the Needs of Young People with Learning Disabilities Who Experience, or Are at Risk of, Sexual Exploitation*. Barnardo's.

Gladman, A. (2016) *A local response to child sexual exploitation*. Available at www.themj.co.uk/A-local-response-to-child-sexual-exploitation/204038, accessed on 17 September 2016.

Griffiths, S. (2013) *The Overview Report of the Serious Case Review in Respect of Young People 1,2,3,4,5 & 6*. Rochdale Safeguarding Children Board. Available at www.rochdaleonline.co.uk/uploads/f1/news/document/20131220_93449.pdf, accessed on 8 July 2016.

The Guardian Online (10 February 2013) *Frances Andrade killed herself after being accused of lying, says husband*. Available at www.theguardian.com/uk/2013/feb/10/frances-andrade-killed-herself-lying, accessed on 20 August 2016.

The Guardian Online (14 September 2014) *Ukip accused of politicising child sex abuse scandal by blaming Labour*. Available at www.theguardian.com/politics/2014/sep/14/ukip-politicising-child-sex-abuse-claim-blame-labour, accessed on 6 December 2016.

Guðbrandsson, B. (September 2013) *The CAC/Barnahus Response to Child Sexual Abuse and the Council of Europe Standard Setting*. 13th ISPCAN European Regional Conference on Child Abuse and Neglect, Dublin. Available at www.bvs.is/media/barnahus/Dublin,-sept.-2013.pdf, accessed on 4 September 2016.

Heal, A. (2003) *Sexual Exploitation, Drug Use and Drug Dealing: The Current Situation in South Yorkshire*. Available at www.lgcplus.com/Journals/2015/05/05/r/b/q/Sexual-Exploitation-Drug-Use-and-Drug-Dealing-the-Current-Situation-in-South-Yorkshire.pdf, accessed on 6 November 2015.

Heal, A. (2006) *A Problem Profile – Violence and Gun Crime: Links between Sexual Exploitation, Prostitution and Drug Markets in South Yorkshire*. Available at www.lgcplus.com/Journals/2015/05/05/v/c/c/Violence-and-Gun-Crime-Linking-Sexual-Exploitation-Prostitution-and-Drug-Markets-in-South-Yorkshire.pdf, accessed on 6 November 2015.

Her Majesty's Inspectorate of Constabulary (undated) *The Crime Recording Process*. Available at www.justiceinspectorates.gov.uk/hmic/our-work/crime-data-integrity/crime-recording-process, accessed on 27 August 2016.

Her Majesty's Inspectorate of Constabulary (July 2014) *South Yorkshire: National Child Protection Inspection*. Available at www.justiceinspectorates.gov.uk/hmic/publications/south-yorkshire-national-child-protection-inspection, accessed on 28 October 2015.

Her Majesty's Inspectorate of Constabulary (July 2015) *South Yorkshire: National Child Protection Inspection Post-Inspection Review*. Available at www.justiceinspectorates. gov.uk/hmic/publications/south-yorkshire-national-child-protection-inspection-post-inspection-review, accessed on 28 October 2015.

Hillsborough Independent Panel. Available at http://hillsborough.independent.gov.uk, accessed on 24 October 2015.

HM Government (2007) *Working Together to Cut Crime and Deliver Justice*. Available at www.gov.uk/government/uploads/system/uploads/attachment_data/file/243156/ 7247.pdf, accessed on 21 August 2016.

HM Government (2013) *Working Together to Safeguard Children: A Guide to Inter-Agency Working to Safeguard and Promote the Welfare of Children*. Available at http://media. education.gov.uk/assets/files/pdf/w/working%20together.pdf, accessed on 20 July 2016.

HM Government (2015) *Working Together to Safeguard Children: A Guide to Inter-Agency Working to Safeguard and Promote the Welfare of Children*. Available at www.gov.uk/ government/uploads/system/uploads/attachment_data/file/419595/Working_ Together_to_Safeguard_Children.pdf, accessed on 7 November 2015.

HM Government (2016) *Review of the Role and Functions of Local Safeguarding Children Boards: The Government's Response to Alan Wood CBE*. Available at www.gov. uk/government/uploads/system/uploads/attachment_data/file/526330/ Government_response_to_Alan_Wood_review.pdf, accessed on 30 August 2016.

Home Office (2011) *Call to End Violence Against Women and Girls: Action Plan*. Available at www.gov.uk/government/uploads/system/uploads/attachment_data/file/118153/ vawg-action-plan.pdf, accessed on 4 April 2016.

Home Office (2015) *Guidance on Part 2 of the Sexual Offences Act 2003*. Available at www.gov.uk/government/uploads/system/uploads/attachment_data/file/442151/2015-07-03_FINAL_Guidance_Part_2_SOA_2003.pdf, accessed on 22 October 2016.

Home of the Duluth Model (undated) *Wheel Gallery*. Available at www. theduluthmodel.org/training/wheels.html, accessed on 20 August 2016.

Human Rights Act 1998. Available at www.legislation.gov.uk/ukpga/1998/42/ contents, accessed on 4 July 2016.

Independent (29 August 2014) *Rotherham abuse scandal: David Cameron calls for under-fire police commissioner Shaun Wright to 'resign and take responsibility'*. Available at www. independent.co.uk/news/uk/crime/rotherham-abuse-scandal-david-cameron-calls-for-under-fire-police-commissioner-shaun-wright-to-9697594.html, accessed on 6 November 2015.

Independent Police Complaints Commission (12 June 2015a) *IPCC announces decision following Orgreave scoping exercise*. Available at www.ipcc.gov.uk/news/ipcc-announces-decision-following-orgreave-scoping-exercise, accessed on 25 October 2015.

Independent Police Complaints Commission (2015b) *Hillsborough Investigation*. Available at www.ipcc.gov.uk/hillsborough, accessed on 25 October 2015.

Independent Police Complaints Commission (2015c) *Child Sexual Exploitation – South Yorkshire Police*. Available at www.ipcc.gov.uk/investigations/child-sexual-exploitation-south-yorkshire-police, accessed on 25 October 2015.

Independent Training Services. Available at www.ind-training.co.uk, accessed on 18 October 2016.

It's not OKAY. Available at www.itsnotokay.co.uk, accessed on 1 September 2016.

Ivison, I. (1997) *Fiona's Story: A Tragedy of Our Times.* London: Virago.

Jay, A. (2014) *Independent Inquiry into Child Sexual Exploitation in Rotherham 1997–2013.* Available at www.rotherham.gov.uk/info/200109/council_news/884/independent_inquiry_into_child_sexual_exploitation_in_rotherham_1997_%E2%80%93_2013/2, accessed on 21 August 2016.

Johnson, M.P. (1995) 'Patriarchal terrorism and common couple violence: Two forms of violence against women.' *Journal of Marriage and the Family* 57, 283–294.

Johnson, M. and Leone, J. (2005) 'The differential effects of intimate terrorism and situational couple violence: Findings from the National Violence Against Women survey.' *Journal of Family Issues* 26, 3, 322–334.

Laming, W. (2003) *The Victoria Climbié Inquiry: Report of an Inquiry by Lord Laming.* London: The Stationery Office.

Leeds partner agencies (2015) *The Brief.* Available at www.leeds.gov.uk/docs/An%20Introduction%20to%20thebrief.pdf, accessed on 19 September 2016.

Local Government Chronicle Plus (10 September 2014) *Minute by minute: Rotherham chief executive quizzed by MPs – full coverage.* Available at www.lgcplus.com/news/minute-by-minute-rotherham-chief-executive-quizzed-by-mps-full-coverage/5074671.article, accessed on 7 November 2015.

Lloyd. S. (2016) 'She doesn't have to get in the car…': Exploring social workers' understandings of child sexual exploitation and sexually exploited girls. *Child Sexual Exploitation: Learning from Rotherham and Beyond.* Available at www.sheffield.ac.uk/law/research/clusters/ccr/learning, accessed on 22 October 2016.

The Local Safeguarding Children Boards Regulations 2006. Available at www.legislation.gov.uk/uksi/2006/90/introduction/made, accessed on 7 December 2016.

MacPherson, W. (1999) *The Stephen Lawrence Enquiry.* London: The Stationery Office.

Mail Online (26 August 2014) *Revealed: How fear of being seen as racist stopped social workers saving up to 1,400 children from sexual exploitation at the hands of Asian men in just ONE TOWN.* Available at www.dailymail.co.uk/news/article-2734694/It-hard-appalling-nature-abuse-child-victims-suffered-1-400-children-sexually-exploited-just-one-town-16-year-period-report-reveals.html, accessed on 7 December 2016.

McDonald, M., Price, J., Rose, V., Diamond, P. *et al.* (undated) *Pieces of Me. Writing by Young People Who Are at Risk of, or Who Have Experiences of, Sexual Exploitation.* Taking Stock, Sheffield.

McLeod, S. (2016) *Maslow's Hierarchy of Needs.* Available at www.simplypsychology.org/maslow.html, accessed on 12 August 2016.

McNaughton Nicholls, C., Cockbain, E., Brayley, H., Harvey, S. *et al.* (2014) *Research on the Sexual Exploitation of Boys and Young Men. A UK Scoping Study: Summary of Findings.* Barnado's. Available at www.barnardos.org.uk/cse-young-boys-summary-report.pdf, accessed on 3 May 2016.

Merriam Webster Dictionary (2015a). Available at www.merriam-webster.com/dictionary/survivor, accessed on 7 November 2015.

Merriam Webster Dictionary (2015b). Available at www.merriam-webster.com/dictionary/victim, accessed on 7 November 2015.

Merriam Webster Dictionary (2015c). Available at www.merriam-webster.com/dictionary/terrorist, accessed on 7 November 2015.

Michell, P. and Dye, C. (2014) *Boys are sexually exploited too.* BLAST, West Yorkshire Mesmac, Leeds.

Ministry of Justice (2011) *Achieving Best Evidence in Criminal Proceedings: Guidance on Interviewing Victims and Witnesses, and Guidance on Using Special Measures.* Available at www.cps.gov.uk/legal/assets/uploads/files/Achieving%20Best%20 Evidence%20in%20Criminal%20Proceedings.pdf, accessed on 3 September 2016.

Ministry of Justice (11 June 2013) *Victims to Be Spared from Harrowing Court Cases.* Available at www.gov.uk/government/news/victims-to-be-spared-from-harrowing-court-cases, accessed on 20 August 2016.

Ministry of Justice (2015) *The Code of Practice for Victims of Crime.* Available at www. gov.uk/government/uploads/system/uploads/attachment_data/file/470212/ code-of-practice-for-victims-of-crime.PDF, accessed on 11 October 2016.

Myers, J. and Carmi, E. (2013) *The Brooke Serious Case Review into Child Sexual Exploitation: Identifying the Strengths and Gaps in the Multi-Agency Responses to Child Sexual Exploitation in Order to Learn and Improve.* Bristol Safeguarding Children Board. Available at www.bristol.gov.uk/documents/20182/34760/Serious+Cas e+Review+Operation+Brooke+Overview+Report/3c2008c4-2728-4958-a8ed-8505826551a3, accessed on 12 July 2016.

National Crime Agency (23 April 2015) *Independent Review of South Yorkshire Police Operations Clover, Mark and Monroe.* Available at www.nationalcrimeagency.gov.uk/ news/604-outcome-of-independent-review-of-south-yorkshire-police-operations-clover-mark-and-monroe, accessed on 25 October 2015.

National Crime Agency (24 June 2015) *Rotherham Investigation Update.* Available at www.nationalcrimeagency.gov.uk/news/639-rotherham-investigation-update, accessed on 25 October 2015.

National Crime Agency (undated) *Crime Threats.* Available at www. nationalcrimeagency.gov.uk/crime-threats, accessed on 9 October 2016.

National Institute for Health and Care Excellence. (2009) *Child Maltreatment: When to Suspect Maltreatment in Under 18s.* Available at www.nice.org.uk/guidance/cg89/ chapter/Introduction, accessed on 7 November 2015.

Ofsted (November 2014) *Metropolitan Borough of Rotherham: Inspection of Services for Children in Need of Help and Protection, Children Looked After and Care Leavers and Review of the Effectiveness of the Local Safeguarding Children Board.* Available at http://reports.ofsted.gov.uk/sites/default/files/documents/local_authority_ reports/rotherham/053_Single%20inspection%20of%20LA%20children%27s%20 services%20and%20review%20of%20the%20LSCB%20as%20pdf.pdf, accessed on 28 October 2015.

Palmer, T. (2001) *No Son of Mine!* Barnardo's.

Panorama (1 September 2014) *Stolen Childhoods: The Grooming Scandal.* BBC. Available at www.youtube.com/watch?v=HQ4fTXnXwK0, accessed on 15 October 2016.

Panorama (15 June 2015) *Stolen Childhoods: The Legacy of Grooming.* Available at www. youtube.com/watch?v=Wgi4b1X2dd0, accessed on 15 October 2016.

PACE (2016) *Parents Speak Out: Crucial Partners in Tackling Child Sexual Exploitation.* Available at http://paceuk.info/wp-content/uploads/Parents-Speak-Out-final. pdf, accessed on 17 October 2016.

Pearce, J. with Williams, M. and Galvin, C. (2002) *It's Someone Taking a Part of You: A Study of Young Women and Sexual Exploitation.* London: The National Children's Bureau.

Pearce, J. (2009) *Young People and Sexual Exploitation. 'It's Not Hidden, You Just Aren't Looking.'* Abingdon on Thames: Routledge.

Police ICT (undated) *National Intelligence Model.* Available at https://ict.police.uk/national-standards/intel, accessed on 6 June 2016.

Prensky, M. (2001) *Digital, Natives, Digital Immigrants.* Available at http://marcprensky.com/writing/Prensky%20-%20Digital%20Natives,%20Digital%20Immigrants%20-%20Part1.pdf, accessed on 22 October 2016.

Regulation of Investigatory Powers Act 2000. Available at www.legislation.gov.uk/ukpga/2000/23/contents, accessed on 4 July 2016.

Rotherham Metropolitan Borough Council (2015a) Commissioners. Available at www.rotherham.gov.uk/commissioners, accessed on 6 November 2015.

Rotherham Metropolitan Borough Council (2015b) *Enough Is Enough.* Available at www.rotherham.gov.uk/enough, accessed on 6 November 2015.

Rotherham Post-Abuse CSE Steering Group (2015) *Victim's Approach to Child Sexual Exploitation.* Unpublished.

Rotherham CSE screening tool. Available at www.rscb.org.uk/safeguarding/downloads/file/59/child_sexual_exploitation_screening_tool_and_guidance, accessed on 7 December 2016.

Saied-Tessier, A. (2014) *Estimating the costs of child sexual abuse in the UK.* NSPCC. Available at www.nspcc.org.uk/services-and-resources/research-and-resources/2014/estimating-costs-of-child-sexual-abuse-in-uk, accessed on 4 August 2016.

Senior, J. (2016) *Broken and Betrayed: The True Story of the Rotherham Abuse Scandal by the Woman Who Fought to Expose it.* London: Pan MacMillan.

Serious Crime Act 2015. Available at www.legislation.gov.uk/ukpga/2015/9/contents/enacted, accessed on 4 July 2016.

Sexual Offences Act 2003. Available at www.legislation.gov.uk/ukpga/2003/42/contents, accessed on 22 October 2016.

Stephens, E. (2016) Conceptions on victim complicity. University of Sheffield Symposium (8 July 2016) *Child Sexual Exploitation: Learning from Rotherham and Beyond.* Available at www.sheffield.ac.uk/law/research/clusters/ccr/learning, accessed on 22 October 2016.

The Advocate's Gateway. Available at www.theadvocatesgateway.org, accessed on 23 October 2016.

The Star Online (16 January 2015) *Ed Miliband admits Rotherham child abuse victims were 'terribly let down' by Labour representatives.* Available at www.thestar.co.uk/news/local/ed-miliband-admits-rotherham-child-abuse-victims-were-terribly-let-down-by-labour-representatives-1-7055963, accessed on 24 October 2015.

The Star Online (26 October 2015) *Rotherham Muslim group urges Islamic community to boycott South Yorkshire Police.* Available at www.thestar.co.uk/news/local/rotherham-muslim-group-urges-islamic-community-to-boycott-south-yorkshire-police-1-7537012, accessed on 26 October 2015.

The Star Online (8 February 2016) *Five men face six-week trial over child abuse offences - as sixth defendant pleads guilty.* Available at www.thestar.co.uk/news/five-men-face-six-week-trial-over-child-abuse-offences-as-sixth-defendant-pleads-guilty-1-7720612, accessed on 2 September 2016.

The Star Online (10 August 2016) *'Neo-Nazi' bomb threat to Rotherham Mosque.* Available at www.thestar.co.uk/news/neo-nazi-bomb-threat-to-rotherham-mosque-1-8060487, accessed on 14 August 2016.

The Star Online (17 October 2016) *Eight men found guilty of sexually abusing teenage girls in Rotherham*. Available at www.thestar.co.uk/news/eight-men-found-guilty-of-sexually-abusing-teenage-girls-in-rotherham-1-8185658, accessed on 17 October 2016.

The Telegraph Online (27 August 2014) *Rotherham: In the face of such evil, who is the racist now?* Available at www.telegraph.co.uk/news/uknews/crime/11059138/Rotherham-In-the-face-of-such-evil-who-is-the-racist-now.html, accessed on 7 December 2016.

The Telegraph Online (7 June 2016) *Rotherham child sex abuse inquiry investigates hundreds of 'potential suspects'.* Available at www.telegraph.co.uk/news/2016/06/06/rotherham-child-sex-abuse-inquiry-investigates-hundreds-of-poten, accessed on 1 October 2016.

The Times (23 May 2013) *Abuse trial that shamed the British legal system.* Available at www.thetimes.co.uk/tto/law/article3772541.ece, accessed on 2 September 2016.

The Times (4 February 2015) *Rotherham: politicians and police 'abused girls'.* Available at www.thetimes.co.uk/tto/news/uk/crime/article4343753.ece, accessed on 6 November 2015.

The Times (7 June 2016) *Rotherham Abuse Inquiry will run for eight years.* Available at www.thetimes.co.uk/article/rotherham-abuse-inquiry-will-run-for-eight-years-xbmrpmcp9, accessed on 2 September 2016.

United Nations Convention of the Rights of the Child 1999. Available at www.unicef.org/crc, accessed on 6 August 2016.

United Nations Universal Declaration of Human Rights 1948. Available at www.un.org/en/universal-declaration-human-rights/index.html, accessed on 18 July 2016.

United Nations Office on Drugs and Crime. (undated) *Organized Crime.* Available at www.unodc.org/unodc/en/organized-crime/index.html, accessed on 9 October 2016.

University of Sheffield Symposium. (8 July 2016) *Child Sexual Exploitation: Learning from Rotherham and Beyond.* Available at www.sheffield.ac.uk/law/research/clusters/ccr/learning, accessed on 22 October 2016.

Van der Kolk, B. (2014) *The Body Keeps the Score. Mind, Brain and Body in the Transformation of Trauma.* London: Penguin.

Van Meeuwen, A., Swann, S., McNeish, D. and Edwards, S. (1998) *Whose Daughter Next? Children Abused through Prostitution.* Barnardo's. Available at www.barnardos.org.uk/research/documents/WHODAUGT.PDF, accessed on 7 October 2016.

Weber, L. and Bowling, B. (2011) 'Stop and search in global context.' *Policing and Society: An International Journal of Research and Policy 21,* 4, 353–356.

Wilson, S. (2015) *Violated: A Shocking and Harrowing Survival Story from the Notorious Rotherham Abuse Scandal.* Glasgow: Harper Collins.

Wood, A. (2016) *The Wood Report: Review of the Role and Functions of Local Safeguarding Children Boards.* Available at www.gov.uk/government/uploads/system/uploads/attachment_data/file/526329/Alan_Wood_review.pdf, accessed on 14 August 2016.

Youth Justice and Criminal Evidence Act 1999. Available at www.legislation.gov.uk/ukpga/1999/23/section/41, accessed on 3 August 2016.

Yorkshire Post (5 November 2010) *Gang jailed for 32 years over sex offences against care girls.* Available at www.yorkshirepost.co.uk/news/main-topics/local-stories/gang-jailed-for-32-years-over-sex-offences-against-care-girls-1-3024341#ixzz3poJH3iBr, accessed on 27 October 2015.

Subject Index

For Acts of Parliament and Government
Departments, please refer to the Author Index.

Abduction Warning Notices *see* Harbourer's
    Warnings
Achieving Best Evidence (ABE) interviews
    198–199
adults
    adult services 270–275
    practice issues for staff working with
        169–173
age issues 31–32, 70–72, 101, 121, 169, 271, 272
agencies *see* professionals and agencies
Ahmed, Mushin 51
Al Jazeera 28
alcohol 43, 68, 76, 83, 85, 89, 94, 95, 133, 170,
    171, 199, 270–271
Ali, Hassan 46
Ali, Qurban 195
Ali, Waleed 195
Alter Ego Theatre Company 154
anal rape 80
Andrade, Frances 215
anti-social behaviour 86, 91, 94, 98, 118, 126,
    203
appearance, personal 230–231
area child protection committees (ACPCs) 241
Asian communities 10, 33, 35, 48, 263
    see also Pakistani community

Barnahus model 237–238
Barnardo's 65, 67, 82, 92–93
Barnsley 153
BBC News 28
Bednar, Breck 67
behavioural indicators 149–152, 171
betrayal trauma theory 116–117
Billings, Alan 56
black and minority ethnic (BME) communities
    33, 48, 49, 264
blame *see* self-blame
'boyfriend' model 82–84, 95, 133
Bradford 183
brain, trauma and the 113–114
British Muslim Youth 50–51
British National Party 49

call handlers 183–184
Cameron, David 46
Canadian Broadcasting Company 28
Casey, Dame Louise 13, 18, 23
CCTV (closed-circuit TV) 110, 145, 185, 194,
    265, 267
'check and balance' approach 188
child, use of term 31–32, 70–71
child-centred approach 242–243
'child prostitution' 29, 65, 176
child protection plans 119–120, 165–167
child sexual abuse (CSA), use of term 30, 288

302

Subject Index

child sexual exploitation (CSE) 64–102
defining and identifying 64–82
age 70–72
gender 66–70
online and mobile phone technology
77–80
reward and exchange 72–74
victims' lack of recognition of their
abuse 75–77
violence and intimidation 80–82
vulnerability 74–75
'hotspots' 95, 97, 147, 201–202, 266
indicators 92–100
emotional and behavioural 94–96
environmental 97
physical symptoms 93–94
relating to perpetrators 97–100
models 82–92
'boyfriend' 82–84, 95, 133
families 90
gangs 87, 88–90
online abuse 81–82, 87–88, 112–113,
117, 221
party house 76, 84–86
peer-on-peer exploitation 86–87, 98, 221
survival and independent involvement
91–92
targeting groups in the community 91
trafficking 90, 177, 214, 268–270, 270–271
use of term 29–30, 65–66, 288–289
children
of adult victims and survivors 172–173
having a child as a result of CSA 132–134
Children's Commissioner 159, 237, 238
children's independent sexual violence
advisors/advocates (CHISVAs) 218–219
Climbié, Victoria 62
Coalition for the Removal of Pimping (CROP)
19–20, 42
Communities and Local Government Select
Committee 32, 45
counselling 131, 171, 218
Coventry 247
crack cocaine 25
Crimestoppers 184–185
criminal investigations 176–206
cases where there are no complainants
205–206
dedicated teams and partnership panels
187–188
disruption techniques 201–205
launching investigations: Operation Clover
case study 195–201
sharing information with the police 177–187

analysing information for intelligence
purposes 178–180, 201–202
good practice 182–185
intelligence problems 180–182
responding to received intelligence
185–187
working with victims to prosecute
offenders 189–194
historical complainants 192–194
criminal justice process 209–239
effective support for victims and families
during the process 219–225
needs of the family 225
pre-trial therapy 223–224
recognising the victim's perspective
221–222
before trial 220–221
victim contact 222–223
issues of safety and risk 226–229
post-trial support 233–235
victim exit plans 234–235
preparing the witness for court 229–231
proposed changes 235–238
Barnahus model 237–238
Section 28 pilots 236–237
special measures 231–232
support for witnesses after giving evidence
232
system in England and Wales 210–211
victims' experiences of giving evidence at
court 212–219
cross-examination 215–217
witness rights 217–219
cross-border working 268–270
cross-examination 211, 213–215, 215–217, 230,
231, 232, 236
Crown Prosecution Service (CPS) 171, 210,
211, 217, 218, 288

Davies, Shelley 195
Derby Safeguarding Children Board 140
Derbyshire 141, 145, 188, 264–265, 267
Derbyshire Constabulary 156–157, 157, 182,
183–184, 187, 220–221
Derbyshire County Council 154, 156, 202
Derbyshire Tasking and Coordination Group
188
disabilities, vulnerability and 104–105, 107–108
disruption techniques 201–205
DNA 145, 185, 186, 194, 203, 269
domestic violence 34, 74, 83, 84, 165, 286
Drew, John 56
Drug Action Teams (DATs) 24, 26

drugs 24–26, 27, 58, 59, 76, 83, 85, 89, 94, 95, 118, 133, 170, 171, 199, 270
Duluth model 83
Durham 238

Eastern European communities 33
economic issues 170
emotional and behavioural symptoms 94–96
engagement
  families and carers 161–163, 190
  guidance 189–192
  non-engagement 120–123, 127, 149, 160–161
  safeguarding and 158–163
English Defence League 46–47
environmental issues 97
ethnicity 33–34, 48–49, 263–264, 273
Excellence for Boys project (E4B) 70, 254
excitement, seeking 107, 122, 152, 285

Facebook 79, 87, 97, 112–113, 116
fag house model *see* party houses
families
  child sexual exploitation within 90
  criminal justice process needs 225
  engagement issues 161–163, 190
  impact on families of victims and survivors 40–44, 96, 119–120
  preventative work with children and families 152–155
  safety and risk issues 227
flashbacks 118, 199, 214, 216, 222
forgiveness 228
France 211
Fraser competence 44, 129–130

gaming 78, 87
gangs 87, 88–90
gay sex *see* sexual orientation issues
gender issues 34, 66–70, 77, 88–89, 99, 106, 190
Gillick competence 44, 129
Gladman, Adele 19–24, 26, 42, 59, 81, 84, 85, 91, 95, 108, 109, 110, 119, 123, 124–125, 139, 151, 155, 159, 163, 179, 193–194, 196, 203, 215–216, 216–217, 236–237, 252–253
Greater Manchester 141, 155, 267
grooming process 68–69, 73–75, 76–77, 79–80, 96, 109–110, 110–111, 111–112, 117, 147, 153, 154, 190, 221, 286, 287
  see also child sexual exploitation (CSE): models
groups
  group supervision 169
  targeting groups in the community 91
Grow women's support organisation 201

Hamner, Jalna 19–20
Harbourer's Warnings 146, 162–163, 202–203
Heal, Angie 24–29, 50, 196, 247
Hillsborough Disaster 55
historical complainants 181, 185, 192–194, 210
Holmes database 195–196, 197
Home Affairs Select Committee (HASC) 23, 45, 54, 60
Home Office 19, 26
hotel industry 183, 266, 267–268
'hotspots' 95, 97, 147, 201–202, 266
Hub and Spoke Project 188
humiliation 80
Hussain family 22, 195–196, 263–264
Hussain, Arshid 60, 195, 208
Hussain, Bannaras 195
Hussain, Basharat 195, 208, 288
Hussain, Sageer 195, 288

Iceland 237–238
impact
  consequences of professionals and agencies' failure to act 123–132
    impact of professional responses 124–126
    role of agencies and professionals 128–132
    statutory agency failure 127–128
  on families of victims and survivors 40–44, 96, 119–120
  of grooming and organised child sexual abuse 103–135
  having a child as a result of CSA 132–134
  of trauma 112–119
  understanding non-engagement 120–123
  vulnerability 104–112
    disability and 107–108
    increasing vulnerabilities 111–112
    lack of knowledge of CSE and grooming 110–111
    looked-after children 108–110
Independent Police Complaints Commission (IPCC) 23, 46, 55, 56, 61
independent sexual violence advisors/ advocates (ISVAs) 218–219, 234
infant, use of term 32
information sharing *see under* criminal investigations; safeguarding
Intelligence Reports (IRs) 178
intimate terrorists, use of term 34–35
Ivison, Fiona 41–42
Ivison, Irene 19–20, 41–42

Jay, Alexis 13, 18, 23, 27–28, 44–45, 290–291
'Jonathan' 79, 117, 154

Subject Index

Khaliq, Ishtiaq 195
Kimber, Martin 32, 45, 52
Kingston-upon-Thames 236

Labour Party 46, 53
Lancashire 155
Leeds 154–155, 183, 204, 236
'Lilly 212–213, 230, 232
Liverpool 236
Local Safeguarding Adults Boards (SABs) 170,
    172, 240, 245, 271, 272–273
Local Safeguarding Children Boards (LSCBs)
    66, 99, 127, 128, 140–142, 142–148, 157
    absent or missing children 143–145
    high-risk/significant risk factors 147–148
    identification of vulnerability factors 143
    information gathering 180
    low-risk/early indicators 145–146
    medium-risk/strong indicators 146–147
    see also strategic and senior management
        responses
London 238, 267
Longfield, Anne 237
looked-after children 108–110
Lucas, Ann 25

MacGregor, Karen 195
Malik, Masoued 195
Maslow's Hierarchy of Needs 199–200
mental health issues 31, 92, 95, 122, 133, 168,
    170, 171, 201, 215, 227, 233
Merseyside 141
Metropolitan Police 49
Milliband, Ed 53
mindfulness 159
missing children 42, 43, 85, 95, 99–100,
    109–110, 119, 137–138, 143–145, 161–162,
    185, 186
    definition 144
mobile phones
    examining contents 204
    exploitative use of 68–69, 81
    querying accession of 150–151
    technology 77–80
motherhood, as a result of abuse 132–134, 170,
    172–173
multi-agency partnerships, robust 157–158

National Crime Agency (NCA) 23, 56, 61, 197
National Crime Recording Standards 181
National Health Service (NHS) 32
National Intelligence Model (NIM) 178, 181,
    184, 287
National Intelligence Record (NIR) 178

National Society for the Prevention of Cruelty
    to Children (NSPCC) 60, 66
neo-Nazis 51
non-engagement see engagement
Norfolk, Andrew 22–23, 45, 60, 213–214
normalisation 29, 68, 72, 75–76, 77, 84, 97–98,
    115, 221
Nottinghamshire Police 206

Ofsted 61, 245, 258
Oldham 89
online abuse 81–82, 87–88, 112–113, 117, 221
online learning 148–149
online technology 77–80
Operation Brooke 168
Operation Bullfinch 115
Operation Carrington 58
Operation Central 58, 179
Operation Chard 58
Operation Clover 58, 60, 177, 208, 218, 220,
    221, 222–223, 228, 231, 232, 233, 234–235,
    288
    case study 195–201
Operation Czar 58
Operation K-Alphabet 58
Operation Kappa 58
Operation Liberty 157, 183–184, 187
Operation Retriever 156–157, 182, 218,
    220–221, 228
Operation Stovewood 197
oral rape 80
organised crime, definition 289
Orgreave Colliery, miners' strike 55
Oxford 64, 115, 247

Pakistani community 35, 39, 45, 47, 47–51, 263
panic attacks 199, 214
parenthood, as a result of abuse 132–134, 170,
    172–173
Parents Against Child Exploitation (PACE) 42,
    44, 154–155
party houses 76, 84–86
peer-on-peer exploitation 86–87, 98, 221
peripheral services 266–268
perpetrators
    indicators 97–100
    see also criminal investigations
personal appearance 230–231
personal, social, health and economic
    education (PSHE) 153
physical symptoms 93–94
police see criminal investigations; criminal
    justice process; professionals and
    agencies; individual Operations; individual
    police forces

305

Police National Database (PND) 182
post-traumatic stress syndrome 115–116, 117–118
pregnancy 9–10, 93, 132–134, 172
professionals and agencies
consequences of failure to act 123–132
impact of professional responses 124–126
role 128–132
statutory agency failure 127–128
psychological abuse 41, 84, 115–116
psychotherapists 237
puberty 106

quality assurance 262–263

racism 49–50, 51, 273
Rafiq, Naeem 195
Rantzen, Dame Esther 159
Read, Chris 47
reward and exchange 72–74, 91–92, 111
risk assessment tools 92–93, 98, 99, 138–139, 140–142, 145–148, 179
Risky Business Project 20–21, 22, 25, 27, 33, 53, 55, 57, 58, 157–158, 179, 180, 196
Rochdale 64, 89, 111, 118, 247
Rotherham
consequences of statutory agency failure in 39–63
families of victims and survivors 40–44
financial costs 60–62
Pakistani community 47–51
perpetrators 58–60
professionals 57–58
Rotherham Metropolitan Borough Council 51–55
South Yorkshire Police 55–56
town and people of Rotherham 44–47
Local Safeguarding Children Board 141, 145, 146, 250, 257, 267
trafficking in 270
Rotherham Metropolitan Borough Council 45–46, 47, 49, 50, 51–55, 57–58, 60–61, 61–62, 124, 180, 197, 246, 247, 249–250, 267, 271

Safe and Sound 157, 188, 220
safeguarding 136–175
criminal justice process 226–229
definitions 241–242
effective planning and review 165–167
effective practice 148–158
information sharing 156–157

knowledge and skills to recognise early indicators 148–149
preventative work with children and families 152–155
questioning young people's behaviour and interrogating 'facts' 149–152
robust multi-agency partnerships 157–158
strategic overviews 155–156
engagement issues 158–163
addressing non-engagement 160–161
families and carers 161–163
Local Safeguarding Children Board guidance 142–148
absent or missing children 143–145
high-risk/significant risk factors 147–148
identification of vulnerability factors 143
low-risk/early indicators 145–146
medium-risk/strong indicators 146–147
practice issues for staff working with adults 169–173
children of adult victims and survivors 172–173
risk assessment tools 138–139, 140–142
staff supervision and support 167–169
therapeutic responses 164–165
understanding and applying thresholds 138–140
see also Local Safeguarding Children Boards
Section 28 pilots 236–237
self-blame 87, 115, 125, 149–150, 221, 222
self-harm 94, 95, 118, 170, 199, 231, 232
Senior, Jayne 22–23, 25, 26, 57
sexism 52, 247
sexting 87, 265
sexual assault referral centres (SARCs) 218
Sexual Exploitation Risk Assessment Framework (SERAF) 92–93
Sexual Harm Prevention Orders 203, 226
sexual health services 151–152
sexual orientation issues and gay sex 67, 68, 69, 76, 79, 105, 106, 117, 253–254, 263, 286–287
Sexual Risk Orders 203, 226
sexualised behaviour 94, 95
Sheffield 48, 56, 177, 268
Skype 88
slavery, modern 177
SMART plans 166
social workers 43–44, 49
South Yorkshire Police (SYP) 24–25, 26, 27, 45, 48, 49–51, 54, 55–56, 57–58, 60–62, 124, 176, 179–180, 180, 224, 246, 247, 267
see also Operation Clover

Stone, Roger 45, 53
strategic and senior management responses 240–277
    adult services 270–275
    challenge and accountability 249–255
       understanding issues locally 251–255
    cross-border working 268–270
    legal and policy framework 241–243
    Local Safeguarding Children Boards
       issues affecting effectiveness 244–246
       role and functions 243–244
    organisational and professional cultures 246–248
    policies and procedures 255–258
    quality assurance 262–263
    raising awareness and working with different communities 263–266
    staff support and supervision 260–262
    training 258–260
    working with peripheral services 266–268
strategic overviews 155–156
stress hormones 118–119
survival and independent involvement 91–92
survivor, use of term 30–31
survivors *see* victims

Taking Stock project 112–113
'Tanya' 9–12, 17, 18, 43, 99–100, 123–124, 137–138, 161–162, 173, 199, 219, 291
targeting groups in the community 91
taxis 38, 48, 52, 91, 266, 267
terminology 29–35
terrorist, use of term 34–35
'testing' by children 130, 159, 223
Thacker, Joyce 45–46, 53–54
The Star (Sheffield) 28
The Times 22, 45, 60
therapy 164–165
    pre-trial 220, 223–224
Thrive model 184
trafficking 90, 177, 214, 268–270
trauma
    impact of 112–119
    therapeutic responses 164–165
    see also criminal justice process
trials *see* criminal justice process
TripAdvisor 183
trust issues 9–10, 11, 18, 67–68, 100, 113, 124, 129–130, 171, 181, 189, 192–194, 198–199, 220, 223

U Create 265
United Kingdom Independence Party (UKIP) 46

victim, use of term 30–31
Victim Engagement Teams (VETs) 200–201, 222–223
Victim Support 219
'victimless' prosecutions 194, 206
victims
    historical complainants 181, 185, 192–194, 210
    impact on families of 40–44
    lack of recognition of their abuse 75–77
    statistics 39
    working with victims to prosecute offenders 189–194
    see also criminal justice process
Victims' Information Service 236
video links and recordings 212–213, 218, 229, 231, 236–237, 237–238
violence and intimidation 80–82
virginity 110, 115
vulnerability 74–75, 104–112, 183
    disability and 104–105, 107–108
    identification of vulnerability factors 143
    increasing vulnerabilities 111–112
    lack of knowledge of CSE and grooming 110–111
    looked-after children 108–110

Wakefield 142, 188
Wall Street Journal 28
West Yorkshire 141
West Yorkshire Police 179, 183, 185–186, 192–193
Whied, Mohammed 195
Witness Support 219
witnesses see criminal justice process
Women's Aid 77
Wright, Shaun 45–46, 56

Yorkshire 155
young person, use of term 31–32
Young Women's Christian Association (YWCA) 201
YouTube 87, 116, 265

Author Index

Alter Ego Theatre Company 154
Anonymous (Girl A) 111, 114
Anti-Social Behaviour, Crime and Policing Act 2014 203
Association of Independent LSCB Chairs 251–252

BBC Online News 51, 67, 89, 182, 195, 267, 288, 290–291
Beckett, H. 88, 273
Bedford, A. 115, 247
Berelowitz, S. 33, 69–70, 80, 88, 107, 127–128, 254–255, 273, 274
Birmingham City Council v Sarfraz Riaz and Others 2014 148
Birmingham Mail Online 263
BLAST 67, 70, 76, 140, 154, 254
Bowling, B. 49
Brown, S. 93, 98, 105, 140, 141, 142, 174

Canadian Broadcasting Company 50
Care Act 2014 170, 171, 283
Carmi, E. 168
Casey, L. 23, 39, 43, 43–44, 47, 51, 52, 53, 54–55, 56, 57, 59, 60, 143, 179, 180, 247, 250, 263, 271, 278
Channel 4 81–82
Child Abduction Act 1984 202, 203

Child Exploitation Online Protection (CEOP) 78, 87, 88
Children Act 1989 70, 124, 202, 203, 241
Children Act 2004 241, 242
Children and Young People Now 54
Children's Commissioner 237
Children's Commissioner's Inquiry *see* Berelowitz, S.
Clutton, S. 92
Coles, J. 92
Coming Out of the Darkness conference 112, 119, 120
Commons Select Committee 45, 258
Community Care 80
Cooper, F. 129, 130
Coventry Safeguarding Children Board 247
Crimestoppers 184–185
Crown Prosecution Service 115, 218, 223–224

Daily Mail Online 88
Daily Post Online 69
Dalby, N. 93, 99, 140
Data Protection Act 1998 180
Department for Communities and Local Government 46, 51
Department for Education 65–66, 66, 70, 136, 144, 246, 286
Department for Education and Employment 124

Author Index

Department for Work and Pensions 201
Department of Health 66, 124, 170, 240
Derby Safeguarding Children Board 183–184,
  203–204
Derbyshire Safeguarding Children Board 157,
  183–184, 187
Drew, J. 56, 61, 247
Dye, C. 140

Eaton, J. 93, 99, 140
Equality Act 2010 70
European Convention on Human Rights 210

Firmin, C. 122
Franklin, A. 107, 108
Freedom of Information Act 28

Galvin, C. 92
Gladman, A. 252–253
Griffiths, S. 91, 118, 247
The Guardian Online 46, 215
Guðbrandsson, B. 238

Heal, A. 26, 33, 48–49, 62, 290
Her Majesty's Inspectorate of Constabulary
  60, 181
Hillsborough Independent Panel 55
HM Government 32, 148, 178, 210, 240,
  241–243, 243–244, 246, 249
Home of the Duluth Model 83
Home Office 29, 67, 124
Human Rights Act 1998 61, 211

Independent 46
Independent Police Complaints Commission
  (IPCC) 55, 56
Independent Training Services 153
It's not OKAY 159
Ivison, I. 41–42

Jay, A. 30, 39, 42, 43, 49, 51, 52, 53, 54, 55–56,
  56, 58, 59, 60, 91, 124, 127, 141, 143, 176,
  196, 201, 204, 247, 250, 257, 263, 272–273,
  278
Johnson, M.P. 34, 41, 77, 84

Laming, W. 62, 290
Leeds partner agencies 183
Leone, J. 34, 41, 77, 84

Lloyd, S. 277
Local Government Chronicle Plus 32
The Local Safeguarding Children Boards
  Regulations 2006 243–244

McDonald, M. 112–113
McLeod, S. 199–200
McNaughton Nicholls, C. 67
MacPherson, W. 49
Mail Online 50
Merriam Webster Dictionary 30, 34
Michell, P. 140
Ministry of Justice 198, 200, 235–236
Myers, J. 168

National Crime Agency (NCA) 56, 197, 289
National Institute for Health and Care
  Excellence (NICE) 32

Ofsted 61

PACE 225
Palmer, T. 67
Panorama 17, 27, 28, 270
Pearce, J. 92, 115
Police ICT 178
Prensky, M. 77

Raws, P. 107, 108
Regulation of Investigatory Powers Act 2000
  194
Rotherham CSE screening tool 141, 143, 145,
  146
Rotherham Metropolitan Borough Council
  46, 47
Rotherham Post-Abuse CSE Steering Group
  189–192

Saied-Tessier, A. 60, 132
Senior, J. 57, 109–110, 132, 158–159
Serious Crime Act 2015 176–177
Sexual Offences Act 2003 29, 65, 69, 176
Smeaton, E. 107, 108
Stephens, E. 116

The Advocate's Gateway 219
The Star Online 51, 53, 106, 227
The Telegraph Online 50, 197
The Times 46, 61, 213–214

United Nations Convention on the Rights of the Child 1999 31, 223
United Nations Office on Drugs and Crime 289
United Nations Universal Declaration of Human Rights 210
University of Sheffield Symposium 43, 99–100, 116, 137–138, 161–162, 173, 219

Van der Kolk, B. 112, 113–114, 114, 117–118, 118–119
Van Meeuwen, A. 65, 66

Weber, L. 49
Williams, M. 92
Wilson, S. 110–111
Wood, A. 245, 251

Yorkshire Post 58
Youth Justice and Criminal Evidence Act 1999 218, 236

Adele Gladman is a Safeguarding Children trainer and consultant who led the Home Office funded pilot in Rotherham from 2001–2002. Formerly a solicitor, she has worked with services across the UK to improve outcomes for children and vulnerable adults within safeguarding and legal structures.

Angie Heal has worked in the public and independent sectors in adults and children's services, and criminal justice. She was a Strategic Analyst for South Yorkshire Police from 2002–2007.

Both Adele and Angie gave evidence to the Home Affairs Select Committee for the Rotherham case in 2014, and they continue to assist with ongoing investigation and enquiries.

Not My Shame

T.O. Walker

Paperback: £8.99 / $14.95
ISBN: 978 1 78592 184 1
eISBN: 978 0 85701 294 4
72 pages

"And suddenly I am flooded…terror, shame, despair, horror, disgust."

"How can I talk about things I can't pin down?"

With subtlety and sensitivity, this powerful graphic novel draws the reader into the experience of trauma and dissociation caused by sexual violence. It reveals the intrusive traumatic memories and distress experienced by a victim of childhood sexual exploitation in her adulthood and follows the process of coming to terms with her past through therapy and art. Positive and hopeful at its heart, it demonstrates her ability to be a good parent irrespective of mental health struggles and explores the importance of relationships with people in the present.

Tackling complex issues including the nature of traumatic memory, self-harm, victim-blaming, racism in the police, health and education services and the media's impact, this graphic novel reveals how the past can be triggered by the present and how victims of sexual abuse can be excellent parents and successful in life in spite of this.

T.O. Walker is an illustrator, educator and activist.